DATE DUE

MR 29 02			
AP 19 02			
AP 3 03			
AP 10 07			

DEMCO 38-296

Blue Dreams

Blue Dreams

Korean Americans and the Los Angeles Riots

Nancy Abelmann and John Lie

Harvard University Press
Cambridge, Massachusetts
London, England
1995

Library of Congress Cataloging-in-Publication Data

Abelmann, Nancy.
Blue dreams : Korean Americans and the Los Angeles riots / Nancy
Abelmann and John Lie.
p. cm.
Includes bibliographical references and index.
ISBN 0-674-07704-0
1. Korean Americans—California—Los Angeles—History—20th
century. 2. Riots—California—Los Angeles—History—20th century.
3. Los Angeles (Calif.)—Ethnic relations.   I. Lie, John.
II. Title.
F869.L89K616   1995
979.4'94004957—dc20
94-23034
CIP

To our parents
Rena and Walter Abelmann, Jane and Harry Lie

Contents

Preface

In this book we narrate the Korean American story in the context of the Los Angeles riots of 1992 and simultaneously place American ideologies on trial. We probe the transnational dimensions and diversity of Korean Americans in Los Angeles. In turn, Korean Americans' situations and voices challenge cherished assumptions about the United States and its minority populations. These concerns—the transnational character of the Korean diaspora, the heterogeneity of Korean Americans, and the critique of American ideologies—constitute the main themes of *Blue Dreams*.

The transnational perspective necessitates transcending received boundaries and frameworks. Indeed, any adequate account of Korean Americans needs to take seriously the interpenetration of South Korea and the United States. Although scholarship on Asian America must challenge the presumption of irrevocable links between Asian Americans and their ancestral homelands, it should not neglect either pre-immigration backgrounds or post-immigration networks. This is especially crucial for Korean Americans, many of whom are first-generation immigrants. They inescapably bring the experiences of their homeland and their ideas about what the United States is like into the vestibule of their new society. In many cases, they continue to maintain political, economic, cultural, and personal ties with South Korea. Limiting our analysis to an American frame of reference would seriously distort our understanding of this community and its diverse values, beliefs, and actions.

Consider, at an ostensibly trivial level, the question of what most Korean Americans call the L.A. riots: *Sa-i-gu p'oktong* (4-2-9 riot). In Korean political history, integer chains mark significant uprisings, demonstrations, and political turns; for example, the March First Demonstration (1919) against Japanese colonial rule is known as *Sam-il undong* (3-1 movement), while the Student Revolution of April 19, 1960, is called *Sa-il-gu* (4-1-9). To be sure, even naming is not simple or unified among South Koreans or Korean Americans. When we spoke to a friend in Seoul and told him that we were writing a book on the 4-2-9 riots, he retorted: "Oh, you mean the 4-2-9 *uprising*." The Korean dimension was equally striking in the mourning for Eddy Lee, the only Korean American to die in the riots. The frequently reproduced image of a young man holding Eddy Lee's tasseled black-and-white photo was reminiscent of South Korean demonstrators mourning political martyrs. The Korean dimension, moreover, is not restricted to Koreans or to Korean Americans. A European American National Guardsman posted in Koreatown, reflecting on his tour of duty in South Korea, remarked how the streets reminded him of Seoul. Framing the L.A. riots is a transpacific venture; we need to transcend national borders to understand Korean Americans.

In reconnecting Korean immigrants to the Korea they left behind, *Blue Dreams*—the color associated with dreams, hopes, and aspirations in Korea is blue, like the clear blue sky—highlights invisible, even repressed, threads: modern Korean history, class and status hierarchies in South Korea, and resources and hopes that immigrants have brought to the United States. The transnational Korean diaspora alerts us to the enormous diversity of the people essentialized into the easy receptacle of "Koreans" or "Korean Americans." Many reports on the riots, for example, identified Korean Americans as prosperous ghetto shopkeepers. Yet not all Korean Americans are entrepreneurs, nor are they all successful. Further, the stereotyped image of the Korean American entrepreneur, which validates the ideal of the American dream, breaks down against the recalcitrant reality of Korean immigrant lives in the United States. Some Korean dreams have turned into American nightmares, oneiric blue into ominous blues.

The diversity and division among Korean Americans, even within Los Angeles's Koreatown, elude facile generalizations. The timing of immigration, for example, is a widely accepted marker of differentiation among Korean Americans. More striking, as we shall see, are class divisions. Effaced in the presumption of a strong national and cultural identity and the post-riot call for ethnic and community solidarity, class differences—income, educational, or status inequality—remain a conspicuous feature among Korean Americans in Los Angeles. While some bask in their wealth, others eke out a living; dreams are both realized and deferred in the United States.

Immigrant dreams and nightmares place dominant American ideologies on trial. Korean American experiences highlight persistent class divisions and structural obstacles to minority advancement. Nowhere is the distance between ideal and reality greater than in the dominant media framing of the "black-Korean conflict." The popular account of the interethnic conflict reifies essentialized views of the two ethnic groups and fails to make sense of the concrete structures of opportunity they face. Facile ethnic and cultural generalizations are drawn, and class divisions within each group are passed over in silence. Although we do not deny that tensions exist between African Americans and Korean Americans, we criticize the dominant "black-Korean conflict" frame by considering its place in the American ideological crucible. In so doing, we challenge comfortable views of American society and its minority populations.

In elaborating these themes—the transnational dimension of the Korean American story, the diversity of Korean Americans, and the challenge to the dominant American self-understanding—*Blue Dreams* scrutinizes the ideological assumptions underlying the popular portrayal of Korean Americans, the American dream, and the "black-Korean conflict." To narrate the Korean American story inevitably forces us to deal with the causes and consequences of the L.A. riots, the history and structure of the Korean diaspora in the United States, the political economy of Los Angeles and Korean American entrepreneurship, and the "black-Korean conflict." Yet we should state at the outset that readers seeking a comprehensive analysis of the L.A. riots or an in-depth ethnography of the "black-Korean conflict" will not find it here. Instead, we offer a broad sketch of the crossroads of Korean and American ideologies and realities as they manifested themselves among Korean Americans after the 1992 L.A. riots.

In challenging some of the dominant ideologies about the United States, *Blue Dreams* also criticizes most media reports and analyses. The mass media profoundly shapes popular perceptions and beliefs about pressing social issues—indeed, even in deciding which issues are important (Herman and Chomsky 1988, chap. 1). We found most media accounts of the 1992 L.A. riots and of Korean Americans, in particular, problematic. If we had not, we would not have written this book.

Yet media accounts neither inevitably reproduce dominant ideologies and distort social reality nor always convince the public. Many perspectives and voices are aired in mainstream media reports. There are truths and significant data even in biased reports. And people often question media-propagated facts and interpretations. Nor is the mass media monolithic or the public passive. Further, social scientists do not have a privileged access to social reality; journalists often do a better job of describing and explaining it. In the age of "sound bites," we suffer not so much from the absence of diverse perspectives but from the dearth of sustained syntheses and interpretations. In the absence of alternative frameworks, a dominant frame emerges to "make sense" of various voices, while muffling other voices and interpretations. Our goal here is to provide a sustained alternative interpretive framework.

The voices of Korean Americans in Los Angeles provide a crucial source for this book. We solicited focused responses from about fifty Korean Americans representing a variety of social positions. We interviewed not only riot victims but also Korean Americans of various age groups, occupations, immigration history, and regional, educational, and economic backgrounds. We especially sought people who are routinely neglected in media and academic accounts of Korean Americans in Los Angeles. These include, for example, an extremely wealthy businessman with domiciles in three countries; an unemployed, non-college-educated immigrant from the 1960s; and a young vigilante with a millenarian vision.

Our interviews were framed by their time and place—in Los Angeles, within one year of the riots. We aimed for loosely structured exchanges. We did not have a battery of questions; we made no attempts to standardize our queries' form or style. Conversations occurred over business counters, on building stoops, in living rooms, and so on. Most interviews were conducted in Korean, with English phrases and acronyms; some were conducted in English, scattered with Korean idioms. Our respondents had questions for us, as well. Lie was usually

asked to situate himself: when did you come to the United States? Lie
answered that he had been born in Seoul and grew up in Tokyo and
Honolulu. Abelmann was often asked to explain why she could speak
Korean, and where she had lived in South Korea. Abelmann responded
that she had been born and raised in Massachusetts, but did her dissertation research on a South Korean farmers' movement in North
Chŏlla Province.

We have used pseudonyms except for people speaking or writing in
the public domain, such as politicians, organizers, and academics, or
for those who are quoted in written sources.

Some explanations of the linguistic conventions we follow are in order.
We generally characterize "blacks" as African Americans, "whites" as
European Americans, "Hispanics" as Latinos, and "Koreans" as Korean
Americans. To be sure, it seems absurd to use an abstract and incoher-
ent category like "Latinos." A Latino may refer to a person of either
gender and to people of various "races" as conventionally understood,
national origins, immigrant status, class background, and so on (Muñoz
1987, pp. 36–37; Portes and Rumbaut 1990, pp. 137–139; Shorris 1992,
pp. xv–xvii). While some Haitian Americans may be perceived as
"white," others are considered "black." Because Haitians usually speak
French or patois, they are often excluded by other Spanish-speaking
"Latinos." The category of "Latino" may even include people, such as
descendants of the Maya, who would actively resist such a categori-
zation. The problem becomes more intractable when we consider the
estimated one million children of "mixed-race" marriages (Rosin 1994,
p. 12; see also Spickard 1989). These complications underscore that
the categories we use are mandated by the necessity of convenience
and the usefulness of convention; the categories should not be seen as
natural. We consider racial and ethnic categories to be constructed;
they are historical products that are negotiated and struggled over (see,
for example, F. James Davis's 1991 analysis of "Who is black?" in the
United States; see also Waters 1990; S. M. Lee 1993).

We attempt to use the United States to refer to the country in which
Los Angeles is located. Many Koreans and Korean Americans, however, refer to the United States as "America," especially when its symbolic meaning is stressed. Lack of another adjective forces us from time
to time to rely on "American" to characterize the United States. Furthermore, many of our interviewees as well as written sources refer to

South Korea simply as Korea in spite of the continuing existence of two Koreas.

We refer to all U.S. residents of Korean descent as Korean Americans, regardless of their citizenship status. We realize, however, that many people we identify as Korean Americans refer to themselves as "Koreans." David Rieff, in writing about Los Angeles, notes: "Koreans, with their fierce and settled sense of national identity, would usually insist, when asked, that they were Koreans, plain and simple" (1991, p. 238; see also Cha 1977, p. 198.) Contrary to the received Korean practice in which last names are given first, we follow standard American practice because most Koreans who appear in this book are in fact Korean Americans, who themselves conform to the dominant U.S. convention. We have made exceptions for those who have no discernible American connections, however; their names are given with surnames first. In such cases, we have italicized the last name (for example, *Kim* Chi Ha). In transliterating Korean words and names into English, we have followed the McCune-Reischauer system, except for well-known names (*Kim* Il Sung, rather than *Kim* Il Sŏng) and for the pseudonyms we used (Soh rather than Sŏ). All translations from Korean, from both written and oral sources, are ours, unless otherwise indicated.

Finally, although many prefer the term "rebellion," "insurrection," or "civil uprising" to denote the political and conscious character of rioters and looters (see, for example, Oliver, Johnson, and Farrell 1993; Thompson 1993, p. 49), we refer to the upheaval in Los Angeles as it is most widely known: the L.A. riots. We do not attach moral connotations to words such as "riots" or "looters," but rather use them descriptively. Further, we do not assume that "riot" refers to apolitical or senseless action; to call a civil disturbance a riot does not deny its political character (compare Klein 1992, pp. 115–116, 120; Noel 1992, p. 41; Carson 1993, p. 35; Lieberman and O'Reilly 1993, p. A1). The historian E. P. Thompson writes: "It is only the shortsighted historian who finds the crowd to be blind" (1978, p. 398; see also McPhail 1991, p. 225).

In researching and writing this book we received help from many people. Above all, we thank those who spent valuable time discussing their opinions and experiences. Eun Mee Kim was especially helpful in facilitating the early phase of this project. Stan Holwitz, Su-Hwan Im, Ann Lee, Kathleen McHugh, Keiko Sakamoto, Frank Shin, and Bill

Witte kindly supported our research in Los Angeles. We would also like to thank Tina Choi, Kathy and Nelson Graburn, Mahee Lie, and Leslie Salzinger in Berkeley; Steven Deutsch, Linda Fuller, and Greg McLauchlan in Eugene; Ed Bruner, Harvey Choldin, Clark Cunningham, Norm Denzin, Walter Feinberg (and the Program for the Study of Cultural Values and Ethics, University of Illinois at Urbana-Champaign), Alma Gottlieb, JaHyun Haboush, Hu Ying, Bill Kelleher, Jun Hwang Kim, David Plath, Patricia Sandler, and Ron Toby in the Urbana-Champaign area; Norma Field in Chicago; Charles Abelmann, Rena and Walter Abelmann, Eve Epstein, Jim Kim, and Cara Seiderman in the Boston-Cambridge area; Ruth Abelmann and Woody Phelps in New Hampshire; Hiroshi Ishida and Sawako Shirahase in New York; Susan Kim and Jack Lee in Austin; Diego Quiroga in Quito; Keiko Nakayama and Hideki Watanabe in Tokyo; the Murakami family in Osaka; Jane and Harry Lie in Honolulu; and Jean Kyung and Byung Ho Chung in Ch'ŏngju. Eri Fujieda, Miwako Kuno, Sang Ah Park, and Jesook Song provided helpful research assistance. We thank Jane Domier for efficiently producing the maps for this book. We are also grateful to the staff of the libraries at the University of Illinois at Urbana-Champaign, the University of California, Berkeley, and the University of California, Los Angeles, especially the Asian American Studies Reading Room.

We have drawn on an impressive group of scholars writing on Korean Americans. That we disagree with some of their analyses and conclusions should not contravene our enormous respect for their scholarship. Certainly, a 1978 lament—"Among major Asian-American groups, probably less is known about Korean Americans than about any other"—is no longer true (B. L. Kim 1978, p. 177). In particular, we would like to thank Won Moo Hurh, Kwang Chung Kim, In-Jin Yoon, and Eui-Young Yu for sharing their thoughts and writings with us.

Rena Abelmann, Walter Abelmann, Tina Choi, Won Moo Hurh, Ann Lee, Soo-Jung Lee, Rebecca Matthews, Laura Nelson, Eun Hui Ryo, and Karen Winter-Nelson each read the entire manuscript and offered thoughtful comments and criticisms. We are extremely grateful to them.

At Harvard University Press, Michael Aronson was very supportive throughout. Elizabeth Gretz was a superb and scrupulous editor. We are also grateful for Norah Vincent's kind attention to our manuscript. Bruce Cumings and an anonymous referee provided us with enormously helpful suggestions.

The epigraph is taken from John Berger, *And Our Faces, My Heart, Brief as Photos* (New York: Pantheon Books, 1984), copyright © 1984 by John Berger.

Finally, we would like to thank our students at the University of Illinois at Urbana-Champaign, the University of Oregon, and Yonsei University. Our reckoning of the L.A. riots was mediated through our teaching. In the spring of 1992, we were both teaching: Abelmann on the "Korean Diaspora" in Urbana; Lie on "Asian Americans" and "Theories of Ethnicity" in Eugene. Although our students were far away from Southern California, the riots had a tremendous impact not only on Korean American students but on other class members as well. Classroom discussions raised questions we could not answer; students' anguish and anger, sorrow and soul-searching, demanded sustained responses. Intellectual bafflement and emotional urgency initially took us to Los Angeles after the term was over, and we returned again and again to listen to the Korean American voices we heard there. They constitute the heart of this book. As we wrote, our classroom concerns were never far away; we hope that we have answered at least some of the questions we could not answer in the spring of 1992.

Every migrant knows in his heart of hearts that it is impossible to return. Even if he is physically able to return, he does not truly return, because he himself has been so deeply changed by his emigration. It is equally impossible to return to that historical state in which every village was the center of the world. The one hope of re-creating a center now is to make it the entire earth. Only worldwide solidarity can transcend modern homelessness. Fraternity is too easy a term; forgetting Cain and Abel, it somehow promises that all problems can be soluble. In reality many are insoluble—hence the never-ending need for solidarity.

—John Berger, *And Our Faces, My Heart, Brief as Photos*

1

The Los Angeles Riots, the Korean American Story

The focused destruction of Korean American businesses and the dramatic image of armed Korean Americans on Los Angeles rooftops during the L.A. riots piqued public attention. Koreans? Why are they in Los Angeles? Are they hated? Are they hateful? The mayhem of fire, looting, and vigilantism seemed to augur an apocalyptic vision of a race war, a real-life preview of Ridley Scott's film *Blade Runner*. Frank Chin, an Asian American writer, saw Korean Americans with Uzis and AK-47s guarding their own and compatriots' shops, and wondered: "The Alamo in Koreatown was a mini-mall. In the race war that's started, are we all going to choose up sides and appear at the appropriate mini-mall to man the barricades?" (1992, p. 41).

In the media barrage during and after the riots, Korean Americans came to occupy a particular place in the American ideological landscape. They were often invoked to support one point or another about the L.A. riots. Imagined variously as quintessential or exceptional immigrants, as culturally legible or inscrutable, as racist or oppressed, Korean Americans emerged at the crossroads of conflicting social reflections over the L.A. riots. Through the Korean American story, observers decried the "death of the immigrant dream," underscored intra-minority racism, and again and again offered formulaic cultural contrasts between Korean Americans and African Americans. *Blue Dreams* presents the Korean American story against the backdrop of the L.A. riots, media bafflement, and the contentious American debates over capitalism, race, and community.

Making Sense of the L.A. Riots

On March 3, 1991, Rodney King, a twenty-five-year-old African American living in Altadena, California, was speeding down a highway in San Fernando Valley, when he was stopped, shot by a stun gun, and repeatedly kicked and beaten by police officers.[1] What distinguished this episode of police brutality was that the "excessive force" used against King was videotaped by George Holliday, a nearby resident, and repeatedly shown on television news shows throughout the United States. Whether the grainy imagery confirmed suspicions of police brutality and racism or shattered myths of police civility and fairness, very few doubted that the worst offenders in the King beating would stand accused and be duly punished.[2] Yet, on April 29, 1992, twelve Simi Valley jurors—ten European Americans, one Latino, and one Asian American—acquitted all four officers standing trial: Stacey Koon, Laurence Powell, Timothy Wind, and Theodore Briseno.[3]

The dissonance between the manifest guilt and the innocent verdict stunned virtually the whole country. As the *Los Angeles Times* reported:

> Mayor Bradley appeared at a press conference, saying he was stunned, shocked and outraged: "I was speechless when I heard that verdict. Today this jury told the world that what we saw with our own eyes is not a crime." Joseph Lowery, president of the Southern Christian Leadership Conference, expressed fear for the nation. Even in South Africa, he said, white police officers are punished for beating blacks. Benjamin Hooks, the executive director of the NAACP, called the verdicts outrageous: "Given the evidence, it is difficult to see how the jurors will ever live with their consciences." (1992a, p. 45; see also 1992c, pt. 4)

In many parts of the United States, angry demonstrations, civil disobedience, rioting, and looting broke out. In San Francisco, a curfew was declared for the first time since the 1906 earthquake; in Las Vegas, uprisings occurred four weekends in a row; in Seattle, Atlanta, and other cities around the country, demonstrations and disturbances rocked urban centers.[4] Nowhere was the violence more pronounced than in Los Angeles. After three days of what came to be known as the L.A. riots, there were an estimated "58 dead, 2,400 injured, 11,700 arrested, [and] $717 million in damages."[5] It was the worst urban upheaval since the 1965 Watts riots, and perhaps since the 1863 New York City Draft Riots.[6] The social historian Mike Davis commented: "It is becoming clear that the King case may be almost as much of a watershed in American history as Dred Scott, a test of the very meaning of the citizenship for which African Americans have struggled for 400 years."[7]

An event of such magnitude, not surprisingly, became an occasion for multifarious reactions and reflections. Perhaps the only consensus was that something seemed deeply wrong with Los Angeles and the United States.[8] The British journalist Martin Walker remarked: "One of the world's richest cities, for so long the ultimate lure in the land of opportunity, has torn itself apart. America's free market has its costs, its democracy fails to embrace so many of its poor, and the high temple of consumer capitalism has been pillaged by its own excluded worshippers" (1992a, p. 7). *Understanding the Riots,* written by the staff of the *Los Angeles Times,* concluded its narrative with: "Los Angeles had come to symbolize an ugly side of the American dream—hatred among races, a widening gap between rich and poor, the rise in urban violence and the seeming impotence of society's institutions" (1992a, p. 139). Whether one was black or white, Korean or Latino, poor or rich, on the left or right, the L.A. riots were a symptom of a deeper malaise afflicting Los Angeles in particular and the United States in general.

Beyond the universal acknowledgment of this malaise, the understanding of the L.A. riots spanned the full range of the U.S. political spectrum. Perhaps it is the most trite of truisms to say that most people saw what they wanted to see in the L.A. riots. Indeed, many people's analyses were shaped by their preconceptions and political perspectives. For some radicals, they were the beginning of a much-awaited revolution by the oppressed, a "black *intifada*" (Davis 1992a, p. 3); for liberals, they denoted the failure of Republican domestic policy; for some conservatives, they were the outbreak of a paroxysm of violence and nihilism of the underclass. Coming as they did in an election year, politicians jumped to explain the "problems" and offer "solutions."

For progressives and radicals, particularly among African Americans, the "fire" of Los Angeles was not a "riot" but a "rebellion" or even the beginning of a "revolution," not "mindless" violence but an "organized insurrection." The poet June Jordan saw in "fire everywhere" a simmering sentiment for social justice and a hope for a political movement against racism and oppression: "I am beginning to sense a victory of spirit risen from the death of self-hatred. I am beginning to envision our collective turning to the long-term tasks of justice and equal rights to life, liberty, and the pursuit of happiness right inside this country that has betrayed our trust repeatedly. Behold the fire everywhere!" (1992, p. 13). Robin D. G. Kelley, a professor at the University of Michigan, wrote: "As I watched 'on the ground' videotape of the black and Latino poor seizing property and destroying what many regarded as symbols of domination, I could not help but notice the joy and sense of empowerment expressed in their faces. It strengthened my belief that the inner cities are the logical place for a new radical movement in post–cold war America" (1992, p. 796).[9]

More prosaically, the U.S. Representative from South Central Los Angeles, Maxine Waters, said: "The fact of the matter is, whether we like it or not, riot is the voice of the unheard" (Cockburn 1992a, p. 17). The Detroit-based journal *Against the Current* proclaimed: "The first and essential response to the explosion in Los Angeles must be: *This rebellion was justified, as was the 1965 uprising in Watts and those in between*" (1992, front cover). The journalist James Ridgeway concurred: "The looting in the streets of Los Angeles was nothing compared to the massive theft openly conducted over the past 12 years by political officials of the Reagan and Bush administrations" (1992, p. 27; see also Colhoun 1992; Lang 1992; Rothstein 1992).

Yet some African Americans, particularly of the middle class, were deeply ambivalent. While understanding the motivation, some nonetheless remained critical of the rioting and looting. Dympna Ugwu-Oju, a professor at Middlesex County College, asked: "Could I tell [my children] that I understand the senseless actions of those black youths and not misdirect them? Could I tell them that while I do not condone their violence, I forgive it?" (1992, p. 17). An African American manager of a law firm explained: "I don't agree with the looting, but I understand the frustration" (George 1992, p. 13). Myra Bauman, managing partner of a public relations firm, responded: "I don't condone the riots. I understand the riots. I understand them as being a result of people who are looking to vent what is pent-up frustration. In some cases, people who don't have, didn't have clothing or didn't have certain household items. . . . Some who were just simply crying out in frustration" (Los Angeles Times 1992c, pt. 3, p. 9). Gary Phillips, "active for the last 20 years in African American community organizing," wrote:

The wellspring of the riot—police abuse, lack of economic equity, underserved schools, years of neglect—were understood. They were the same conditions that led to Watts 27 years ago. But I had no romanticized view that the people were in the streets taking justice into their own hands. Otherwise, Black-owned businesses . . . would not have been gutted. The oldest continuously operated Black bookstore in America (opened in 1941), the Aquarian Book Shop . . . was burned down because it had the misfortune of being in a strip mall that was looted and then firebombed. . . . The mob ruled, not politics. (1992, p. 3)

Among mainstream liberals, the L.A. riots offered an occasion to criticize twelve years of Republican presidency. Senator Bill Bradley, for instance, reasoned that the "tragedy" of Los Angeles resulted from the public and politicians' "distortion and silence" on "the issue of race and urban America." He stressed the need for a "new democratic movement," which "must start with the acknowledgment that slavery was America's original sin and race remains our unresolved dilemma" (1992, pp. 10, 12). The solution "can occur only by winning over all segments of urban life to a new politics of change, empowerment, and common effort." Similarly, Jesse Jackson noted that "the riots in Los Angeles and elsewhere remind us just how incalculable the costs of neglect are" (1992, pp. 6, 1). Like Bradley, the charismatic African American politician spoke of the need "to rebuild our cities, to invest in people, to provide hope." Bill Clinton, then a Democratic presidential hopeful, echoed Bradley and Jackson in blaming the riots on "twelve years of denial and neglect" by the Reagan and Bush administrations (Walker 1992b, p. 10).

At the other end of the American political spectrum, the conservative writer Mark Horowitz simply found the riots humorous: "Not many people thought the Los Angeles Riot was funny, but I did. I freely admit it. I enjoyed great sweeps of it. I suppose you could say I had a good riot" (1992, p. 16). More ominously, Patrick Buchanan sounded an apocalyptic note. Comparing the looters to Brown Shirts and Red Guards, he warned that "what we saw in Los Angeles was evil exultant and triumphant" (1992, pp. 11, 14). While Bradley and Jackson spoke of racism and poverty, Buchanan invoked "a religious war going on for the soul of America." In contrast to the progressive prescription of anti-racism, empowerment, and the economic rejuvenation of inner cities, Buchanan's remedy was religious: "The war for the soul of America will only be won with basic truths [which] are spelled out explicitly in the Old and New Testaments."

Most conservatives, like Buchanan, condemned what they perceived as the mindless anarchy and pathological violence of the poor. They attempted to find the source of the riots in the moral depravity of the rioters and the larger society. The California Senator John Seymour, who was later defeated in the 1992 U.S. Senate election, observed: "Finally, there must be a return to family values and community respect" (McNelis-Ahern 1992, p. 15). In keeping with his bashing of the television program *Murphy Brown* for positively depicting a single mother, Vice President Dan Quayle said of the riots: "I believe the lawless social anarchy which we saw is directly related to the breakdown of family structure, personal responsibility and social order in too many areas of our society" (Rosenthal 1992, p. A1). President George Bush, after his spokesperson Marlin Fitzwater blamed the riots on social welfare programs since the 1960s, noted: "What we saw in Los Angeles is not about civil rights. It is not about the great cause of equality that all Americans must uphold. It is not a message of protest. It has been the brutality of a mob, pure and simple."[10]

No doubt the memory of the burning flames in Los Angeles played its part in overturning twelve years of Republican rule, as most voters emphasized the sluggish economy over "family values" at the polls. Yet it should be noted that poverty and inner-city problems remained virtually taboo topics in the 1992 presidential election campaign. The national debate on the origins and meanings of the L.A. riots reached no specific consensus or conclusions (see Georges and Joseph 1992; Gooding-Williams 1993; Kang et al. 1993; Kō and Rī 1993; Madhubuti 1993).

The Riots in Black and White

The 1992 Los Angeles riots were originally reported as a reprise of the 1965 Watts Rebellion. The 1965 civil disturbance, which resulted in 34 dead, over 1,000 injured, and nearly 4,000 arrested (the vast majority of them African Americans), epitomized the twin failures of liberal social reforms and moderate civil rights movements (Edsall and Edsall 1991, p. 50; see also Fogelson 1969; Henry 1990, pp. 54–59). As televised images of African Americans rioting and looting—"Burn, Baby,

Burn!"—became etched in the American memory, Watts came to signify "black race riots," which raged across the United States in the
1960s (Feagin and Hahn 1973). While these riots revealed rising expectations of urban African Americans and their frustration with the
Johnson administration and the "nonviolent" civil rights movement,
they also prompted Republicans to unleash "a full-scale assault on liberal social policies" (Edsall and Edsall 1991, p. 51). The "race riots" thus
set the stage for burning political debates over race, city, poverty, and
welfare—central issues in the United States since the 1970s.

The disparate responses to the 1992 riots represented, at first glance,
a continuation of the debates unleashed by the 1960s "race riots." For
many, the 1992 L.A. riots reconfirmed the 1968 Kerner Commission
report, which stated: "To continue our present policies is to make
permanent the division of our country into two societies; one, largely
Negro and poor, located in central cities; the other, predominantly
white and affluent, located in the suburbs and in outlying areas" (National Advisory Commission on Civil Disobedience 1988, p. 22). The
Economist expressed its opinion on its editorial page: "An apparently
racist verdict, followed by black riots, seems to have confirmed both
blacks and whites in an instinctive distrust of each other" (1992a,
p. 13). *Time* wrote: "As Los Angeles smolders, black and white Americans and the country try to comprehend the verdict and the future of
social relations" (Church 1992, p. 18). In discussing the beating of the
truck driver Reginald Denny during the riots, Lance Morrow commented: "The truck-driver video accomplished the amazing task of
nullifying the Rodney King video. . . . On that level of discussion, if
Americans choose to stay there, there can only be a gridlock of rage:
blacks make demons of whites, whites make demons of blacks" (1992,
p. 68; see also Los Angeles Times 1992b, p. 9).

Yet the facile imagery of the black race riot, 1992 as a reprise of
1965, belied what was obvious to most eyes: the multiethnic composition of looters and victims. Indeed, the L.A. riots have come to be
widely characterized as "the nation's first multiethnic urban riot."[11]
Along with the Denny beating, "the pictures of Korean boys with Uzis
keeping watch from a rooftop and the shots of several buildings in full
frame, constituted the main iconography of the first 36 or so hours of
the riot" (Decter 1992, p. 18; see also Palumbo-Liu 1994). As television
viewers and journalists in Los Angeles came to appreciate the multiethnic character of the L.A. riots, simple parallels with the 1965 Watts

upheaval no longer seemed adequate.[12] It turned out, for example, that one of the "white" police officers, Theodore Briseno, was part Latino (Skerry 1993, p. 9). No longer were African Americans the only rioters; Latinos constituted over half of the arrested (Lieberman 1992, p. B3; Lieberman and O'Reilly 1993). Many of the victims were not "white"; Korean Americans were the single most visible group of victims. More than half of the 3,100 Korean American businesses in Los Angeles suffered damages, totaling $350 million (D. H. Kim 1992, p. 1). When the L.A. riots are viewed as essentially "black and white," a variation on the saga of "race" in the United States—slavery, civil war, Jim Crow, civil rights—Korean Americans and other ethnic populations are rendered invisible and irrelevant.[13]

The Curious Role of Korean Americans

The multiethnic reality of Los Angeles struck us forcefully on one of our first days of fieldwork in Los Angeles. When a Korean American man addressed in English a seemingly African American guard at a mini-mall in Koreatown, the guard replied in Korean: "I am Korean; don't speak to me in English." The son of an African American military man stationed in South Korea and a South Korean mother, he in fact preferred to use Korean. On the same day, a middle-aged Korean American we had just interviewed in his jewelry shop encouraged us to interview his sister-in-law. A long drive took us to an affluent suburb and a sprawling home, where a Korean American woman was giving orders in Spanish to a Latina maid who was taking care of the woman's four children. Losing our way home around the interminable surface streets of Los Angeles, we stopped at one of the few unburned and unlooted "swap meets"—modeled after open-air markets in South Korea—to ask for directions. When Abelmann, a European American woman, asked one of the seemingly Latino guards in English, he spoke in Korean to a middle-aged Korean American woman, "Come here, she is asking a question." When Abelmann then asked again, this time in Korean, the woman was unfazed and simply gave her directions in Korean. In Los Angeles, nothing seemed obvious; certainly things were not black and white.

The broadcasted images of the multiethnic riot featured Korean Americans in unexpected places and in surprising poses. The prevalence of Korean-language signs near downtown Los Angeles—indeed, the very existence of Koreatown—must have been news for some viewers. More striking, armed Korean Americans on rooftops and in cruising vehicles overturned the stereotype of meek and diffident Asian Americans.

For those who explored beneath the surface of the L.A. riots, then, the curious but crucial role of the Korean Americans became inescapable. Some saw a simmering and seething interethnic conflict between African Americans and Korean Americans as one of the significant stories behind the riots. They noted that the ferocity of African American anger against the "Rodney King verdict" could be understood only in the context of the earlier light sentence against Soon Ja Du. Du, a Korean American grocer, shot and killed Latasha Harlins, a fifteen-year-old African American girl, after an in-store squabble over a shoplifting charge. The shooting, in cold blood, was videotaped by an anti-theft camera. "Latasha Harlins. A name that was scarcely mentioned on television was the key to the catastrophic collapse of relations between L.A.'s black and Korean communities" (Davis 1992a, p. 5; see also Kō and Rī 1993, pp. 34–35). Richard Rodriguez wrote: "We cannot settle for black and white conclusions when one of the most important conflicts was the tension between Koreans and African-Americans" (1992, p. M1). Thus the "black-Korean conflict" was sometimes presented as one of the key factors of the L.A. riots. Many Korean Americans, as we shall see, disagreed vehemently; we too criticize the "black-Korean conflict" frame in Chapter 6.

Like the responses to the L.A. riots, media portrayal of Korean Americans varied widely. In accounts decrying the mob violence, Korean Americans emerged as the model minority, immigrant entrepreneurs who had realized the American dream. The conservative author William Murchison wrote: "For Korean merchants the looters reserved a special fury. I should ask parenthetically, isn't it time our society showed some concern over the well-being of these honest, hardworking, lovable people, the Koreans, who prosper in the black ghettos only to arouse their customers' wrath when they prosper too well?" (1992, p. 12).

In contrast, Korean Americans played a more ambiguous role in other accounts, as part exploiter and part victim. John Edgar Wideman offers what might be a canonical progressive interpretation of Korean Americans' role in the L.A. riots:

Koreans arrived determined to be merchants, buying failing businesses in Hispanic and black neighborhoods. The function of such
businesses in the larger economic picture is to snatch back the few
dollars that trickle down into the hands of the working poor, the
unemployed, mothers on welfare, the elderly on social security,
exploiting segments of the public that big business no longer
deems worth the trouble to service. Since labor is expensive,
Korean businesses tended to be family concerns. Long hours, hard
work, minimal overhead, streamlined services were survival strategies. Korean businesses monopolized the cash coming into the
community and eventually turned a profit, prospering and expanding while the neighborhoods supporting them languished. An
explosion was inevitable, a systemic failure whose symptom, not
cause, was racial animosity between Koreans and other people of
color. (1992, p. 155)

Even in Wideman's considered response, however, Korean Americans
merely fill a particular niche in his interpretation of the L.A. riots.[14]
With a few exceptions—such as the lawyer Angela Oh's appearance on
Ted Koppel's *Nightline* after a campaign waged by Korean Americans—
Korean Americans were virtually shut out of the mainstream media in
the United States. They were widely discussed but largely silent.

None of the portraits of Korean Americans across the American
ideological spectrum captured the complex realities of Korean American lives. In part this was because writers mobilized Korean Americans
for one or another interpretation of the riots. There are, of course,
glimpses of truth in many of these accounts. Yet we must be mindful
both of the transnational dimension of Korean Americans and of their
irreducible diversity. In turn, understanding their situations and listening to their voices challenges some of the dominant assumptions about
the United States.

2

Reckoning via the Riots

We have suggested that the L.A. riots became a national point of reflection; here we suggest a parallel reckoning among Korean Americans. In 1990, approximately a quarter of the nation's 800,000 Korean Americans lived in Southern California (Yu 1993, p. 144).

Korean Americans in Los Angeles responded to the destruction of the riots, their representation by the media, and government intervention in many ways. The voices and stories in this chapter are not limited to the riot victims, but encompass Korean Americans of various social positions. The voices and vignettes that follow portray Korean American diversity in Los Angeles and reveal a creative tension between U.S. and South Korean ideologies and meanings.

At the heart of Korean Americans' riot responses is a contest over the meaning and direction of the Korean diaspora.[1] This struggle engages both the U.S. ideological landscape and the South Korean memory-scape, the sense of what has been left behind in the homeland. The prevalence of borderland ideologies of culture and nation—idioms that traverse place and time—is striking. In other words, these responses speak to the transnational reality of multiethnic Los Angeles.

Two refrains punctuated many of our interviews: "You know Koreans; you know what I mean" and "you know [South] Korea." They underscored South Korea as a ubiquitous presence in riot reckoning. These refrains signaled that the speaker had touched on matters where the "a to z" of it was a shared cultural terrain; the nods and the *"ye ye"* (yes, yes) they anticipated allowed the discussion to move forward. Yet in spite of the seeming fixity of South Korea and Korean identity, we will see that places and identifications are unstable. In this vein, James Clifford asks: "What does it mean, at the end of the twentieth century, to speak . . . of a 'native land'?" (1988, p. 275); and Stuart Hall suggests that ethnicity "is located in a relation to a whole set of notions about territory, about where is home and where is overseas, what is close to us and what is far away" (1991, p. 22). Immigrations, immigrant lives, and ethnic identities belie easy characterization. Immigrants arrive in complex political, economic, and ideological contexts; immigrant lives inhabit multifarious spaces at several crossroads; and ethnicities are always in flux. In short, migrations, immigrant lives, and ethnicities are born and nurtured amid a stream of political ideologies, material goods, and media images flowing across national boundaries.[2]

Transnational Narratives on the Riots

We begin with three Korean Americans who explain the riots through both U.S. and South Korean idioms and ideologies. The following sketches—of Choi, a retailer serving the Latino community whose store was spared in the riots; Park, a former retailer and currently a full-time community "activist"; and Lim, an import-export business tycoon—remind us that Korean Americans are heterogeneous.

Choi, a college-educated clothing wholesaler, moved easily between American and South Korean ideological frameworks. He prided himself on his keen knowledge and understanding of the players in the riots. His dialogue moved from perspective to perspective, presenting a wide-ranging catalogue of riot causes and in effect calling for sympathy for all participants through his empathetic portrayals of merchants, looters, bystanders, police, and others. He finished almost every thought with: "Now if I were standing in other shoes, let me tell you what I would think." As he stretched the limits of empathy, his wife giggled at what seemed to be his typical conversational style. It wasn't hard to identify a sermon-like quality in his ruminations, and indeed he spoke at some length about his pastor's plea for understanding in his post-riot preaching. As a church-going Christian, Choi is among the Korean American majority; a glance about his suburban home revealed the markings of a Christian abode in South Korea, including carvings of Jesus and a prominently hung framed velveteen copy of the Last Supper.

Accounting for African Americans' failings by contrasting them with Korean Americans, Choi invoked both South Korean maxims of progress and South Korean ideologies of cultural identity. Although many Korean Americans noted the failings of their own community leadership, he instead stressed the dearth of African American leaders: "They have no hope for work—no leaders, no hopes, no dreams. There are no leaders to give them dreams. Even though they know the system and the language, after two or three years we are doing better than they are. They need the idea of 'if you try you will succeed' [hamyŏn toenda]; they need dreams." Hamyŏn toenda is a popular maxim in South Korea, found printed on an array of surfaces, including small banners and plastic trophies that rest on student desks, hang in offices, and even decorate living rooms. It is one of a number of aphorisms that have cheered accelerated economic growth, intense labor exploitation, and tortuous educational examinations in South Korea. Choi continued that, devoid of vision and hopes, African Americans are entirely powerless in the face of "whites" because they have no homeland consciousness (kohyang ŭisik). His perspective emerges from his personal identification with South Korea, his persistent identity as a proud Korean in the United States. He comments: "Every black I meet I ask them where they are from and none of them, none of them, say Africa or name an African country, Algeria, Kenya, or wherever. . . . They all say the United States. Now you ask Koreans [where they are from] and they will all say Korea. That is the problem [with African Americans]." Borderland or hyphenated identities have been alien to many Korean Americans, even as they traversed South Korean and American idioms and identities.[3] After the riots, however, many Korean Americans reconsidered their "natural" identification with South Korea.

For Choi, the American dream and a homeland consciousness are necessary complements. In South Korea, dreams of success have been powerfully nationalized through the country's aspiration to become, and its success in becoming, a world economic player. In turn, the Korean concept of hamyŏn toenda finds its ideological double in the American dream. In this way, national identification—not with the United States, but with South Korea or an African nation-state—is seen as the key to such success. This narrative's ironic twist—immigrant success nationalized via the homeland—demonstrates a persistent theme of this book: the transnational context of diaspora lives and ideologies.

A memorable interview with Park revealed, as in our discussion with Choi, a convergence of U.S. and South Korean cultural frames. Park, who is in his early thirties, was active in the local militia that emerged in the riot mayhem; he was also a central member of a group of young men interested in "protecting" the Korean American community, a group regarded by many Korean Americans, he explained, as "crazy" and "illegal." Many objected that his group allows—and he admitted "encourages"—minors to carry guns. They have taken up such activities as boycotting distributors of "Black Korea," the infamous song by Ice Cube in which Korean Americans are repudiated and targeted for retaliation (J. Chang 1993). A paragon of macho bravado, Park boasted of his, albeit unidentifiable, television appearance in a brawl with an African American. Defying easy classification, however, he proceeded immediately to stories of African Americans who sang his praises during his days of riot patrol. Park confessed little interest in Korean affairs. He is indifferent, for example, to the cause of Korean reunification, but proclaims Korean superiority and is devoted to spearheading security activities on behalf of Korean Americans.

Unwilling to talk to any media representatives, Park agreed, through a beeper phone call, to meet us for "only one reason," which he revealed toward the end of our three hours together: because we had mentioned *illyuhak* (anthropology) over the phone. As many people do in South Korea, he took *illyuhak* (literally, human-group-study) to mean the study of the history of the peoples or races of the world. He wanted to tell us his version of that history: "Believe me, it has nothing to do with the fact that you are professors or that you can speak Korean." He had wanted to publish his theory of world history in the local Korean-language newspaper, but he had been politely told that it would cause a scandal, or even "another riot." He reminisced that when he had immigrated to the United States as a young man he had dreamed of becoming a *paksa* (Ph.D.), but a decade later he lamented that he had been unable even to finish high school.

We met Park, who explained that we would find him dressed in military fatigues, at a bake shop exactly like those in Seoul. His brusque quip to the young woman at the counter—"what do you have here anyway?"—didn't seem out of place in this setting. Over milk and confectioneries, the standard bake shop fare, Park began to map out—in words and in a series of busy diagrams—the history and future of the world. His *illyuhak* or ethno-history glided across centuries and continents, mapping winners and losers in world history. In it we recognized both an assessment of ethnic Los Angeles, particularly the labor relationships among African Americans, Latinos, Korean Americans, and European Americans, and an essentialist cultural portrait of "superior Koreans." He reviewed the relationship between "whites" and "Indians" (Native Americans): "The Indians weren't willing to work for the whites; they tried to fight back. They were beaten up and they died [out]. . . . This is where the blacks came in. They were brought in as slaves when the Indians wouldn't work." In passing he remarked that like Native Americans, Koreans also tried to resist, but ended up becoming colonized by, the Japanese. Proceeding from the arrival of slaves, he sketched parallel relations among Korean Americans, African Americans, and Latinos in the contemporary United States: "Blacks won't work hard—they won't work at minimum wages for Koreans, but Hispanics will." He predicted that within two hundred years, African Americans, like Native Americans before them, would die out; Latinos, by contrast, would rise up and become politically powerful like blacks today. As for the Koreans, "they will end up like whites, and whites will end up like Indians in some two hundred years." And so Park prophesied Korean Americans becoming like European Americans, and Latinos becoming like African Americans.

Against the tide of his fantastically racialized narrative, Park offered a utopian aside: "What *should happen* is 'We are the world' [a reference to the World Aid song lyrics]—forget about these colors [races]." Quickly, though, he went on to discuss Koreans' superiority, their unbelievable accomplishments over the last twenty years in both South Korea and the United States. He joked, though, about the success: "Koreans are labor slaves, but because Americans live better, the slaves do also. . . . We look rich because we live above our means; we don't look like slaves."

At first glance a rather fantastic millennial fable, Park's sketch delineated African Americans' unwillingness to work for Korean Americans in the same stroke that portrayed Native Americans' resistance to European Americans. As for European Americans, Park minced no words: "Whites think other people are like rats—they have a superiority complex." For Korean Americans, however, he reserved a twilight zone in the race war, between domination and enslavement. Park's soliloquy on the U.S. multiethnic labor structure is not totally enigmatic. His discussion reminded us of Korean millennial visions during the colonial era (1910-1945), which imagined the coming of an age when Korea would reign over other nations. In South Korea, where grand histories of the world à la H. G. Wells or Arnold Toynbee have been popular, such accounts are not entirely exceptional.

Like the clothing wholesaler Choi, Park also takes on the African American plight; both reckon the U.S. racial equation through transnational idioms. Our discussions with Choi and Park may not sound like direct riot responses in that they are not simple retorts to the largely African American and Latino destruction of Korean American property. Considered, complex, and transnational, however, they are typical of the ruminations we encountered in the months following the riots. When after two hours we moved to end our discussion with Park, he insisted that we chat together longer: "We will probably never meet again in this world so let's take every minute we can." He ended by suggesting that "everyone is a philosopher, but it is just that not all of us can write things down; almost everybody has a version, a philosophy, of the world historical story leading to the L.A. riots."

Lim, a wealthy immigrant who made his money in import and export before immigration and who maintains a domicile in Seoul, also comfortably straddled transnational spaces in his riot reckoning. Like Choi and Park, he addressed the plight of African Americans, but went further in implicating Korean Americans in the riots beyond Choi's homespun migrants or Park's labor slaves.

Lim, whom we met over lunch at an upscale hotel coffee shop in glittery Century City, assessed the causes of the riots by simultaneously asserting that "Koreans had nothing to do with it" *and* offering a lengthy explanation of why *"Koreans* had it coming." He believed that "the Koreans in South Central had it coming for twenty years." He marveled that the riots took so long to happen: "If it had been Koreans living in a place like South Central—and outside businesses came in—believe me Koreans wouldn't have waited twenty years. Things would have exploded after a few years. The United States is a patient country, a very patient country—people really put up with things. Blacks have a great deal of perseverance." In an entirely different vein, however, Lim argued that Koreans had absolutely nothing to do with the riots—it was only the happenstance of which areas were guarded that affected the Koreans: "The blacks were headed for the rich white neighborhoods like mine [Century City]."

Over chicken pot pie, one of Lim's culinary favorites dating back to his early days as an immigrant, "Korea" and the "United States" emerged as neighboring districts, as if L.A.'s Koreatown were a ward of Seoul.[4] He wanted us to understand that one cannot begin to talk about the riots without knowing the backgrounds of "these people," the Korean American merchants in Los Angeles. In stark contrast to Choi, he described the great chasm between "Koreans in the United States" and South Koreans: "If people think that there is a distance between blacks and Koreans, it is nothing compared to the distance between Koreans here [United States] and there [South Korea]. If they think blacks blew up at Koreans in South Central, watch what would happen if all of them [Korean Americans] went back to Korea today." He suggested that Korean immigrants are by now unwelcome in South Korea. "The Koreans in the United States," he stressed, "are all people who have been looked down upon in Korea." Failures at home, Lim's immigrants arrive in the United States with their eyes still fixed on South Korean compatriots and cohort groups, from whom they seek redemption and clamor for respect.

Lim does not hesitate to count himself among those looking back, but of course he isn't a retailer in South Central Los Angeles.

Do you know why people in Korea come here? Many people don't talk about this. They leave to *show people*, to *show people* that they can make it. That is the whole problem [in the riots]. Koreans here only care about what people back home think so they just want to get rich the quickest way possible—two years, not twenty—they don't care one bit about contributing to this [U.S.] society. They don't know anything about the United States and its problems. That is where you get these guys driving their Mercedes to South Central and infuriating the blacks. . . . Part of this whole problem is the [South] Korean government: it only praises immigrants who give money back to Korea. So there is no consciousness about what a good immigrant is—someone who contributes to American society.

Explaining that "there is no one who knows they can make it in Korea who comes [to the United States]," Lim was convinced that the entire immigration—and by extension, the riots—could only be understood by acknowledging that the point of all reference continues to be South Korea. His sister-in-law, who joined us for lunch, verified his claims. A South Korean citizen and resident of Seoul who is educating her children in the United States, she periodically took part in the conversation to stress that nowadays Korean Americans are "beggars" (*kŏji*) or poor people in the eyes of South Koreans.

At the heart of the immigration, Lim continued, is that in South Korea "those who aren't born well are full of themselves"—lower-class people are always putting on airs. He explained: "[In South Korea] if a person is 'born well' there is absolutely no reason for such pretension."[5] Thus he portrayed the immigration as the revenge of the excluded, and diaspora identity as but revenge's accomplice. Repeating the expression—"those who aren't born well are full of themselves"—over and over, he went so far as to profess that every mistake he has made in his own life can be traced to this aphoristic folly: "Even though I know about this [tendency] it still hasn't stopped me from failing." Continuing with even greater dramatic flair, he ventured to say that this bravado will only cease when the current generation dies: "The frustration [of having been put down] lasts an entire generation." He predicts that, even after the riots, Korean Americans will continue to do anything to be able to show that they are making it. Hence he assaults the South Korean image of the "good [Korean] immigrant" who continues to contribute to the homeland. South Koreans will continue to emigrate because "the Korean land mass will never satisfy all Koreans' aspirations." Although he described an immigration of frustrated people of humble birth, he also noted that most Koreans in the United States would not go back to South Korea even for money, "even an instant $2,000." They would not want to return, he explained, to the pollution, crowds, and headaches of Seoul. His immigrant image shifted between hapless victims of a rigid South Korean social order and brazen opportunists who "got what they deserved in the riots."

In the narratives of Choi, Park, and Lim, we find a diversity of class positions, idiomatic conventions, and riot interpretations. They are borderland narratives that challenge received views of the riots and of Korean Americans. In keeping with their allusions to the Korean past, many Korean Americans placed the L.A. riots, at least in part, in the annals of Korean history. For some this response was merely reflexive or even subconscious; for others it was self-conscious.

The Lens of the Past

Korean American discussions of the L.A. riots present a rich play of national memory and ethnic identity. Korea's twentieth-century history offers a repository for reflection on the riots. The riots are rendered as but another chapter in age-old stories. In the process, ethnic or national portraiture is posited as a reflection of this past.

One 1970s immigrant constantly repeated throughout our discussion that the roots of the riots were "deep." He complained that no one understood, that none of the depth had surfaced in any of the reporting he had read. Our discussion had wandered far from the riots when he suddenly remarked—as if he too were surprised—that "the story is so deep, it even goes back as far as the *pundan* [the North-South division of Korea]." Until then, he had stressed the complexity of twenty or thirty years of Korean immigration; now the narrative stretched back to 1945, and he worried whether his account might throw us for a loop, whether we might have to entirely refashion our analysis. His evocation of the division is meaningful because his entire family is still in North Korea; he also noted that hundreds of thousands of the North Koreans who made it south have left South Korea. Similarly, a mid-thirties male immigrant of ten years likened the situation of Korean Americans to the Korean division. At the new upscale Koreatown Plaza, he suddenly pointed to an elderly man in the foyer: "See that grandfather over there—he lived through the colonial period, a time when he couldn't freely say what he wanted to say. Then came Syngman Rhee [President of South Korea, 1948–1960] and the division of Korea; people didn't know what democracy or communism was. How can people like that [grandfather] pick a side to stand on?" Stressing the *pundan* as an externally imposed national tragedy, he went on to note that "once again [with the riots] Koreans have found themselves between 'sides' [blacks and whites]." Narratives thus moved smoothly between a United States present and a Korean past.

As those we interviewed recalled the flames and fear of the riots, the most frequent historical allusions were to wartime. Older Korean Americans who "knew war [in Korea or in Vietnam]," a Korean shorthand for drawing generational lines, said that the 4–2–9 *p'oktong* (the L.A. riots) was like "war." In the days before the retrial of the police officers in 1993, the liquor store owner Jay Shin "monitored his store from the mall's parking lot, surrounded by men who were armed," and told *Boston Globe* reporters: "I've been in Vietnam, the Korean War, and I've owned a liquor store in South Central L.A. . . . So I guess I've been in danger all my life" (Gorov and Mashberg 1993, p. 15).

In several interviews we had barely begun before our respondent told us: "Those days were exactly like it was for me in [such and such a] war."[6] One Korean American veteran of the Vietnam War and a shopkeeper since the early 1970s began talking about the ethnocentrism of Korean soldiers in Vietnam. Suddenly, however, his discussion turned to South Central Los Angeles and the riot days, highlighting the same ethnocentrism. Counselors for riot victims suggested that the Korean War was a frequent benchmark for comparison; the consensus was that the riots were worse, much worse than anything they had experienced in the war, although as one of the counselors pointed out, "Most of them were children during the war." The counselors were told repeatedly that while the Korean War was experienced as a nation, the riots did not touch the entire community. This feeling of isolation seemed to be most pronounced for the liquor store owners in South Central Los Angeles; it was less so for swap meet merchant victims who worked alongside dozens of similarly looted Korean American stalls.

For some, the riots conjured up historical memory beyond division or war, touching on colonial memory. One man said that the more he thought about the riots the more he was reminded of the great Japanese Kantō earthquake in 1923, when Korean immigrants [colonial servants] were scapegoated and thousands were killed after the quake (Weiner 1989, chap. 6). "We [Koreans] were caught between the Japanese people and the government then, just like we are today between blacks and whites." A recent college graduate was exhilarated by the Korean American lawyer and activist Angela Oh, who, while discussing the riots, "talked about our oppression from the Japanese and that there are people still alive who lived through it." For this young man, Oh's public presentation of Korean history made sense as a response to the riot destruction of Korean property. As another Korean American college graduate told us: "My family lost a prosperous factory during the colonial period. You see, [this legacy of destruction] is all inherited; yes, it's all inherited."

Allusions to the Korean past often entailed reference to historically derived cultural traits or national character.[7] In South Korea, notions that "Koreans are this or that" are a commonplace of popular and even political discourse; frequently, these shared national traits are seen as legacies of Korea's historical fate, especially colonialism and war. They are, however, often contradictory and vary enormously from one person to the next.

Yang, a wholesaler who began ten years ago in the United States "making sandwiches for Mexicans," defended his Korean American wholesaler neighborhood during the riots as a member of an armed Korean American patrol. He spoke at some length about the national character (kungminsŏng) and "heart" (maûm) of different peoples and nationalities, offering essentialized ethnic portraits. "There are different kinds of people, meat eating, vegetable eating, and so on." At his sandwich shop he tried to teach Latino customers about Korean history and stressed the importance of "sharing histories." Yang explained that Koreans "have a remarkable ability to persevere under difficult circumstances." Asking, "Do you know why Koreans eat so quickly?" he explained that this Korean trait is a wartime vestige. Similarly, a Korean American owner of a dry cleaner, "the 'highest' of businesses with *very* 'high' [class] people," claimed: "We are a nation that has lived through many hungry periods. So we have learned to work hard. We like doing everything quickly—quick, quick, quick—eat quickly, succeed quickly, get rich quickly." Yang suggested that the even greater war experience of the Vietnamese has made them even less patient. Predicting that Vietnamese Americans will succeed Korean Americans in South Central Los Angeles, just as Korean Americans succeeded Jews, he warned: "When the Vietnamese go into South Central it will be an entirely different matter: they will not put up with things the way we Koreans have—their country has been at war for thirty years."

Yang's cultural descriptions are not merely footnotes to the future of South Central Los Angeles but an interpretation of ethnic or racial tensions that surfaced in the riots. He was, however, careful to downplay the "black-Korean conflict" as a cause of the riots. Yang stressed that "to know a language and its structure is to know the culture: Japan and its *perapera, shinshin* [examples of onomatopoeic words], Korea and its guttural phrases [he dramatized these by throwing his shoulders back and sticking his chest out], Russia. . . . Now the relationship between language and culture—that's a subject worth researching, a really hard one." For Yang, racial tension in Los Angeles is the story of people who cannot talk to each other. Dramatizing his point by shifting his body back and darting a suspicious look in our direction, he explained:

"When all people can do is look askance at each other and wonder what the other is thinking about them, their imaginations start to run wild—it all takes on a life of its own having *nothing* to do with reality." In this way, his dialogue moved seamlessly from linguistic cultures to cultural tensions in the riots. His dialogue, fast-paced and confident, turned on Korean Americans who are "willing to take it"—the hardships of South Central shopkeeping and the recent destruction—because of wartime memories, including their inscription on eating practices.

For those familiar with contemporary South Korean society and the post-colonial production of cultural identity, Yang's comments are familiar. Reckoning what is Korean is a contested national venture in South Korea. A teen immigrant and son of a dry cleaner celebrated the courage of Korean Americans who returned to South Central Los Angeles to rebuild after the destruction: "They have the courage to survive; this is the pattern of Korean history—Japanese rule, invasions over and over—but we always come back. A long time ago—I'm not sure if it was a poet or a politician—someone [in Korea] said that the Korean people are like weeds, that if they are stepped on, they rise right back, and that is the way it is."

Interchangeably, Korean unity and solidarity or disunity and divisiveness were invoked in assessments of both the strengths (unity) and the failures (disunity) of the Korean American response to the riots. In the context of an ideologically divided nation, "unity" and "disunity" refer to both the local and the global. These proclivities are rendered meaningful in another context as well: the Japanese colonial era rhetoric, which charged that Korea's ancient divisions (the Three Kingdoms), its political factionalism, and its inability to "meet" the West successfully destined Korea for colonial subjugation. "Korean disunity" and "factionalism" as markers of Korean self-identity are powerful colonial vestiges (Henderson 1968, chap. 9). In this vein, a second-generation immigrant who had studied Korean history at a U.S. university recalled an "ancient Korean expression" his father had taught him—"united we are strong, divided we fall"—and proceeded to recount Korea's ancient political divisions, the Three Kingdoms and the story of their "unification," and the persisting problem of the North-South division.

Pang, a merchant who organized a militia group to protect a cluster of Korean American–owned stores during the riots, challenged this rhetoric of disunity, noting its historical roots: "People say we [Koreans] cannot unite or come together. But all of this [the response to the riots] shows just how well we Koreans come together." He continued that South Korean regionalism persists in the United States where Korean Americans from Honam (the South and North Chŏlla provinces) tend to "stick together." He was, however, careful to explain that the regionalism is the product not of cultural or national traits but of a contemporary South Korean politics of exclusion that thwarted the development of the Honam provinces: "While regionalism can in part be explained by the fact of the Three Kingdoms, it was really Park [President *Park* Chung Hee, 1961–1979] who created it." In this way Pang contested facile cultural identifications, querying their historical production and waxing optimistic about the unified riot response of Korean Americans.

As we have seen, for some Korean Americans the riots slid into the Korean national epic or into personal dramas. Other Korean Americans, however, chose to situate the riots and their beforemath and aftermath squarely in an American trajectory. In this vein, Angela Oh declared: "What is happening right now is not Korean history, it is American history" (D. Lee 1992b, p. 12). These seemingly mutually exclusive responses, however, often resided comfortably side by side.

Debating the Diaspora I: Koreatown, South Korean Nationalism, and American Ethnicity

In summoning Korean idioms and ideologies, the debate over the diaspora refers to South Korea, particularly to South Korean fashioning or imagining of the (South) Korean nation. In the interstices of many diaspora visions we find the contested contours of South Korean nationalism. In other words, the ways in which Koreans or Korean Americans think of themselves often express the idioms and sensibilities of the ways in which the Korean nation is imagined. Among Korean Americans there are competing ideas on the Korean diaspora vis-à-vis Korean political struggles; indeed, they date to the earliest days of immigration, as we will discuss in Chapter 3.

As Korean American spaces in Los Angeles multiply and suburbanize, a matter we take up in Chapter 4, enclaves emerge that defy easy characterization. Indeed, sheer numbers allow Korean Americans to bypass non-Koreans if they so choose. Save for slight shifts in architectural convention, some Los Angeles locales appear to be South Korean sites. Furthermore, one can find such spots in the L.A. suburbs as easily as in Koreatown. And yet the riots served to spotlight the "American" in "Korean American," shattering for many any pretense of ethnic insularity. Some Korean Americans sounded a clarion call to a new era. Elaine Kim, professor of Asian American literature, wrote: "What they [Korean immigrants] experienced on 29 and 30 April was a baptism into what it really means for a Korean to become American in the 1990s" (1993a, p. 219). She continued that in an "Asian American legacy of violent baptisms," the riots are to Korean Americans what internment was for Japanese Americans (p. 234). Angela Oh struck a similar chord, designating the riots "our [Korean American] rite of passage into American society" (Mydans 1993b, p. 9).

Korean American responses, as we have seen, were by no means uniform. The defense of, and the devastation in, Koreatown forced a contest over the definition of this urban space. Although Korean Americans are a residential minority, Koreatown is a symbolic center for Korean Americans in Los Angeles, and even in the United States. While the riots forced an awareness of the United States as the home of the Korean American diaspora—as one person said, "Like it or not, this is our community, we have to make our mark here"—the nature of this awareness and its corollary agenda varied enormously among Korean Americans. Riot-related events and responses led some to call for a (South) Korean center; others came to champion Koreatown as a multiethnic community.

Post-riot ruminations over what to call Korean Americans in Korean delineate the contours of this diaspora contest. Beyond mere semantic details, various Chinese character–based terms[8] for people of Korean ancestry who reside in the United States symbolically define the diaspora community. The 1993 Korean-language statement on "the background of the founding of the Korean American Research Center [KARC]," a progressive research center devoted to the study of Korean Americans and Koreans, announces that the riots brought the clear message to Korean Americans that they must shed their "guest consciousness" and "traveler consciousness." The authors of the statement appeal to Korean Americans to discard their identification as South Korean political subjects. Moreover, they call for Korean Americans to "live with dignity as leaders in social change and as masters of [U.S.] society." The notion of "master" (chuin) here simply opposes "subject [of rule]." The research center's Korean name, Miju Tongp'o Sahoe Yŏn'guso (U.S. Resident Brethren Society Research Center), employs *tongp'o*, or brethren, as opposed to *kyop'o*, which is tinged with the flavor of "Koreans living abroad"—"Koreans in America" rather than "Korean Americans."

> We can see that the terms we [Korean Americans] generally use, *kyop'o* and *kyomin*, represent the attitude that Korean Americans should quit American society and just be the master of their Korean American society. These Japanese-style expressions reflect the perspective of the homeland [South Korea], considering Korean Americans as [South] Korean subjects. We can find this consciousness of "travelers abroad" or "people away from home" promulgated at important events such as the establishment of overseas Korean political offices. Compared with these expressions we use "Korean American community" (*miju tongp'o sahoe*) to mean *hanp'itchul* (one [group] of the same blood) or *han'gyŏre* (brethren).[9] So for Korean Americans to play leading roles in American history and social change . . . we need to begin by embracing the right perspective and proceed in a direction that respects the experience and cultural legacy of the multiethnic community. The expression, "when in Rome do as the Romans do," is for guests or travelers. Now Korean Americans (*miju tongp'o*) are the masters of this land (*ttang*). (Korean American Research Center 1993, pp. 1–2)

In this way, the term *tongp'o* marks a symbolic call to identify with the diaspora community as an agent of political and social change *in* the United States. Although our discussions seldom touched on such semantic points, they addressed these concerns both through assessments of the pre-riot diaspora identity and through calls for post-riot reform.

The struggle over redefinition in fact began in the earliest moments of riot response, in part spurred by the lack of any obvious Korean American organizations or leaders to respond to the riots. Korean-language reporting on Radio Korea became—in the total absence of state services—a sort of two-way walkie talkie through which businesses in need and a cadre of self-appointed militia communicated (Kō and Rī 1993, pp. 51–57). David Kim, legal counsel for Radio Korea, told a *Los Angeles Times* reporter: "They [callers who were given airtime on radio broadcasts] were emotional. They were irrational. Sometimes they erred, but they were all we had. There is absolutely no doubt, that they helped us survive" (Wilkinson and Lee 1992, p. A15). In this remarkable media activism, in which the media extended its role beyond representation, Radio Korea's sudden function was also a powerful reminder that there was no obvious leading organizational "voice" or service infrastructure among Los Angeles's Korean Americans. While Radio Korea saved the day, the leadership of the official Korean American political organ—the Haninhoe—was in shambles. It was not even meeting at the time; its prominent building had become a symbol of community disarray.

Radio Korea found itself at an ideological crossroads, torn between a new activist front and conservative leadership that arrived intermittently from South Korea. The Radio Korea parking lot, a sea of Mercedes Benz, Lexus, and BMWs where members of the upper management were pampered as they stepped in and out of chauffeur-driven cars, looked like a Seoul corporate headquarters. Radio Korea went so far as to urge listeners to call mainstream media offices and complain about the scapegoating of Korean Americans—they even announced the phone numbers on the air. This emergency transgression of normal media behavior, while an exciting new development for some at the radio station, represented dangerous, inappropriate activity for others. There were struggles over the news content and, more important, over the balance of the division between South Korean and Korean American news. Younger reporters who were committed to Korean *American* affairs welcomed this media activism and the chance to report on the community; others felt threatened by this turn away from a focus on homeland news.[10]

The question of diaspora identity and the symbolic nature of Korean American spaces, whether South Korean colony, ethnic enclave, or multiethnic space, came under examination with the visit of South Korean politicians after the riots. Alongside American presidential hopefuls, the South Korean presidential candidates for the December 1992 election rushed to Los Angeles. They promised South Korean relief money and pledged diplomatic engineering to ensure U.S. relief for the riot victims. Some Korean Americans believed that these were merely political ploys in the scramble for votes. While they were appalled at this political show, others welcomed the involvement or even lamented that it did not extend far enough. For still others,

beyond the reality of much-needed financial disbursements to riot victims, the support from South Korea took on special significance. In the
context of the changing meaning imparted to immigration, in which
the United States no longer guarantees social mobility—to be elaborated in the next chapter—the South Korean attention was crucial.
Indeed, as many Korean Americans became keenly aware of the riots
themselves as a final blow to the positive images of immigration, the
South Korean response became larger than life. In this context, Korean
Americans sought to gauge: Was it a supportive or condescending
response? The gaze of brethren or strangers? Or did it matter anyway?

Min, a highly educated Korean American shop owner, charged:
"[South Korean politicians] are 100 percent for themselves." He
laughed, recalling how quickly they arrived on the scene: "Korea has
absolutely no relation to any of this. It is crazy to think it does. The
politicians were just using us, but that brings me to another matter: we
need to be Korean American, not Korean." Through the meandering
course of our discussion, he repeated: "We are not Koreans, we are
Korean Americans."

Baek, a wholesaler in downtown Los Angeles, discussed the absurdity of the South Korean government's posturing after the riots,
launched into a discussion of the recent call for Korean American
political representation, and denounced nationalist politics: "It is absurd
to think of Korean representatives [South Korean politicians in the
United States], I mean people who say they are going to represent
Koreans. I'm embarrassed for Korean politicians who—just like during
the '88 Olympics with the boxing—think that everything to do with
Korea is good." Baek steadfastly rejected Korean nationalism, which he
finds extreme, embarrassing, narrow, and at odds with his universalistic
Christian faith. He stood out in unhesitatingly and repeatedly referring
to himself as a minority (sosu minjok), thus rejecting South Korean
political figures and the call for Korean American politicians to "represent Koreans." His interjection about the 1988 Olympics in Seoul
refers to a fight between a South Korean coach (and several other
South Koreans) and a New Zealander referee over a decision that went
against a South Korean boxer.[11] Baek called for "reflection" (pansŏng) in
the Korean American community: "If people hit me I feel the pain, but
if I hit others, I don't necessarily feel their pain. This is true of business
also: when I'm selling, if I remember how it is to be a buyer, it helps.
We need to reflect on the fact that we ignore blacks. If you straighten

your arm to here [arm outstretched] you think you cannot go any further, but with a strong 'perspective-on-things' you should try and extend it further—only then will it be really straight."

Other Korean Americans, however, welcomed the promise of financial help from their South Korean compatriots, and some demanded political and emotional support from South Korea as well. For them, the South Korean retreat from the matter (eventually no formal government action was taken) was sorely disappointing, if not shocking. Soh, a second-generation Korean American, conceived his homeland, where he had spent a year and several summers, differently. While he too denounced the South Korean politicians, he was dissatisfied with the extent and nature of South Korean civilian concern.

> At first the donations from Korea really brightened my day. The Koreans here [in the United States] raise huge amounts of money every time there is a natural disaster in Korea, and you know how there are disasters there all the time—floods, demos, and riots. What did we get from Korea? Just a remark about how well we live and how we deserve it [the riots] and collections [only] in the hundred thousands [of dollars] and that's it! I know we have to give stuff back to Korea too. I think that, but the "good life" here is something we worked for and we can't help Korea until we help ourselves. More than money, at this point we need emotional support from Korea. The politicians who came—they are idiots, real idiots. I mean with the exception of Kim Dae Jung [laughter]—after all my father is from Kwangju [Kim is from the same region]—but even Kim isn't so great after all those house arrests [for dissident political activity].[12]

The give-and-take of Soh's Korea and Korean America—the borderlands of "floods, demos, and riots"—concerns people, not states. He wanted money, emotional support, and recognition that the "good life" was won through hardship, like that of his immigrant parents. Although he felt that most of his life had been "a waste"—absorbed in frivolous social activities—Soh had thrown himself into community action since the riot days and had recently decided that simply to go into his parents' business would be "disgraceful." "Of course" he would still take care of his parents "as a Korean son should." He conceded that "things might not get better [in the United States] in my lifetime, but

I don't want my kids living in Korea. I mean they wouldn't be able to do anything; they wouldn't know what's going on. So while I'm hyped up [from the riots] I might as well get involved." His cross-generational ruminations, surprising utterances from a man in his early twenties, projected the changing contours of the diaspora into the twenty-first century.

One victim spoke of South Korean support matter-of-factly: "After all, they are of the same blood. We have sent lots of money; they need to support us." Another man in his thirties suggested: "The [South Korean] government should send $100 million because of all the capital flow from immigrants to people in Korea"—a direct reference to the transnational economies linking the Korean diaspora and South Korea. Shim, a member of an informal delegation that traveled to South Korea shortly after the riots to explore the possibility of more South Korean relief resources, was saddened to find that the media and political spotlight had been ephemeral. In South Korea he found newspaper cartoons suggesting that the riot coverage had merely served to deflect attention from local political scandals at the time. He said that initially many Korean Americans were happy that the riots were "big news" in South Korea—"for a while it gave people here the sense that they were really important." He continued, however, that "instead of resources [in South Korea] we [the informal delegation] found the attitude, 'You who betrayed your country—why do you ask for help now?'" The betrayal spoke again of the diminished appraisal of emigration in South Korea, underscored by the very occurrence of the riots. In keeping with his call for a minority consciousness, Shim noted that such disappointments "go far in divorcing people from ideas of Koreatown-as-extension-of-Korea."

Ryu, a merchant and longtime immigrant, however, maintains that even after the riots, Los Angeles will remain a "colony" of South Korea. His perspective is a striking contrast with the long-standing claim of some activists in South Korea who proclaim that South Korea is a colony of the United States: "The Koreans in the United States have been a colony, not a community. This is partly because of the telecommunications revolution—after all we live in the same time zone, and the newspapers arrive on the same day. But, with the riots, people were reminded, 'Oh yeah, we live in America.' Koreans in America, though, have no philosophical ideas about what to do about it; people continue to only be interested in Korea." Although Ryu calls for a

Korean American "community" in contrast with a colony, he thinks that Korean Americans are not ready for this because, in spite of South Korea–United States technological simultaneity, many Korean Americans continue to live in a time warp, caught in the moment they left Korea.[13]

Chun, a middle-aged ex-Marine and Vietnam veteran who was wounded in riot crossfire, doesn't envision Koreatown as a South Korean colony. Instead, he imagines an ethnic enclave. For him, the riots were a rebirth, prompting a new vision of the Korean diaspora: "Yes, I was born again." He and his wife plan to return to South Korea for retirement, but only after he has contributed to making Koreatown a secure neighborhood.[14] He knows that his generation must do the job: "It is impossible for my children's generation to do this—they don't even speak Korean." He dreams that many suburban Korean Americans who fled to the suburbs because of downtown dangers will return to Koreatown. To this end, in February 1993, Chun used his own money to contract for safety patrols in Koreatown. In a public appeal, he wrote [in Korean]: "Those of you who have not had your life threatened by a gun wound probably will not understand the spirit in which I want to spend enormous personal funds to begin this crime patrol. I am beginning this as an individual, hoping that no more will people like [Edward] Lee [who died in riot crossfire] lose their lives, or people like me have their lives threatened by gunshots." Although the patrol began as a contract with an American company, he hoped that eventually it would become a patrol "supported purely by our own power." "As it is said, 'If you unify you live, divided you die'; we want to show various nationalities our Koreatown solidarity." He imagines a place where Koreans will gather "again." That Chun and his wife plan a return migration to South Korea suggests the complexity of this nationalized vision: though committed to fortifying Koreatown for the next generation, they themselves do not intend to spend their future there.

Young, a former student activist in South Korea who arrived in the mid-1980s, complained about a nationalized vision of Koreatown. He was particularly dismayed by the perspective of a man who had joined a self-appointed militia unit during the riots: "The consciousness of many Korean Americans considers the communities here as merely an extension of [South] Korea. This is the kind of vision portrayed particularly by the ex-Marine types who [during the riots] would burst onto KT [a Korean-language television station in Los Angeles], saying

'this is our land' [uri ttang] and babble on about 'Korean power' and all
sorts of crazy things." Young objects to the nationalistic bravado expressed in claims such as "this is our land" or calls for "Korean power."
These phrases and sentiments are deeply rooted in South Korea, in-
stantly conjuring up the rhetoric of the South Korean state and military, particularly at the time of his 1980s student activism. For him,
then, these are the trappings of a right-wing nationalism, a composite
of catchphrases and imagery unmistakable to any 1980s Korean *pan-
jŏngbu* (antigovernment) sympathizer. For Young, this rhetoric also
represented the ongoing, albeit waning, South Korean consular control
of Koreatown, including their "many spies" and continued South Korean government indoctrination of Korean Americans in Los Angeles.
He prefers that Korean American spaces be U.S. minority spaces and
hopes that through the riots Korean Americans will realize that "we are
different from Korea," and that "this [the United States] is where we
need to protest." At his place of employment, he protested the hanging
of the South Korean flag—a flag that he noted was quickly put away
when President Bush passed through Koreatown immediately after the
riots—and the singing of the South Korean national anthem. "Korean
power"—the essence of national flags and anthems—and "an American
minority space" inhabit different ideological universes: South Korean
rightist nationalism and the American civil rights movement.

   Is there, however, no convergence of sentiment between Young and
the ex-Marine militia man whose television appearance so riled him?
Or between the Korean American Research Center's call for Korean
American identity and the notion of "our [Korean] land"? In the transnational borderlands of American *and* Korean American ideologies,
realities impede simple classification. It is difficult to identify clear
opposites and enemies or obvious progressive and conservative positions. In the final moments of our first of several encounters in which
Young stressed the importance of U.S. minority identification, he emphasized that "the North-South division [of the Korean peninsula] is
behind everything I have said to you today." Although he did not
elaborate, he implied that the Korean diaspora and the Korean division
themselves are inextricable from U.S. immigration, the culture and
character of the South Korean military, anticommunism and authoritarianism, and the consular control of Los Angeles's Koreatown. While
the ex-militia man would also probably have no dearth of sentiment
concerning Korean reunification, Young would not be likely to share

his fervent anticommunist sentiment, a cornerstone of South Korean state nationalism. In South Korea and the United States, "reunification" and other nationally defined projects span a range of political and ideological positions.

To the suggestion that the Korean North-South division is tied to diaspora concerns and that unification struggles will politicize Korean Americans, one political organizer quipped: "So Korea gets united? What are we going to do? Go and live in a United Korea? Yeah, sure!" He continued sarcastically: "Like we are going to have an impact on the reunification process. As soon as government officials start talking, Korean Americans will completely lose interest."

Yet some Korean Americans see a strong link between local struggles and South Korean politics. Such visions are transnational, but different from the perspectives that sanctioned an appeal to the South Korean government for aid. Representing counter (state) nationalism, this is a far cry from the ex-Marine's "Korean power" or the South Korean flag as a government symbol hanging in a U.S. office. From such a perspective, Hahm, who also came as a student immigrant, is hopeful about the consciousness inspired by the riots: "Korean Americans will realize that the fate of their community is intimately tied to the fate of Korea, that if Korea isn't democratized this community will not be able to stand. My hope is that more Korean Americans will find a stake in the antisystem [antigovernment] struggles in [South] Korea and in the unification movement." Here Hahm suggests that the riots will inspire sentiment against both the South Korean and the U.S. state, that people will see that the lack of Korean American community leadership is in large part related to South Korea's formal and informal control of the community. He said that anti-American sentiment would arise from both direct and indirect contact with the U.S. government as a result of the riots.

At the headquarters of a Korean American group deeply identified with antisystemic and reunification struggles in South Korea, we found not the South Korean flag but the signs and symbols of South Korean counter-state or radical nationalism. These included photographs of deceased revolutionary nationalists from the colonial period, canonized representations of the leader of the late nineteenth-century Tonghak Peasant Rebellion, videos and books on people's struggles in South Korea, and icons of Korean popular history and resistance, including masks and traditional musical instruments. In a similar vein, the Center for Korean Youth Culture (CKYC), founded on March 7, 1992, advertises itself as "youths seeking healthy culture" who aim to learn about "our cultural community." The community they call for is not racialized, but instead contests American capitalism through the voice of antisystem movements in South Korea. "Denouncing the individualistic, pleasure seeking, and consumption oriented values, CKYC promotes collective and productive values and wishes to cultivate cultural values of cooperation and coexistence" (Korean Immigrant Workers Advocates of Southern California 1992, p. 12). This call for a precapitalistic community represents an extremely nationalized scenario: the vision is akin to contemporary cultural nativism in South Korea, which aims to revive Korean traditional culture and social arrangements against Western [U.S.] capitalism, cultural forms, and values. What appears, then, as a particular diaspora voice in a U.S. context is in fact an antisystemic voice from South Korea in which the "United States" is an object against which "Korean" culture is realized.

Hahm's concern with antisystemic struggles in South Korea, however, is not incompatible with his hope for "the birth of a minority consciousness [among Korean Americans]." The two political projects converge in the meanings they attach to the United States. The U.S. intervention in Korea and the American racialized state are respectively implicated in Korean and Korean American politics. Hahm hopes that Korean Americans' twin disappointments in the riot response of the U.S. government and the "disorganized" Korean American community will expose the "imperialism of the United States" and the South Korean political control of Koreatown.

The position of Young Koreans United (YKU), a global diaspora political movement, is similar. In an article on their 1993 telegram campaign against the presence of U.S. troops in South Korea, a YKU member explains: "Korean Americans see a direct connection between the presence of U.S. troops in Korea and the lack of funds for domestic programs which was clearly indicated by the events in Los Angeles last April" (Chung 1993, p. 4). For Hahm, then, the stark resignifying of the United States—which did not defend Korean American life or property—"should" affect consciousness such that Korean Americans will recognize the unity of the "U.S." in Korea and the "U.S." in Korean America. Minority consciousness, he explains, will come from the forced realization that Korean Americans are not a privileged minority, "just below or better than whites."

The question of Korean Americans' standing in a U.S. ethnic hierarchy appeared again and again in our discussions with Korean Americans. We were told repeatedly about a newspaper report of a survey in which Americans were asked to rank fifty nationalities. "Korea," which many imagined would be high, if not the highest, on the list, was among the "least favorite" countries.[15] The riot experiences and their representation in the media seemed to confirm these shocking survey results. Hahm, however, was hopeful that through these results Korean Americans would come to understand themselves as the victims of U.S. racist institutions and practices. Others suggested in a related but somewhat different vein that Korean American racism must be acknowledged. The KARC founding statement discusses the origins and effects of Korean American racism: "The racist policies of the American ruling powers permeate Korean Americans as well. . . . 'We [aren't quite as good as whites], but are superior to blacks and Latinos' is exactly what this is about . . . the result of uncritical acceptance of the [United States] ruling logic [ideology]." An immigrant of twelve years similarly explained: "Our national weakness is that we have been living thinking that we come right after whites—clean, gentle, and so on—so we've discriminated against other races. Here [in the United States] Hispanics—we call them [all] 'Mexicans'—work for us, they do our dirty work, so we discriminate." Running a dress shop catering to Latinos, she suggested that Korean American rejection of minority consciousness is the flip side of racial or cultural superiority. Transnational musings on the significations attached to South Korea are thus intimately tied to the question of Korean American ethnic identification.

In two Korean American sermons preached within days of the riots we find a subtle divergence in the speakers' visions of Korean American identity. Although both sermons challenged Korean American congregations to dismantle metaphorically the barriers between "neighbors," a close look reveals somewhat different political sensibilities and appeals. While Paul Yung, one of ten ministers at a large Korean American church, urged from his pulpit not to ask, "Who is my neighbor?" Samuel Lee challenged his much smaller congregation to "realize our [and our neighbors'] common struggles and destinies as human beings." One plea demanded empathy that does not inquire about the particulars of the riots; the other called for consideration of social and political realities.

Paul Yung, whose congregation includes thirty families who became victims in the riots and the family of Edward Lee who was killed in riot crossfire, tells the story of the Samaritan who stops to aid a man who has been robbed and beaten and takes him to an inn, promising the innkeepers that if they take care of the man he will pay all of the expenses. For the first time, Yung explains, "this passage gave me comfort instead of a guilty conscience."

> Why? Because there was no choice. I had to be identified with the person who was robbed. We [Korean Americans in the riots] are the ones beaten without knowing any reason. We are just traveling along this life and we are robbed all of a sudden. We are beaten harshly. We are helpless, and that is why this text became a passage of comfort and new strength. (Castuera 1992, p. 19)

Yung asks his congregation to help those who have been robbed, but he urges them not to wonder about "how you and each person are involved in this riot":

> And Jesus is saying to us who are asking, "Who is my neighbor?" don't ask any questions about their racial background. Don't ask any questions about their cultural background. Don't ask any questions about why they got into that environment, and don't ask any questions about how you and each person are involved in this riot. All you need to do is just to go to the people who need your help and be a neighbor rather than asking, "Who is my neighbor?" (p. 22)

Although in the final passages of his sermon Yung sounds a note of racial harmony—"I believe somehow our African-American communities will restore their areas, but it won't matter unless we look into their faces and can tell that this is my brother and sister" (p. 24)—his sermon does not demand a critical Korean American reckoning over the riots. Rather, he asks that people suspend their queries as they turn to people who have been robbed as the Korean Americans have been.

In his sermon "One Circle," K. Samuel Lee strikes a very different chord, saying that "we must bring about radical changes both in our society and in our individual lives" (Castuera 1992, p. 82). He urges that people not draw circles around themselves "under the disguise of security and protection," and that they "clean up" their prejudices.

> We must change our racial attitudes and stereotypes. We must
> change even our individual lifestyles. So often our lifestyles con-
> veniently create another circle of separation from others, espe-
> cially from those who live distant from us economically, socially,
> or culturally. . . . We must realize our common struggles and des-
> tiny as human beings with a common vision for a better world. . . .
> I hope we clean up not only our streets, but also ourselves. I hope
> we clean up our own prejudices, biases, apathies, and insensitiv-
> ities, even to the point of changing our own lifestyles. (pp. 82–83)

Although Yung and Lee both make a Christian call to "love thy neighbor," Yung downplays difference, while Lee takes it up.

We have reviewed an array of positions: the Korean American Research Center's appeal for Korean Americans to become masters in a
multiethnic society, Ryu's claim that Koreatown is a South Korean
colony, Chun's born-again vision of a safe Koreatown, Young's call for
minority space, Hahm's evocation of a community of transnational
struggles, Paul Yung's sermon on a community of the robbed, and
Samuel Lee's vision of "one circle." These voices represent divergent
directions for Korean Americans and their symbolic community,
Koreatown. The continuum between Koreatown as a South Korean
colony ("our land") and Koreatown as an American minority or multiethnic space stretches across a broad field of ideological and political
difference.

Debating the Diaspora II: A Shattered Covenant
with the United States

After the U.S. government abandonment of Korean Americans during
and after the riots, the United States took on entirely new meanings for
Korean Americans. The refashioning of the image of the United States
is central to the contest over the Korean diaspora.

Yu, a female proprietor of a small accessories stall in one of the few
swap meets still standing in Koreatown, said that "nowadays *nobody*
wants to come [to the United States], *nobody* at all." Two months after
the riots, business was still slow, and several women sensed a "menacing
attitude"—"watch out or it will happen again"—from their mostly Latino customers. Yu and two other female stall managers who gathered
in the tiny space of her stall—some four feet square—all proclaimed

that they hated the United States, that they wanted to go back to South Korea, but they could not: "Even if you come here with lots of money, it all gets tied up in payments—house, car, and so on—it's different from Korea, you can't leave." The U.S. government holds no appeal for Yu, who has come to realize that it does "absolutely nothing for minorities": "Of course the Korean government should take care of this [the riot damage to Korean Americans] because most people are Korean citizens. I have absolutely *no interest*—even though I know I could—in getting an American citizenship because it doesn't mean a damn thing in the United States. In the United States, the ideology is 'whites-are-the-best.' This government does absolutely nothing for minorities so there is no point to citizenship."

After her impassioned comments, a discussion ensued on the meaninglessness of American citizenship. A Korean American mental health counselor has commented that the "second stage" of the riot response, after the immediate shock and anger of loss, is to regret having come to the United States in the first place. Men in particular, the counselor explains, experience a pervasive helplessness: "They are unable to do anything and have no motivation." In response to such apparently laconic men, women are angry, "frustrated that their husbands can't take care of them, and wondering why they are so helpless."[16]

Yu's excursus on the meaninglessness of U.S. citizenship must be understood in the context of a series of grave disappointments for many Korean Americans: the striking absence of police protection during the riots; the delayed—"absurd," as many put it—appearance of the National Guard; the insufficient, piecemeal government relief programs and disbursements; and, finally, government directives regulating the return of certain businesses to South Central Los Angeles, particularly those owned by or employing large numbers of Korean Americans, including liquor stores, swap meets, and pawn shops.

Kang, a college-educated Korean American merchant in his early forties, who gave a sustained "structural" (his word) analysis—"Koreans were doing the wrong businesses in the wrong place at the wrong time"—offered a powerful indictment of the U.S. government's suppression of the riots: "Basically, the orders were to draw a line, to cordon off the affluent neighborhoods, and to tell the looters, 'OK, you play here in Koreatown and South Central.' It was a topsy-turvy time and police orders were all backwards, inside-out, and upside down—Gates [Los Angeles Chief of Police] is not a human being, he's a bastard. The police, well they came out 'big' when it was safe, and retreated in the face of real danger."

Korean American businesses were thus in the "looter's playground," abandoned by the police. Chae, the owner of a swap meet building that burned to the ground during the riots, stands to lose $600,000 if he cannot "go back in." He commented that "the whole thing is a man-made disaster, isn't it?" He continued, "I mean, didn't everyone know it was going to happen, see it coming?" He was active in a grassroots movement of Korean Americans who aimed to sue the city of Los Angeles for not protecting them during the riots. For Chae and others, the covenant had been broken. He also noted, "It just happened to be Koreans who were there at that time; it's the city's fault." The shop owner So Chung told *Village Voice* reporters that there were conscious decisions involved in the betrayal of Koreatown. "Daryl Gates wanted the blacks to let out their outburst toward the Koreans . . . because he knew that the blacks didn't feel very good toward the Koreans. I do believe there must have been some conscious politics, because [the police] just weren't there" (D. Kim and Yang 1992, p. 33). A shop owner suggested that the media showed the looters "how easy it was to loot, calling out the looters; it was a real propellant, as if to say—don't worry, there are no police here." A cartoon in Seoul's progressive daily, *Han'gyŏre sinmun*, portrays the deliberate abandonment of Koreatown. It shows the National Guard behind a row of shields—at first glance they appear to be the South Korean military suppressing student activists—protecting the *"paegin maûl"* (white village), while the *"hanin maûl"* (Korean village) is in flames and a few police officers with guns ask looters carrying baseball bats, "Can't you stop?" (Lim 1992, p. 25).

A young Korean American student said: "The police weren't there for us, it blew my mind." Guarding the remains of a dry cleaners with a friend, he scoffed at the late arrival of the National Guard: "They walked in 'high and mighty'—with their jeeps and everything—saying [to him and his friend] 'go home.'" One Korean American suburban housewife chided: "What a joke about the National Guard—they were nowhere to be seen in Koreatown, that's for sure." A shopkeeper who lost her store was incensed when she learned that the National Guard had been paid $1.7 million in overtime alone for "doing absolutely nothing—the money should have been distributed to us." Jin Lee, one of the leaders of the Korean American Victims of the L.A. Riot, was bewildered that no leader took responsibility for what had happened.

In South Korea, he said, " 'morals [are] very important.' He wondered why none of the city's top officials resigned after the riots" (McMillan 1992b, p. B4).

Korean Americans felt abandoned not only by the state but also by the American people. A nineteen-year-old Korean immigrant student expressed his disillusionment with Americans: "How do I explain it?. . . . I have been here seven months. When I came here I said to my friends, this is gorgeous. This is beautiful. Now my American dream is broken. I'm so disappointed in American people" (Clifford and McMillan 1992, p. A1). The reporter John H. Lee used the Korean word *chŏng*—"it's one part love, equal parts affinity, empathy, obligation, entanglement, bondage and blood"—to describe how he felt as a Korean American during the riots (1992, p. 157). That Koreans Americans have "lots of *chŏng*" is a frequently used self-identification: "If I took the feeling of loss after Olympic Market burned, multiplied it by more than 1,800— the number of Korean-owned businesses racked by rioters—then compounded that feeling with the bitterness that comes from knowing *the destruction was deliberate*—I would come close to describing how Koreans felt about the L.A. Uprising. Never have I felt such soul-yanking *jung* [*chŏng*] as when I reported on the victims' plight" (ibid.). A man whose store was looted in the riots reflected that after twenty-nine years he now wonders how welcome he is in the United States and whether he should leave: "The most important thing for me is the dilemma in my heart. I've lived in the United States for twenty-nine years. I went to college here, and grad school, and got my doctorate here. But now none of my experiences here seem meaningful. I wonder if because I'm Asian, I am not really welcome in American society? I wonder whether I should leave here?" (D. Lee 1992a, p. 9).

One reaction to state abandonment was the Korean Americans' organized effort to protect their streets and stores. This response itself became symbolic because of the media's focus on armed Koreans,[17] an obsession that escalated even one year later during the anxious days of the retrial. Images of armed Koreans, smiling looters, a framed photo of Martin Luther King, Jr., amid riot rubble, and arrested looters laid out on the pavement were among the canonized views of the riots. When in January 1993 we mentioned our research to a European American immigration lawyer with several Korean American clients, he blurted: "I hope you're armed." The media had successfully fixed this image on the riot wasteland.

That armed Korean Americans came to signify a cultural portrait, rather than the last-resort response of a people abandoned by the state, was a source of deep-seated anger.[18] Yang was one of thirty who participated in an all-day business neighborhood patrol that successfully prevented any damage or looting. When the police told the patrol to disarm, they hid their guns. Yang was incensed to think that the police who had abandoned them now dared to disarm them: "The police had nothing to do with this!" One man who participated in the civilian militia to defend Koreatown described the police cowering behind buildings: "They looked on as we approached the looters, and only when we began firing guns did a few of them emerge; they came out and fired off a bit, and then they proceeded to confiscate our guns. They are really bad men!"

Another man could not stop talking about the coverage of Los Angeles's Channel 7—the object of many Korean Americans' ire—which made Korean Americans look like hoodlums (kkangp'ae). "In fact Koreans never once shot anyone, it's not in our 'national character' to shoot straight and kill." He continued that many of the "fearsome Koreans" were in fact brandishing toy guns, whatever they could garner to scare off the looters. Im, a Korean American housewife who turned her hand to show us bite marks from a run-in with a Latina customer in a shop she had managed several years ago, said bitterly: "They depict us like crazy people holding guns, but they have no idea of how many Koreans died doing business—people struggling to make it, people who had finally made it, students from Korea about to return, young people, old people."

Ha, a recent college graduate and a son of entrepreneurs, took to the streets with a gun he purchased during the riots. His emotional story, a blow-by-blow account of the anger that moved him to risk his life, reveals the profound impact of the abandonment that many felt during the riots' destruction of Korean American enterprises. At the time of the riots he was living in a four-hundred-unit apartment in Koreatown, "an incredibly integrated building—[take] a look at the apartment roster and you find Kim next to Hernandez, Park next to Sanchez." He enjoyed the "exciting interracial life," laughing as he recalled the Latino bouncers at Koreatown bars who say in Korean "show me your ID," and the Latino chef at one of the best Korean restaurants. "Until the riots I thought everything was great":

The greatest shock for me was the Hispanic looting of Korea-town—you know it was the Hispanics who did most of it. It was shocking—they were the very same people that I live with, drive by, walk by, talk to, the very same ones who were looting the stores. And here they were, a baby carriage full of looted goods in one arm and a baby in the other—it freaked me out. I kept thinking: "I'm not going to sit here and let this happen." Every thirty minutes I got a telephone call—friends, relatives in the United States, relatives in Korea—telling me to stay at home.

When Ha ventured outside to buy supplies, figuring he might be at home for a spell, he discovered the fortresses of Korean American middle-aged men—"cars, guns, bats, sticks, knives, whatever"—at the main entrances to Koreatown. The next thing he knew, a "black male in a tow truck" was speeding for the blockade, and he ducked to hear gunshots and shouts, among them "you—excuse me for swearing—fucking Koreans." He couldn't get over it all: "The Koreans, about to lose everything they had worked so hard for. . . . Frustrated, angry, and sad, that's how it was for Koreans: their life savings, hard work, a lifetime." About these men of the barricade, he stressed: "Make no mistake, they really knew what they were doing." He explained that ex-ROK (Republic of Korea) soldiers are tough, with their "Uzis and sawed-off shotguns." With no one helping the Korean Americans, Ha was overwhelmed by the irony of the many Korean Americans arrested for breaking the curfew and carrying weapons. He felt "helpless" at the destruction and the breakdown of all services as the television announced not to even bother calling 911.

> With no help from *anyone* we needed to help ourselves. I felt so low at home. All I could think was "whatever I have to do, I won't take it anymore." What's worse, the looters were arrogant, laughing as they went. The TV showed Koreans begging, hands together in prayer, begging the looters to leave their stores alone, to no effect. Many of the Koreans were beaten, women and young sons, sons who give up a lot of their time [to work in the family business].

Purchasing three guns, Ha set out to help the middle-aged men at one of the larger Korean American–owned supermarkets, but the men sent him home, telling him that he was "too young." When he returned home and saw himself "with my gun, having purchased a gun—I opened it, examined it—and thought, 'I was so mad—I could have gotten killed, I could have killed someone.' "

The anger of the riot days was only the beginning of a saga of profound disappointment in the political organs of the United States (cf. Kwoh, Oh, and Kim 1993). After the riots, Korean American victims came face to face with U.S. government bureaucracy in ways that many of them never had before. The small size of their businesses had minimized their contact with U.S. institutions and, for many, with the English language. The morass of forms, government letters, and edicts was an unfathomable onslaught. Suddenly they had been thrust into a sea of acronyms: SBA (Small Business Administration), FEMA (Federal Emergency Management Agency), and so on—empty letters for most immigrants. Beyond the already formidable language barriers, the bureaucratic system and ideology encoded in these English words was alien.[19] We spoke with a couple whose son had been injured in crossfire while manning a nearby Korean American establishment. At their apartment in Koreatown, the father of the newly immigrated family poured a basketful of envelopes on the small, portable Korean-style table—the only piece of furniture in the room—that we were gathered around. The envelopes—phone bills, insurance company statements, hospital bills, letters from the city and the state, informational literature, and so on—were unintelligible and threatening to them. Victims' counselors explain that government forms incur victims' wrath: "They [victims] feel 'We have nothing, everything is gone. Why do I have to fill out all these forms to show that everything is gone?' "

For the well-established businesses with proper records, bookkeeping, and insurance coverage, the forms and red-tape byways were not insurmountable. Circumstances were different for those with informal arrangements, underreported incomes, and fly-by-night insurance policies that fizzled away after the riots.[20] The unorthodox or illicit practices of many small businesses were revealed after the riots because of the detailed documentation required in order to gain access to public relief or private insurance coverage. Some Korean Americans criticized those who were remiss; others defended these legal transgressions. Park, the Korean American who was deeply involved in the militia units during the riots, went so far as to suggest that Korean Americans should not be taxed: "White people have been here for four hundred years, we've only been here for twenty years. In the beginning did whites pay taxes? We work hard—it's impossible for us to pay taxes, we can't afford it." Others explained that U.S. regulatory practices were ill suited to the cash economy of Korean American enterprises. In such arguments, both transnational practices and ideologies were contested: as an enclave Korean economy in a U.S. city versus Korean American businesses in a U.S. economy; and as burgeoning capitalists living out the American entrepreneurial dream versus minority shopkeepers/ laborers struggling in the interstices of racist American capitalism.

The government, once a "protector," suddenly brandished the many arms of its bureaucracy and, for some, reared "its ugly head." One man noted that the riot aftermath had been a sobering lesson in the American "power structure," as he came to realize "that the mayor and the governor are not on the same level." A group of six female victims, gathered on the steps of the makeshift Koreatown quarters of the Korean American Victims of the L.A. Riot, were shocked to learn that moments earlier a representative of the Small Business Administration—who had set up shop next door in a church annex—had told us that the press had been misreporting Korean American dissatisfaction with the SBA and that people were "very happy with SBA's response to their demands." A mental health counselor working with Asian American riot victims commented: "They thought they would be protected by the government [relief], and when they weren't they felt abandoned. Their 'basic trust' is gone; yes, their trust is *really* gone." One shopkeeper from South Central Los Angeles, who "will never be able to go back in" because she did not own the store, describes her angry encounter with a psychological counseling center: "I didn't really go to get help. I mostly went to argue with them. And I went to see if they had anything to offer that I could tell others about. I was so mad at their attitude: that at the base of all this [Korean American anger, disappointment] is psychological problems. I had a fit, screaming at them, telling them that there are real problems, asking them what can they do about it? *Finally* the therapist admitted that there is *absolutely nothing, absolutely nothing!*"[21] She also screamed at a state employee who called from Sacramento to survey her losses: "I know I am paying for this call with my taxes. Why waste all this money on these phone calls? What are you doing for us?"

Mental health workers serving victims explained that their patients' overwhelming sentiment was: "You can't help me. The only thing that will help me is money. Only if I get money will my problems be solved." Determined to address the ongoing emotional trauma, mental health personnel made multiple visits to shop owners and found that eventually there was a sudden release of tension, tears, and stories of helplessness. Several counselors noted that the PTSD (post-traumatic stress disorder) model does not really fit the case of the Korean American merchant victims because many of them continue to live and work amid the source of the trauma.

One counselor was almost in tears as she detailed the "unbelievable story" of one merchant victim. For her and other care givers the story demonstrated the profound injustices of the American government— the "first, second, third, and even fourth victimization" of those who sustained riot damages. First were the riots themselves, followed by PTSD. In this particular case, the story of "a well-educated couple, both from really good families, who opened a large market only recently with family money and savings," the store owner managed to safeguard some of the store's goods in his home before the store was looted and eventually burned to the ground. When authorities discovered merchandise at the owner's home, they charged him with arson, suggesting that he had destroyed his own store. He was imprisoned and bail was set at $500,000; reduced to under $50,000, the money was put up by relatives in Seoul. When his insurance company learned about the arson charges, they sued him. There was still more: the owner had secured a small SBA loan for rebuilding; completely broke, he and his family used some of the money to pay bills, but this was discovered by the SBA and he was fined. Finally, the owner's children were ostracized even in the Korean American community; other children were told not to play with them.

The counselors explained that, although unreported at the time,[22] this story was circulating in its every detail among Korean American merchants. One counselor added that this victim was being made "a scapegoat"—an example to show the others that they had better not demand very much from the U.S. government. Another counselor commented that she could not stop herself from feeling that this was also "my problem," and she spoke about the "problems of transference: these people of the same nationality [minjok]; it is extremely difficult to maintain an emotional distance from them." Counselors stressed how important it was for them to gather for debriefing—"as we are with you now"—so that they could maintain some perspective and not be over-whelmed.

Lee, whom we met in a dollar-a-plate Chinese restaurant in the heart of Koreatown, complained bitterly of the government bureaucracy and political system. An auto mechanic in his late fifties, he had lost his job through the riots, and referring to receiving state money, he professed: "I've become a beggar for the first time in my life—I'm embarrassed." Immigrating "because America was good, they helped us in the Korean War, and the GIs were good," he finds himself now in the mire of government bureaucracy. He said ironically: "FEMA has done a beautiful job, beautiful, thanks, wonderful job, proud of it." He spoke primarily in Korean, peppered with English phrases when referring to the U.S. political process. He said that employees like himself were not covered:

> There are not just one or two problems—where should I begin? The problems are at the state, federal, and local level. [President] Bush's programs are said to do well by the riot victims—appreciate it, very nice. The government programs want me to search for a job, but I don't need to search for a job. If I had a tool box [which would cost $20,000], no problem; without it, no way. There is something wrong with that program, that program which insists you search for a job. It just wastes my time—so I pretend [to be searching for a job]—I have to do it. They need to pass a bill to change it, it's wrong. Or they should give me a job from the government. I had a hearing—they cut off my benefits. It's all go by-the-rules—food stamps, housing authority—it needs to be straightened out. . . . I will end up homeless. I am mad. I told all my relatives, everybody I know, to vote for Clinton.

Lee is sure he will never be able to purchase a set of tools again and wishes he could become a bilingual receptionist in a government office, making the life of new immigrants easier than it has been for him over the last twenty years: "I could be a bilingual receptionist, but nobody will give me that job. The problem has been that there are no Koreans working at the court house, social security office, no Koreans at all; all other nationalities but Koreans are represented. . . . I'm going to go to the district congress and ask for help. I'm not looking for a nice job—any job!—hopefully reception. We have no representation!" Lee's repeated plea to work as an interpreter, a bilingual receptionist, sounded bitter criticisms of the U.S. government: the dearth of Korean American representation, the insufficient response to employee victims like himself, and government ignorance of the real lives of working people.

Korean Americans' encounter with the American political system came to a head over the state regulation of liquor stores in South Central Los Angeles. Although most Korean Americans agree that a large number of liquor stores makes for an undesirable situation, they disagree as to whether Korean American enterprises should be restricted or allowed to reopen freely. The very term "liquor stores" is contested, because many are primarily grocery stores that sell some liquor; as one person put it: "After all, 7-Eleven isn't a liquor store." Concerned parties are working to change the image of these establishments. They instruct the stores, for example, not to place the liquor company advertisements so prominently in the store front. There are few simple answers, and many people are of several minds as their calculations shift from the structural to the particular, the political to the personal—"I feel stuck in the middle," said many. Hwang, a second-generation Korean American, suggested: "It is ethics—the liquor stores should be closed down—versus principles—the fate of the Korean families that depend on them." Pitting ethics against principles makes for ambivalent calculations over a tortured subject.

> It is opportunistic for South Central to seize on it [the devastation of Korean American enterprises] this way. I advocate for the Korean side a bit more strongly. I can really understand what they [those who lost their businesses] are going through—the basic American dream, isn't it? I mean, these are not sex shops, they are legitimate businesses, many of them ten to fifteen years old. We are denying them what they deserve. My parents are college educated, they were professionals back in Korea. *The city, state, and federal government are all missing the whole point*—they say they understand, but it is all false promises. . . . Maxine Waters [Congressperson from South Central Los Angeles] and all those who are trying to keep Koreans out [of South Central Los Angeles]—if that isn't being racist, prejudiced, I don't know what is. . . . They [African Americans] are always complaining about white men oppressing them, and now they are doing the same thing [oppressing Korean Americans]. Koreans now have no faith in the justice system.

They have been victimized twice, first losing their stores, and second getting no help.

Hwang conceded: "I'm conservative, I guess, but I'm also liberal, but isn't that what business is all about—supply and demand?" His convictions that honest businesses, the old-fashioned way, are the stuff of "the American dream," and that the creed of U.S. capitalism, supply and demand, is the warp and woof of immigrant stories left him angry at the double victimization of merchants. A self-proclaimed "conservative," for him the riots and their aftermath threatened all the tenets of textbook America, its democracy, justice, and so on. He couldn't imagine that Korean Americans wouldn't simply be compensated for their losses without "any problem," noting: "If you lose something you have the right to get it back." Another Korean American victim who worked in South Central Los Angeles said: "We've made lots of money in this lawless universe [South Central Los Angeles]. Why shouldn't we be able to live well in the middle class?"

One merchant who does not regret emigrating—"no matter how much Korea develops it cannot become like America—its size, wealth, freedom"—suddenly offered an excursus on capitalism and communism, hinting at the chimera of capitalist superiority in the United States: "Think of North Korea—you get everything. It's [U.S. capitalism] not all that different from communism. There [North Korea; communist countries] you are forced to work; here you are forced to work. Yeah, you have 'freedom,' but you have to keep making money to pay the rent. Some even say that the United States is more severe than communist countries—just look at the freeways in Los Angeles at 6 A.M.!" This comment, which ruptures cold war silences, is quite remarkable when we note that this man left South Korea in the late 1970s, is old enough to remember the Korean War, and is quite successful, with two daughters in Ph.D. programs at prestigious U.S. universities.

Visions of capitalism aside, the American covenant has been broken for many Korean Americans. In each instance, the idealized image of the United States—epitomized in its democratic political and economic institutions—seemed to shatter. For some, "I hate the United States" and "I want to go home" became the refrain; for others, the post-riot aperture for a new, radical minority politics seemed hopeful.

*   *   *

We have seen that reckoning via the riots emerges as a series of contests over the transnational character of the Korean diaspora and over the promise of the American dream. It is essential to situate these responses in a transnational universe of meaning spanning ideological production and co-production in South Korea and the United States. Further, riot reflections appear in a mediated universe as local realities are telecommunicated across boundaries and languages. Finally, the contests underscore the production of differences—political, ideological, economic, and cultural—among Korean Americans. In a sense, the riots shook the landscape—political and personal—calling forth the unspoken. It is from that wellspring that this chapter's voices emerge.

3

Diaspora Formation:
Modernity and Mobility

Korean Americans' reflections on the riots reveal enormous diversity in politics, ideology, and idiomatic flair. Furthermore, the Korean memoryscape emerges alongside the American ideological landscape. Riot responses cannot be wrested from the meanings Korean Americans attach to immigration itself. The riot reckonings in Chapter 2 leave no room for imagining South Korea and the United States as distinct or fixed spheres. Korean immigrants inhabited transnational spaces before emigrating from South Korea, and they continue to do so after immigration. Most South Koreans have a relative, or at least a classmate or good friend, in the United States. We do not mean to diminish the profound rupture experienced by the Korean immigrant who leaves Seoul for Los Angeles or a regional South Korean city for an American small town. Emigrants' contacts with the United States, however, do not begin on the eve of emigration, nor do their connections with South Korea end at the beaches of Los Angeles.[1]

In this chapter we explore the structure and meaning of the Korean immigration to the United States. Mindful of political economic contexts, we focus on emigration as a twin quest for modernity and social mobility, which are elements of a transnational cultural universe, not fixed signifiers.

The Diaspora Legacy

Modern Korean history has been transnational throughout. The correspondent protagonist of Ty Pak's short story "A Second Chance"

muses on Korean history as a diaspora saga. During the Korean War
the correspondent is sent to cover a settlement of Korean farmers in
Manchuria and loses himself in their collective history:

> He [the correspondent] could have died for them, stayed there for
> the rest of his life working with them. Every cell in him tingled
> and reverberated with the story of the race—the vagabondage
> that originated from Central Eurasian steppes, trekking and me-
> andering across the mountains and deserts of two continents, the
> persecutions, discriminations, genocides that hounded them ev-
> erywhere they went and kept them on the move, the narrow
> escapes, constant packings-up and marchings-on, panting runs,
> exhausted droppings on the road, children smothered in their
> cries, the uneasy settlement of the peninsula coveted by the hos-
> tile nations, Chinese, Russian, Mongolian, Manchu, the thousand
> years of invasions, national emergencies, midnight alarms, vigils,
> widows' keenings. The ten millennia of Korean history paraded
> past him like a grim tableau. The whole time he was there, he
> lived in a trance-like state of exaltation. (1983, pp. 114–115)

The global Korean diaspora includes communities throughout East
Asia, Soviet Central Asia, Australasia, the Middle East, Europe, and the
Americas, which by 1982 accounted for 10 percent of the global Korean population (Light and Bonacich 1988, p. 107). This displacement
is not new: at the end of Japan's colonial reign in Korea (1945), 11
percent of the Korean population lived abroad.[2] Indeed, all Koreans are
mired in dislocation as the North-South division engulfs them in a
diaspora of sorts, displaced from families, homeland, and landmarks. As
the division persists as a geopolitical reality, so does the symbolic
legacy of colonial period dispersals remain alive in the political and
ideological workings of contemporary South Korea.

In South Korea, images of displaced colonial period Koreans are
disparate: the etching of a young Korean labor recruit in Southern
Japan—"Mother I want to see you; I'm hungry; I want to return to my
homeland"—carved on a wall of a coal mine (Cha 1982); the tragedy
of the wianbu (literally, comfort women), sexual serfs for the Japanese
military (Lie 1992b); guerrilla resistance soldiers in China participating
in the Chinese Communist Revolution;[3] civilian agricultural settlers in
Manchuria; the officials of the Korean provisional government pro-

claimed in Shanghai in 1919; and the independence movement leader Syngman Rhee, later South Korea's first post-Liberation president, at Princeton University and in Hawaii. These vignettes encompass Koreans of different ages, classes, genders, residences, religious affiliations, and political and ideological orientation.

In spite of this diversity, the South Korean memory of colonialism has until recently been carefully fashioned through elaborate commemorative activities and institutions and through the rigorous and uniform educational system. In the 1980s, however, vibrant and far-reaching revisionist historiography resurrected this diversity in South Korea. These efforts have transcended facile formulations of a nation victimized in one uniform pattern and instead have considered the varied experiences and displacements of colonialism. By the late 1980s there were numerous books detailing the colonial period *ch'inilp'a* (Japanese sympathizers) as well as the leftist anticolonial struggles at home and abroad (Abelmann 1990; Eckert 1991). Because the South Korean state, in its inception and legitimation, represents a particular lineage of the colonial period nationalist struggle, these works continue to have political significance.

While North Korean legitimacy hails from what has been officially understood in South Korea as the hagiography of *Kim* Il Sung's guerrilla activities in Manchuria (Wada 1992),[4] South Korea's sovereignty began under President Syngman Rhee, who spent much of the colonial era in the United States, with a Princeton Ph.D. and non-Korean wife.[5] The historiographical contest in contemporary South Korea—one in which the role of the United States in Korean history is paramount— looks for the colonial period origins of present-day political struggle. The legacy of diaspora independence struggles looms large in South Korea's current political and historiographical contests.[6] The displacement of Koreans as poor laborers, educated elites, political moderates, revolutionaries, and sexual serfs reflected the social and political currents and rifts of the entire Korean population.

The North-South division brought enormous population dispersal: 3.5 million northern Koreans made their way south between 1945 and 1950 (C. S. Kim 1988, p. 30). The vast majority migrated in 1945–46, either because they were ideologically unsympathetic to communism or because they were members of the former landlord class destined for downward mobility or even death. It is widely appreciated among Korean Americans that northern exiles are overrepresented in the

United States.[7] Their earlier displacement contributes to their decision to emigrate.[8]

Though numerically insignificant, occasional movement across the Korean 38th parallel, the most densely militarized spot in the world, where one-and-a-half million troops face each other (Roh 1990, p. 15), continues to receive headline coverage in South Korea: South Koreans to North Korea, the sensationalized "defection" of North Koreans to South Korea, and the specter of North Korean spies.[9] All movements across this heavily patrolled *hyujŏnsŏn* (armistice line) are registered by hypersensitive military and media authorities.[10] Most remarkable, though strictly a South Korean affair, was the 1983 Korean Broadcasting Service "reunion telethon," in which refugees from the North appeared on television with childhood photos and refugee stories in desperate attempts to find long-lost family members (C. S. Kim 1988). Planned for 95 minutes, the program was so well received that it ultimately ran for 64 hours over eight days. Because many of the still separated refugees seemed to be poor, their stories unleashed powerful images of the division's ongoing personal costs.[11]

The legacy of these colonial period displacements and struggles is a transnational repository of Korean and Korean American identity shared across national boundaries. Although not all colonial and wartime dispersals led directly to emigration—in fact, few did—emigration to the United States is in part born in the dislocations of this era. Diaspora struggles have also been and continue to be inextricably bound to domestic politics and identity. Bearing in mind that Koreans in the United States are but one community of the global diaspora, let us turn to the beginning of Korean immigration to the United States.

The Colonial Crucible of Immigration, 1900–1945

The rise and eclipse of the earliest Korean immigration to the United States is emblematic of the entire century, both for its transnational political-economic structures and its local meanings.

The earliest Korean immigration to the United States, though by now remote, remains an important legacy. Beyond a smattering of Korean students and diplomats, as well as twenty-odd ginseng merchants, some seven thousand Koreans made their way to Hawaii between 1903 and 1905 to labor in sugar plantations (Patterson 1988, pp. 9–10). During the post-1905 period of Japanese aggression and

colonialism, emigration consisted of approximately one thousand picture brides from 1910 to 1924 and some nine hundred political exiles,
students, and intellectuals during and after this period (Yu 1983, p. 23;
see also Yang 1984; Yim 1989; Chai 1992). The resounding themes in
this early immigration are the convergence of modernity, particularly
as symbolized by Christianity, and mobility, in both a social and an
economic sense.

The largely male immigration to Hawaiian sugar plantations occurred at the crossroads of the economic circumstances in Korea, U.S.
Christian missionary efforts in Korea, the Japanese encroachment in
Korea, and the ethnic politics of Hawaii plantations. The U.S. missionary Horace Allen arranged for a labor immigration with Hawaii
plantation owners, who sought Korean labor to force down wages and
break the labor unrest of their predominantly Japanese work force
(Patterson 1988).

The early eclipse of this immigration again reveals a convergence of
transnational factors. Facing mainland U.S. anti-Japanese exclusion
movements and the increase in Japanese labor migration from Hawaii
to the continental United States, Japan exerted diplomatic pressure to
halt Korean labor emigration to slow Japanese moves to the mainland.
"American policy became aligned with Japan's desire to control Korea."[12] Indeed, a 1907 U.S. government rule only recognized Korean
passports issued by the Japanese Foreign Office (Houchins and Houchins 1976, p. 136). The U.S. immigration policy went even further in
limiting and effectively prohibiting Asian immigration. After the 1904
Chinese exclusion laws, the 1917 Immigration Act further restricted
Asian immigration with the creation of a "barred zone," the so-called
Asia-Pacific triangle.[13] The 1921 Quota Law set the number of aliens
who could enter the United States to "three percent of the foreign-born
persons of that nationality who lived in the United States in 1910"
(INS 1990, app. A.1-5). It ended the immigration of Asians whose U.S.
communities were sparse and small. Most crucial was the first permanent limitation on immigration, the "national origins quota system"
of the 1924 Immigration Act. Together with the 1917 promulgation,
these acts proscribed Korean immigration until 1952 (INS 1990, app.
A.1-6).

These early labor immigrants, while representing diverse class origins,
were predominantly Christian city dwellers (Patterson 1988, p. 105;
Moon 1976, p. 12). Driven to urban centers by poverty, famine, and

political turmoil and unrest, similar forces destined them both for conversion to Christianity and for emigration (Patterson 1988, p. 111). Central to the emigration was their geographical and cultural displacement and their exposure to missionaries (Patterson 1988, p. 109). The successful Christianization of Korea—upwards of a fourth of South Koreans were Christian by the early 1990s—can in part be explained by the early and continued equation of Christianity with the West and modernity.[14] In addition, Christianity became widely associated with anticolonial nationalist struggles. This image is in part sustained by the memory of the largest anticolonial uprising, the 1919 March First Movement, and its Declaration of Independence: many signatories, all primarily religious figures, were Christian.[15] Korea's majority, however, did not embrace Christianity then or today.[16]

The emigration of Mary Paik Lee to the United States in 1905 is emblematic. The Lees were a Christian family, converted by early missionaries. She describes the childhood afternoon in Korea in 1905 when Japanese officers came to her home wanting "everyone to move out so that they could use our home to house their soldiers" (M. P. Lee 1990, p. 6). Her family picked up and left for the nearest large port city, Inch'ŏn, where Hawaiian sugar plantation owners were recruiting workers, and later that year they set off on the SS *Siberia* for free passage to Hawaii (M. P. Lee 1990, p. 7). Similarly, in another early immigrant story, the emigration to Hawaii followed many prior sojourns. Morris Pang, born in 1878, stole away in his youth for Russia to seek his fortune; when Japan and Russia went to war in 1904, he says, "we had to leave or risk the chance of being killed" (1974, p. 117). The roads to Korea were blocked so he traveled on an English ship for Japan, and three months later returned to Korea penniless. "It was then that we heard of a man who was talking a lot about the opportunities in Hawaii." And so Pang made his way to Mountainview, Hawaii.

Picture brides formed the second-largest group of early immigrants, following the largely single male labor immigration.[17] The Japanese government granted visas to picture brides in order to "calm political passions [anticolonial] among Koreans [overwhelmingly male] overseas" (Houchins and Houchins 1976, p. 140). Photos traveled both to and from Korea, and stories abound of brides who were shocked to find their husbands ten and fifteen years older than they had expected; the photos had lied in the transpacific passage.[18]

Not all Koreans, however, set off to the United States to labor or to marry. Younghill Kang's 1949 *The Grass Roof*, a fictional account of an aspiring intellectual's childhood in Korea and passage to the United States on the eve of Korea's colonization, reveals the America encountered by upper-class Koreans. The protagonist learns of America, "the home of those queer missionaries," from a young mentor at a "school of new learning": "What glamour he cast over the great colleges in America, which held all that the West had ever thought or known. . . . An American education was for the few, he preached; those few would reap the golden reward. He made me see that the road of a scholar's future prominence lay toward America like the shortest distance between two points . . . in a straight line."[19]

Whether laborer, picture bride, or scholar, the center of the colonial period U.S. diaspora was the nationalist activity channeled through the Korean-American church and various political organizations.[20] A speech on the third anniversary of the March First Movement in 1922[21] reveals the immediacy of the Korean plight. Apologizing for his faltering Korean, a young Korean American pleads: "Let us consider Korea as our dying mother. . . . We ought to be ashamed to look at the reflection of our faces in the mirror and we ought to consider ourselves as the most ignoble and the most despicable creatures under the sun unless we do something to relieve her" (Patterson and Kim 1977, p. 102). Women were also active, forming their own groups and journals in the anticolonial diaspora struggle. A picture bride, for example, proclaimed the patriotic duty of women: "Sisters! Stop dreaming in a family which is actually an invisible prison. . . . Our utmost tasks are to free ourselves of bondage, to build our wealth, to enlist as soldiers, and to obtain an education. . . . We should educate ourselves so that we can gain equality with men [in the independence movement] and be second to none in responding to our national duty" (Yang 1984, p. 20).

We find among early Korean immigrants the same complexity of diaspora identity and politics that emerged in the voices after the L.A. riots. In accordance with the ideological and tactical differences in the global diaspora independence struggle, Korean Americans experienced deep-seated political divisions.[22] Not unlike the 1990s, generation emerged as a salient dividing line; Helen Givens's study noted: "The second generation was being affected by American customs and culture, even though their parents attempt to stimulate loyalty to Korea, by continuing to use the language and to agitate for national independence of the mother country" (1939, p. 49). Matters of loyalty, lan-

guage, and the mother country are prominent here as they were in Los
Angeles in 1992.

Post-Liberation I: Encounter with the U.S. Military

In the post-1945 era, liberated from Japanese rule, Koreans once again
sought the United States as an emigration destination. In the colonial
period, Christian missionaries offered the primary American contact; in
the post-Liberation era, the United States was a predominant political,
economic, and cultural influence in South Korea. The central conduit
of U.S.-Korean relations was the American military. Most Korean emigrants until the post-1965 period were military wives and students,
representing opposite poles of the South Korean status hierarchy.

Mark Gayn's account of his travels in Korea in the fall of 1946—a
year and some months after the August 15, 1945, liberation from Japan
and the September 7 arrival of 25,000 American soldiers (Cumings
1984, p. 27)—offers a remarkable window on immediate post-
Liberation South Korea. Gayn writes of Korea as "the blackest, the
most depressing story I have ever covered. As an American I was
ashamed of the facts that I kept digging up . . . of the concerted effort
to prevent the American people from learning what was happening in
Korea" (1981, p. 433). He reports on the reactionary nature of the
occupation, guided solely by fear of change, revolution, and communism, save for an occasional enlightened officer or recruit. "We appear
uncertain whether we had come to liberate or to occupy" (p. 352).
Gayn documents the U.S. military reinstatement of conservative pro-
Japanese personnel who suppressed progressive local Korean organizations and movements. One official told him: "People we now use to
govern Korea are rightists who happily did Japan's dirty work. There
are now men in the Korean police force who actually were decorated
by the Japanese for their cruelty and efficacy in suppressing Korean
nationalism."[23] During this era, a popular saying still touted today
warned: "Don't rely on the United States, don't be deceived by the
Soviets; Japan will rise again."[24]

Beyond political ideology, Gayn was shocked by the ignorance and
cruelty of U.S. military personnel. The lieutenant who met him upon
arrival "spoke of Koreans with contempt. He said they were dirty and
treacherous . . . 'Psychological warfare,' the lieutenant said. 'That's the

only way to show these gooks [derogatory slang for Asians] we won't stand for any monkey business' " (1981, p. 349).

The dawn of Liberation faded quickly into the debacles that Gayn documents and the devastation of the Korean War (1950–1953). How many American viewers even know which Asian war is the stage for M*A*S*H—one of the most popular U.S. television series of all time?[25] The Korean War resulted in over three million Korean deaths (Halliday and Cumings 1988, p. 200). It was a brutal war in which kin and friends fought against one another. South Koreans usually refer to this war as *Yuk-i-o* (6-2-5), the date of the first North Korean attacks. Although villages in South Korea are replete with visceral markers of the war, including homes that were burned, sites where massacres took place, and the individuals who espoused leftist ideologies, post–Korean War cold war politics silenced or effaced many of these memories (cf. Kendall 1988, p. 54). Over the last decade in South Korea, however, people have begun to question the received wisdom on the post-Liberation era. As memory is unleashed, the history of post-Liberation Korea and of U.S. intervention is literally being rewritten. The growing anti-Americanism in South Korea, which we explore in this chapter's final pages, stems in part from the reconceptualization of *haebang chikhu*, the period immediately following the Liberation.

As part of the profound impact of the American occupation and military, GIs carried the United States to South Korea. The U.S. military stayed after the war, and some 40,000 troops were in South Korea in the early 1990s. Over the years an estimated one million U.S. servicemen and women have been stationed in South Korea (Hellman 1984, pp. 83–84). A brush with the U.S. military is not a rare experience—most South Koreans have a story or two, some of them hideous. Noting the scaffolding of power with which the Americans arrived, however, is only a beginning.

The dominant U.S. and South Korean historical memory has recorded the United States as colonial liberator and Korean War savior, but the day-to-day contact with GIs has been gritty and varied, more complex than coveted GI giveaways: "candies, chocolate and chewing gum" (Kang 1976, p. 26). In the public domain, at least until the 1980s, decades of cold war and pro-American political regimes successfully etched an image of the United States as savior and liberator. The Korean American attorney Sook Nam Choo, a teenage immigrant in

1971, recalls: "Every day on our way to school, we had to pass through a park named after General MacArthur. There was a gigantic statue of him, in tribute to his landing at Inchon (Inch'ŏn) in 1953. We naturally viewed Americans with admiration and thought they were our benevolent protectors. I used to look up at that statue and wish I could someday visit America, that rich and freedom-loving country" (E. Kim and Otani 1983, p. 34). Across the Pacific, on the outskirts of Koreatown in Los Angeles, Korean Americans find another MacArthur Park.

The primary loci of South Korean engagement with the United States are the U.S. military bases, or, more precisely, the zones, called *kijich'on* (military base villages), that grew around them to serve the soldiers' material, sexual, and other needs and desires (Cumings 1993; Enloe 1990). South Korean women who work as bar maids and prostitutes sometimes marry GIs.[26] Stories about *yangkalbo* (foreigners' whores) appear widely in popular literary works; they provide a ready forum for criticizing crass, uneducated, and violent American military men.[27] In a 1979 short story, "Chinatown," South Korean children peer at "GIs in T-shirts" who are throwing knives at a nearby base: "Whenever a knife whistled to the black spot dead in the center of the target, the men howled like animals and we gulped in terror." In the next horrifying moment: "The knife ripped through the air toward us. We flattened ourselves with a shriek in front of the wire fence surrounding the base. . . . The chuckling GI was pointing at something a short distance behind us. . . . A black cat lay rigid on its back with its legs in the air, the knife stuck in its chest" (O 1989, p. 220). In the story's final episode, the *kkamdungi*[28] ("darky," a racist epithet) flings his South Korean prostitute/lover to her death in the street, making an orphan of their child.

Approximately 28,000 South Korean women married Americans between 1950 and 1972 (I. Kim 1987, p. 330). They make up the largest group of Koreans to emigrate from 1945 to 1965;[29] Herbert R. Barringer and Sung-Nam Cho estimate the numbers at over 50,000 by 1980 (1989, p. 112). From 1965 to 1981, half of the Koreans naturalized were spouses of U.S. citizens (Barkan 1992, p. 74). Resulting from this marriage immigration, the sex ratio of Korean immigrants was significantly skewed over a long period; in 1964, for example, 82 percent of immigrants were female.[30] Any picture of post-Liberation Korean immigration that ignores this significant group of women and the chain of further migrations that they cause in the post-1965 era blinds us to the profound class divisions among Korean Americans (I. Kim 1987, p. 334).

These marriages conjure up images of the union of South Korean and American peripheries: the poor farm girl from a South Korean village who makes her way to the bars and brothels of the "base villages," and the poor U.S. recruit from one of America's rural states—the movement from one pocket of poverty and discrimination in South Korea to another in the United States. A widely repeated anecdote in South Korea tells of the illiterate American GI who needs the South Korean military recruit assigned to his unit to transcribe his letters home. During fieldwork in North Chŏlla Province villages, Abelmann found that her presence ignited stories of long-lost sisters and cousins, as farmers dug out tattered envelopes with return addresses in English they could not make out.

Although theirs is a story much more diverse than a series of stock narratives suggests, many South Korean military wives have led difficult lives in the United States (Moon 1978; Song 1989; Yoo 1993). Daniel Booduck Lee remarks that these women have been subjected to the "most insidious social barriers of classism and racism" (1989, p. 348). Their lower-class backgrounds and lower education levels—many have not graduated from junior high school—contrast sharply with those of their elite contemporaries: student migrants (B. Kim 1977, p. 102). Such class discrimination among Korean Americans is revealed in a "typical statement" of a South Korean military wife who knows no other Korean Americans, although many reside near her: "Of course, I love to see our people and eat our own food that I crave and talk about our past in Korea. . . . But I don't want to see them, because I don't want to be looked down on by them. I've suffered and waited for the day when people would say I am a wonderful housewife. But it never came to me" (Moon 1978, p. 103).

Contemporaneous with the military brides were the students who left South Korea for what one early student immigrant called "the greatest country in the world: the richest, most powerful country." The dreams of the elite who left war-devastated South Korea for a U.S. education are not hard to imagine. Prior to 1965, over 10,000 South Koreans studied abroad, many in Japan at first, but over the years largely in the United States. Their opportunity was resented by those who stayed behind. During his 1966 visit to South Korea, the novelist Richard Kim, an exemplar of the successful intellectual immigrant, met with harangues such as this one:

> I know lots of students who went to America. Like you. And they don't come back. I am not mad at you. I am not mad at them, either. I don't blame them. If I could get away, hell, I wouldn't come back either. But I know I can't. . . . I know those rich boys and kids with influential connections who slip out . . . just go to the American consulate and take a good look at more bleary-eyed college kids milling around applying for a passport. Just stand outside the Bando hotel at noon and watch the lucky ones boarding the buses to the airport to fly out of the country, and watch those who are sending them off, sick with envy. Every kid I know wants to get out. (1966, pp. 115–116)

The majority of student immigrants eventually stayed in the United States, while others returned with an "American story" (cf. H. Lim 1978, p. 9). It is not uncommon to encounter South Koreans who cultivate the tastes—culinary, musical, cinematic, aesthetic, and so on—of the American era and region of their stay abroad: a rural southern fifties, or a midwestern sixties, fried chicken or beef steak. These temporal and regional Americas have been an important conduit of American images. That the elite in many circles have established civilian contact with the United States, that many elite careers have come to fruition in the United States, and that U.S. degrees and institutions of higher learning confer legitimacy in both the public and the private spheres in South Korea are central to understanding how the United States secured a place in the plans and dreams of a sizable number of Koreans during and after the 1960s (Bark 1984). Over the decades, the South Korean student presence in the United States has steadily increased; by 1991–92 South Korea's 25,720 students represented the fifth-largest group in the United States behind its East and South Asian neighbors: China, Japan, Taiwan, and India (Gonzales 1993, p. H6).

Military brides and students constituted a two-tiered immigration for the 1950s and the 1960s, representing the lower and upper reaches of South Korean society. One 1970s Korean immigrant underscored the severity of the immigration's class differentiation, suggesting its continued importance: "If people hear that you went to get a degree at Harvard that is one thing, but if you went because your sister married an American, then you are merely *paju munsan* [the names of two U.S. military bases, referring to those who immigrate via the U.S. military]." The college reflections of a 1970s immigrant attorney who came to the United States to live with her sister, a widow of an African American GI, similarly reveal the stark contrasts in the differentiated immigration:

> When I was in college, I met some Korean women from exclusive private colleges in New England. . . . Once, we went around the table introducing ourselves, and they said, "My father is . . ." instead of "My name is. . . ." Korean young women would tell me proudly how many servants they had in Korea. They had attended international schools in Seoul I never knew existed. I was shocked that there were people in Korea as rich as they were, and they were shocked that there were people there poor like me. When I told them that I had seen people who had starved or frozen to death along the road on my way to school, they didn't believe me. (E. Kim and Otani 1983, p. 36)

Post-Liberation II: Material and Media Encounters

South Korea has been saturated with the material trappings of the United States, objects of both fear and envy. In a fictional account, childhood memories are inextricable from the material and sexual trappings of the U.S. military presence during the Korean War:

> . . . the bread the retreating American soldiers left behind at the school playground, the C-ration cans the GIs threw at us from the passing trucks . . . the prostitutes for the U.N. Forces called "the U.N. princesses" . . . the miserable meals of "piggie soup" (the garbage from the U.S. mess halls boiled again after removing coffee-grounds, cellophane paper, broken razor blades and other inedibles) . . . the Lucky Strike cigarette packs with big red circles. (Ahn 1989, pp. 8–9)

One of the most visceral signs of military presence has been the ever-changing stock of American food products that have made their way onto the black market. Until recently, every marketplace in Seoul and regional cities had vendors who sat behind carefully constructed pyramid-shaped mounds of canonized American foodstuffs, one or two of each, which some South Koreans could afford in small quantities at great cost: Spam, marshmallows, Hershey's Kisses, M & M's, cornflakes, canned fruit cup, ham, Taster's Choice coffee, and so on. These products are further shrouded with stories of the so-called *"Kimch'i* [a spicy Korean dish] GIs"—Korean American GIs—who are said to have retired as millionaires from dealings in this black market economy. In part, the United States has been fashioned in the South Korean imagination through these alimentary channels. The American consumption ideal, however, has not been received without reservation.[31] In *"Yang-gwaja kap"* (The Box of American Candy), Yŏm Sang-sŏp's 1948 Korean short story, the professor protagonist worries that the sugar-coated GI culture will devour South Korea, and exclaims to his wife: "Throw that candy box away. While you enjoy these sweet candies and play with the beautifully decorated box, it will bring the bad content of America into this house" (Kang 1976, p. 28).

Through military and civilian contacts, the United States became at once an object of material longing and materialistic scorn, a heroic savior and a reactionary intruder.[32] Material desire and moral approbation, longing and disdain, have been twin responses to many of the trappings of American culture. A 1976 survey in South Korea asked people to name the major positive and negative traits of the United States. Each positive trait had its near-twin counterpoint, perhaps identified by the same respondents: 22 percent identified military aid during the Korean War as positive, while 13 percent identified territorial division as negative; 20 percent considered economic aid positive, while 14 percent considered American materialism negative; and 12 percent championed frontier spirit as positive, while 20 percent and 16 percent decried American individualism and moral decadence, respectively (H. Lim 1978, pp. 11–12). These are not fixed positions with adherents who espouse one or the other, but rather reside together both in the South Korean collective imagination and in private memories. It does injustice to the full-bodied nature of the South Korean engagement with the United States to assume that images of the United States are fixed or one-dimensional.

Material longing is a long-standing feature of immigration dreams.

One Korean American woman recalls her childhood in the late 1940s and early 1950s and the Western world of her piano teacher:

> I went to that house to learn piano. The father was a doctor, the mother a pianist. Their oldest daughter had gone to the United States, and each lesson I would stare at the photo of their daughter standing in the kitchen of her American home. The piano teacher's house was a Western-style house; ours was a Korean-style house [hanok]. Their house had a piano, ours didn't. The kitchen in the photo of the U.S. was all white and shiny. The piano teacher's family lived well; they gave me cocoa. Now they all live in the United States; they all graduated from good colleges.

A piano, a bright and shiny kitchen, and cocoa: the teacher's Western-style house was a Western landscape. Although the goods vary, the longings have been constant over the years. One recent young immigrant anxiously awaited his departure for the United States, "the land with great toys—mini cars by Matchbox and Legos"; for another, his farming mother's promise of color television in the United States became a family mantra.

American movies—mostly entertainment films and Westerns—have brought another America: the glamour of Hollywood and its adages, "rags to riches," "go West young man," "gentlemen prefer blondes," and so on.[33] The bitter irony of these images sounded loud and clear in post-riot reflections in Los Angeles, and in L.A. lives in general. The anthropologist Renato Rosaldo suggests that the Philippines spent "nearly a half century in Hollywood (American colonial rule)" (1989, p. 197); the same can be said of South Korea. One Korean American merchant spoke at length about a photo of the actress Terry Moore[34] that he came across in *Silver Screen* as a junior high school student in a regional city in South Korea.

> She was posed in a steel helmet with her long hair against a long army jacket. The scene was snowy hills. Now I know that it was a really sexy pose, but then I just thought she was so pretty. I wrote a letter to her and sent it to the magazine. My uncle who lived with us at the time had studied at Tokyo Imperial University [during the colonial period] so my English was better than most

students'. She sent a letter to me and enclosed many photos and promotional materials. I brought them to school and the kids all swarmed around me.

This was "one of the most memorable events" of his childhood. He revived this youthful memory while talking about his experiences as a journalist in Vietnam.

Another immigrant dreamed of America through the saga of Scarlett O'Hara: "America? It was a place in novels I'd read, and films I'd seen. . . . It was Scarlett O'Hara and *Gone with the Wind*. I was going to live at Tara and meet Rhett Butler, I guess."[35] Speaking about his "otherwise politically radical" father, one Korean American explains: "But he had a special love for the United States. It was founded by highly intelligent men, was incredibly wealthy, was a democracy, and even had produced Elvis Presley and Marilyn Monroe. He had a wonderful time watching Gregory Peck and Charlton Heston duke it out in *The Big Country*."

These material and media encounters should not be taken lightly. The visceral presence of the United States that leaves its indelible mark on Korean cityscapes and personal material longing is a powerful marker of modernity and an inextricable aspect of immigration.

South Korea's Vietnam Interlude

In the mid-1960s, another U.S. military exploit in Asia—Vietnam— extended the U.S.–South Korea military engagement. South Korea sent troops to Vietnam from October 1965 to March 1973. The Defense Ministry reported 312,853 troops sent, 4,678 killed, 5,000 wounded, and 41,000 enemy deaths at the hands of South Korean troops (Sterngold 1992, p. 6; Han 1978, p. 893). The story of South Korean troops in Vietnam has been neither well documented in historical accounts nor openly discussed in South Korea (Suk and Morrison 1987). Thus it was newsworthy in both South Korea and the United States when two feature-length multimillion dollar movies were released in 1992: *White Badge* and *Farewell to Songha River*.[36] Not only did South Koreans and Americans fight side by side in Vietnam, but the U.S. military "saw" Korea in Vietnam; the misunderstandings, mishaps, and misdeeds of the Korean War were reproduced in Vietnam. One

Korean American veteran stressed that "the U.S. lost the Vietnam War because they mistook Vietnam for Korea."

South Korea's Vietnam legacy is relevant because a significant number of immigrants to the United States are South Korean Vietnam War veterans, who made their way to the States either directly from Vietnam or later from South Korea (Bonacich, Light, and Wong 1977, p. 55; see also Barkan 1992, pp. 118, 122). One veteran told us: "Once you leave Korea and eat off of Americans, you don't want to go back [to South Korea]." Another left Vietnam in 1969, traveled around the world, and ended up in Los Angeles, which he found the "most depressing" of all the cities he had seen; he then moved on to Canada, but made his way back to California in the 1970s, starting a shop in South Central Los Angeles. The central role played by Korean American Vietnam veterans in the informal militia during the riot days marks an interesting turn of fate: having immigrated as an extension of their combat under U.S. military command, a gesture in part in memory of their U.S. military service during the Korean War, they found themselves defending the Korean American community as it was abandoned by the public organs of the United States.

Military involvement in Vietnam provided an opportunity for South Korea to repay the United States for its contributions during the Korean War. It also secured the continued commitment of American troops to protect South Korea in the event of a North Korean attack.[37] Additionally, as an anticommunist war in Asia, Vietnam had particular meaning for South Koreans who, still only a few years away from their own war, inhabited a singularly anticommunist state.[38]

Beyond the diplomatic motivation for South Korea's participation in Vietnam, the war resulted in a remarkable boost to the South Korean economy (estimated to account for 4 percent of the GNP at its height in 1967 and totaling one billion dollars).[39] In 1970 "we can do it too" was a popular slogan in South Korea, referring to the enormous economic benefits that Japan reaped from the Korean War (S. Kim 1970, p. 522). For military men, the salaries and money-making opportunities resulted in personal fortunes: "Vietnam became Korea's El Dorado, a place Koreans could go to earn their fortune or seek adventure."[40]

Popular support for this troop assistance, however, was neither unanimous nor continuous. In 1967 South Korean opposition leaders charged that "the Korean government had 'sub-contracted' Korea . . .

and was thus fighting essentially a mercenary operation at the cost of Korean blood" (Lyman 1968, pp. 575–576); and the opposition candidate ran on a platform against "diplomatic servility" (S. Kim 1970, pp. 526–527). In *White Badge,* one soldier reflects: "I wished I could convince myself of the reasons, even one single reason, why I had to fight somebody else's war in somebody else's land" (Ahn 1989, pp. 213–214). The soldier is not only haunted by the meaninglessness of the Vietnam War but alienated from the economic boom piggybacked on his sacrifices: "The blood money we had to earn at the price of our lives fueled the modernization and development of the country. And owing to our contribution, the Republic of Korea, or at least a higher echelon of it, made a gigantic stride into the world market. Lives for sale. National mercenaries" (Ahn 1989, p. 40). Although contested at the margins, this military partnership and shared affirmation of cold war ideology are symptomatic of the long-standing ties between the United States and South Korea.[41]

The escalation of the Vietnam War and the entry of South Korean troops coincided with a massive increase in the Korean immigration to the United States. In this history, 1965 marks a watershed.

Post-1965 Immigration I: Background

The vast majority of Korean Americans arrived after 1965. Three factors critical for this era's migration were changes in U.S. and South Korean immigration policies, continued South Korean equation of the United States with modernity, and social mobility barriers in South Korea. Although policy changes dictated the numbers and to some extent the character of the immigration, the promise of modernity and mobility in the United States in conjunction with barriers to mobility in South Korea largely governed individual migration decisions. The United States promised national and individual prosperity, democracy, a Christian country, and "modern" family structure and gender relations. These promises came to life for those who faced blocked mobility in South Korea. The meanings attached to mobility and modernity, however, did not remain constant over the post-1965 era, and by the 1980s a series of changes had shifted the pattern and character of immigration. Although many post-1965 immigrants were highly educated and capital bearing, the generalization does not hold constant throughout this period. More recent shifts in the immigration composition are related to reforms in U.S. immigration policy, changes in significations of the United States, and new developments in the structure of social mobility in South Korea.

At the height of the U.S. civil rights movement, the U.S. Immigration and Nationality Act of 1965 abolished the 1924 national origins quota system and the so-called Asia-Pacific triangle, thus removing national origin, race, and ancestry as formal immigration criteria.[42] Designated relatives of U.S. citizens and permanent residents and people with special skills or training were to be admitted on a first come, first served basis. The relative preference categories extended to citizens' unmarried sons and daughters over twenty-one (first preference), permanent residents' spouses and unmarried sons and daughters (second preference), married sons and daughters and their spouses and children (fourth preference), and brothers and sisters and their spouses and children (fifth preference) (INS 1990, p. 37). Excluding immediate relatives (spouses, children, parents) and certain occupational immigrants, an annual limit of 20,000 immigrants per country was set.[43]

Called by some the "brothers and sisters act" (Reimers 1985, p. 94), the 1965 law resulted in an influx of unforeseen numbers of immigrants. From 1985 to 1987, the peak period of South Korean immigration to the United States, over 35,000 arrived annually, making South Korea the third-largest sender nation after Mexico and the Philippines.[44] This dramatic influx leads many Americans to blame national woes on immigrants. The calls to restrict immigration do not easily fall according to conservative, liberal, or progressive fault lines.[45] The journalist Daniel James charges: "California . . . is a basket case, largely because of a flood of immigrants in the 1980s that increased its population by 30.5 percent, to 31 million" (1992, p. 15). The newcomers "provided," he suggests, "the tinder for the rioting in Los Angeles."

In South Korea, a series of government formal actions coincided with the U.S. Immigration and Nationality Act in the United States. In 1962 the South Korean government promulgated an overseas emigration law to control population growth, lower unemployment, and acquire foreign technology (Light and Bonacich 1988, p. 103). The government also organized programs to send doctors and nurses abroad in order to earn foreign exchange, which left the country short-handed, particularly in rural areas (Light and Bonacich 1988, p. 89). In addition, South Korean labor contracts with foreign countries began in the early 1960s. From 1963 to 1974, 17,000 nurses and miners migrated to West

Germany (I. Kim 1981, pp. 53–54), and over half of the medical graduates between 1953 and 1985 from South Korea's prestigious medical
college, Yonsei, were practicing in the United States (Shin and Chang
1988, p. 612). Ironically, many of these professional immigrants have
not been able to exercise their skills and training in the United States.[46]

Post-1965 Immigration II: Class and Meaning

The meaning of emigration differs across the class spectrum, as do the
barriers that motivate the desire to leave. We begin by exploring how
the "modern" is conceptualized via political, religious, and familial systems and styles.

The material and symbolic goods that mark class and status in South
Korea are transnational (cf. Ong 1992, p. 127). A Mercedes, a Stanford
MBA, or consumer durables are shared class and status capital, and as
Stuart Hall notes, global mass culture "is centered in the West and it
always speaks English."[47]

But modernity goes well beyond material goods. The dissonance
between democracy as a marker of modernity in South Korea and
military authoritarian politics under the 1961–1979 *Park* Chung Hee
and 1980–1987 *Chun* Doo Hwan regimes was an important emigration
factor. Under the cloak of what was termed "Korean-style democracy"
(*han'gukjŏk minjujuŭi*), Park's authoritarian military regime was at odds
with many people's aspirations for a middle-class life that included both
personal and political freedoms. Many South Koreans believed their
own country to be "backward" and "undemocratic" (I. Kim 1981, p. 17).
We find a stark gap between political realities and the growth of South
Korea's GNP, with its corollary expansion of the middle class over the
1970s and 1980s. South Koreans wanted personal freedoms to accom-
pany their accumulating commodities: uncensored programs, for example, for their televisions.

Authoritarianism was deeply stitched in the fabric of everyday life:
the curfews, police and military presence, imprisonments, suppressions
of citizen unrest, tear gas, government controls on consumption and
reproduction, and censorship in every aspect of life—literary, intellectual, musical, and artistic (Nelson 1994). The interventionist state was
legitimated through cold war ideology. South Koreans lived under the
double threat of their own state and the terror of a communist inva-
sion. Many worried about another war, a persistent fear that fed on

memories of the Korean War and threatened the security of middle-
class life. The South Korean intelligentsia was particularly dissatisfied
with the political climate, and was active in antigovernment struggles.
One Korean American woman noted: "It is the excluded people who
end up here . . . often it is the intellectuals who feel the most excluded.
Many of the reasons people come [to the United States] are invisible:
the fact that we were divided, the American army. . . . It is all because
we were not an independent country [tongnip kukka]." Through the
migration of professionals and students, many Koreans with antigovernment sentiments and even experience in opposition movements
have come to the United States.[48]

Christianity, as was true earlier in the century, is another fundamental sign of the West and modernity. In the post-1965 era, South Korea's
growing Christian population is overrepresented among immigrants. A
1986 predeparture study found 54 percent of emigrants to be Christian
(non-Catholic Christian, 42 percent; Catholic, 12 percent), contrasting with 1985 figures for South Korea indicating a combined 21 percent.[49] To a large extent, this overrepresentation reveals the largely
Seoul-centered middle-, upper-middle-, and upper-class composition of
the Korean Christian church. In addition, Peter Park reminds us of "the
role of the Christian church in promoting the flow of immigration; the
U.S. immigration policy which makes it easier for ministers to immigrate; the ministry as a career channel for Korean immigrants; and the
material support given by American churches to affiliated Korean congregations."[50] Many South Korean Christians think of the United
States as a Christian country, holding it in high regard as the source of
South Korean Christianity. By extension the United States is also
credited to some degree with the virtues imparted to Christians in
South Korea, including superior morality, enlightened thinking, and
clean living. The prevailing sense of Christians in South Korea is that
they do not smoke, drink, or engage in "backward" religious or family
practices, including shamanism and, for some, traditional ancestor worship. Regardless of the realities of religious practice, Christianity has
also been associated with gender equality in South Korea in contrast to
patriarchal Confucianism's ritual exclusion of women.[51]

Indeed, the Christian church is at the heart of Korean American
life;[52] the staggering number of churches in any Korean American
center brings to mind the evening vista of Seoul, where green and red
neon crosses illuminate every hilltop. By the late 1980s there were

about five hundred Korean American Christian churches in Los Angeles (Yu 1990a, p. 2).

Independent of the particular Christian view of gender relations or Confucian ritual, in the post-1965 era the anachronisms of the Korean family system, authoritarian regimes, and military culture became unpalatable or even terrifying in the South Korean public realm. Gender equality and the isolated urban nuclear family unfettered by the constraints of an extended family signify modernity. For many women, moreover, the traditional patriarchal family—both its gender inequality and its familial obligations—became increasingly loathsome in their private lives. The normative Confucian family structure in South Korea burdens married women with duties to nurture their husband's immediate and extended family. In villages, marriage, particularly to eldest sons, often meant that wives lived with their in-laws, assuming a supporting role in the onerous ritual life of ancestor worship, tending to social relations with the extended patrilineal family, and severing ties with their own families (Janelli and Janelli 1982, chap. 2). The trials and tribulations of the young bride and particularly her relationship with her mother-in-law appear over and over again in the never-ending hardship stories of women (Kendall 1988). Although these requirements have been relaxed both in urban settings and in the countryside in recent years—young couples often reside independent of their parents, the ritual of ancestor worship has been simplified and its frequency diminished, and women often retain close ties with their own families—women continue to assume primary responsibility for the household, child care, and care for in-laws and relatives. After a semester of reading on the Korean diaspora, one Korean American student noted that she could not find the reason for her family's emigration in the literature: while her mother was able to emigrate because of her occupational status as a nurse, the "real" motivation was the oppressive extended family. Family duties can be unwieldy and unpleasant for men as well; eldest sons in particular feel burdened fiscally and emotionally by their siblings and parents. One Korean American laughed as he explained that his parents sponsored none of their relatives to immigrate because they left South Korea to get away from them.[53]

Immigration to the United States is thus invested with yearnings for modernity. But more specifically, it is affected by class position and identification. Although immigration is circumscribed by government policies—only a minority can emigrate—social mobility constraints shape emigration decisions.

A complex set of interrelated factors, including family background, educational attainment, and regional origin, affect class and status mobility. In part, emigration to the United States aims to subvert these barriers as people strive to achieve better material lives for themselves and higher-status positions for their children. Constraints on mobility span the entire class spectrum. There are, however, profound differences among the following immigrant scenarios: the poorly remunerated menial laborer who dreams of an improved salary and less draconian work circumstances; the middle- or lower-middle-class office worker who aspires to educate her children and buy a house; the upper-middle-class professional who feels that forces beyond his control are thwarting his mobility and longs for more; the academic who strives for a cutting-edge research environment; and the capitalist who wants to achieve a cosmopolitan upper-class identity and internationalize his children. Each scenario represents a situation in which immigration promises mobility that is somehow thwarted in South Korea, in real or symbolic terms. There are several important barriers.

The great class and status gap between mental and physical laborers in South Korea is an important factor in social mobility immigration.[54] The labor force shift of the 1970s and 1980s from the agricultural to industrial sectors promoted greater income inequality, depressing the relative poverty of manual workers and farmers (Koo 1984, p. 1031). South Korea's export-oriented industrialization relied on low wages, and the agricultural sector was sacrificed; its children were sent to industrial areas to work for low wages and elusive upward mobility. As late as 1986 South Koreans worked the longest hours in the world at low wages and under terrible work conditions (Lie 1992a). Not only did wages allow just a meager standard of living, but labor unions were tightly controlled and all unrest was severely punished. As South Korea's phenomenal GNP growth was in large part accomplished at the expense of the proletariat, the income disparities between mental and manual labor were exacerbated during the 1970s and 1980s when the laboring class became over 25 percent of the population. If we include those employed in the marginal economy, the lower fringe of the petite bourgeoisie, and the lower echelon of office workers, the numbers are even greater.

As the value of educational credentials escalated,[55] their attainment became critical to maintaining one's class position in South Korea. Although South Korea has experienced remarkable overall increases in terms of educational achievement, capital and other resources have become crucial in the attainment of a college, or even a high school, education. By the late 1980s, the poor child who made it to the head of the class and to Seoul's elite colleges had become an anachronism. The creation of class enclaves in Seoul has contributed to the growth of an informally stratified educational system, in spite of the dominant ideology that mandates the parity of schools everywhere. Escalating school fees and the extensive extracurricular tutoring critical for entrance into the elite educational track make family fortune a prerequisite for educational attainment. In addition, the "envelope problem" in South Korean schools—parents' payments to teachers to ensure privileged or at least neutral treatment of their children—has by now been widely publicized and was a central objection of the Teachers Union Movement (Chŏngyojo) in the late 1980s (H. Cho 1993, p. 26). Further, parents' educational capital—most specifically mothers' abilities to participate in their children's education in both a labor- and an intellectually intensive fashion—has similarly erected yet another requirement for educational attainment.

The United States holds out the promise of a college education and white-collar jobs for immigrants' children. One Korean American woman in Los Angeles described the difference: "Educating [through college] my children in Korea was like a star in heaven [that is, unattainable], but here [in the United States] there was a chance." Chatting with a group of women who lost their businesses in the riots, we heard an uproar of laughter following one recent immigrant's comment that if her children had been stupid she would have never thought of coming, implying that she came because her children had promise. As if to say, however, that it isn't so important to be smart in the United States, another woman remarked: "The United States is such a big land, and after all—if you go for it—anyone can get a Ph.D."

The situation of the rich, however, is different. For them, the United States affords a way of sparing their children the rigors and trauma of the South Korean examination system. It also provides an escape hatch for any less able children who, even with the finest of tutors, are unlikely to gain admission to elite colleges in South Korea.[56]

Even for those with a college diploma, however, other factors limit opportunities for mobility. The income benefits of education are not distributed evenly across the occupational spectrum. Hagen Koo and Doo-Seung Hong point out that managers in the 1970s earned "27,800 won for each increment in education, compared with 18,700 for petite bourgeoisie"; the returns were again skewed between small capitalists and workers (Koo and Hong 1980, p. 616). Similarly, managers are more highly educated than capitalists but earn lower incomes.[57] Increasingly, education does not ensure white-collar employment in large corporations. High rates of unemployment for college graduates— upwards of 30 percent[58] annually—have presented a grave problem for the middle class and are a palpable reminder that education alone does not guarantee an upper-middle- or even a middle-class lifestyle (Koo 1987, p. 109). In special programs marking the first anniversary of the L.A. riots in South Korea, the immigrant dream was repeatedly described as a "place where there would be rewards commensurate with labor and effort."

Beyond the limits in attaining educational degrees in South Korea are barriers for those without the requisite backgrounds and political favor. In South Korea, social networks and political favors have bolstered both corporate growth and individual mobility (E. M. Kim 1988). At all levels of the South Korean employment structure, personal networks have been essential to mobility; a dearth of contacts dooms one's climb up the bureaucratic or corporate ladder.[59] Factors impeding access to the "right" networks include hailing from the Southwestern coast, the economically underdeveloped and politically marginalized Chŏlla provinces (Honam region) (Yu 1990b); not having the valued elite or *yangban* (gentry) background; not being affiliated with one of South Korea's educational, military or even religious power cohorts—the "right" high school, military academy, or Seoul church; and being tainted by oppositional political ties and ideologies, especially a leftist family background. These multiple barriers create class hierarchies that reflect much more than educational attainment. A North Chŏlla Province immigrant and Korean American officeholder in the Honam Association in Los Angeles describes the sequence of barriers his compatriots face as a prelude to their decisions to emigrate:

> The problem with Korea is that once you are stuck at the bottom there is nowhere to go. . . . Our only path is to go to a regional

city, and then to Seoul, where discrimination pushes us out of the
country. . . . People in the Kyŏngsang provinces have been in
power for thirty years—all heads just veer in that direction; Korea
is a heaven for them. We from Honam, we are the ones working
in the markets in Seoul, but we are not among the ranks at the
military academies. We have been cut off for thirty years. It is like
when you cut a plant, it stops growing, and by now there are none
of us even qualified to rise up the ladder. . . . We don't need to live
in a place like that [South Korea], so we come here, to a place of
freedom. . . . So you see, this is the structure of Korea; we have to
come.

Los Angeles, then, is but the next destination in the struggle to overcome circumstances beyond one's own control.

Profound political shifts of the post-colonial era have also exiled
people who fall out of favor. One Korean American woman traced her
immigration to the New Year's day when the room in her house that
had always been reserved for holiday gifts remained empty—her father
had lost his government post.

Beyond particular barriers to class mobility are features of South
Korea's urban geography that render many of the trappings associated
with most people's vision of the urban, middle-class life unattainable:
most notably apartment ownership. Seoul and the South Korean media
are buzzing with the middle class's worries over whether it will be able
to reproduce itself and its lifestyle.[60] Rapid increases in land and housing costs in the 1980s shattered many middle-class dreams (Yi and Kim
1991), and the pressures have been mounting in Seoul. The *chŏnse* or
"key money" system, which requires enormous down payments in the
rental market, makes it difficult for many people even to rent an apartment. While women have long been warned not to marry eldest sons
because of burdensome filial requirements, recently some young women
are being told to marry eldest sons so as to secure housing. Beyond the
housing crunch, Seoul is an increasingly difficult place to live: its population density, pollution levels, and rate of car accidents are among
the highest in the world. By contrast, the United States promises
infinite territory and seemingly easy access to spacious homes and large
cars. These urban conditions have contributed to the changing contours of immigration, in which the entire class spectrum is increasingly
represented.

For those faced with insurmountable hurdles to mobility or fears over class reproduction, emigration offers another avenue, another future. Not all immigrations originate in blocked mobility, of course. For many the promise of U.S. prosperity alone—the ultimate symbol of global modernity—is reason enough. More and more, however, the place of the United States in the global hierarchy—the certainty of its promise—has changed. The protagonist's conviction in Younghill Kang's novel *The Grass Roof* (1947) that "future prominence lay toward America like the shortest distance between two points" is no longer universally shared.

The 1970s and 1980s: Trends and Numbers

Korean immigrants to the United States do not fully reflect the class distribution of South Korea—the upper echelon is consistently over-represented. The medical professional immigration programs, occupational preference programs, the student-abroad-turned-immigrant population, and the finances needed to emigrate have ensured disproportionately highly educated and professional Korean immigrants. The composition of Korean immigrants has been changing, however, since the mid-1970s. Several broad trends in INS (Immigration and Naturalization Service) data demonstrate that the immigration increasingly represents the entire cross-section of South Korea.

Although the numbers of South Koreans admitted under occupational preference—highly skilled and often professional—increased steadily through the early 1970s, their proportion relative to overall immigration declined. The downward shift in the social and economic profile of Korean immigration can in part be attributed to a 1976 act placing restrictions on the immigration of foreign medical school graduates and to the 1976 amendments to the 1965 Immigration Act, which shifted professional immigrants from third to sixth preference (INS 1990, app. A.1-16; I. Kim 1987, pp. 332–333). The increase of Korean immigration from levels hovering under 5,000 to the steady 30,000 to 35,000 annually throughout the 1980s is accounted for not by the 2,000 to 6,000 occupational preference immigrants but, rather, by the phenomenal growth in immediate relatives—not counted in the 20,000 per country quota—and those entering under the various relative preferences. Although 45 percent of South Koreans came under occupational or nonfamily preferences in 1972, this figure was only 6 percent

in 1983 (I. Kim 1987, p. 333). Recent immigration is thus often referred to as a chain migration, snowballing from the citizens and permanent residents already present (Tilly 1990; Yim 1991).

Reflecting these shifts in preference categories, a second important
trend is the steady increase from 1965 to 1972 of Korean immigrants
in INS-designated "high [status]" occupations, followed by a slow decline. Fifty percent were professionals in 1973, but this figure dropped
to 35 percent in 1977 and 22 percent in 1990. Clerical workers, by
contrast, rose from 6 percent in 1973 to 12 percent in 1977 and 18
percent in 1990. Laborers accounted for 4 percent in 1973, 13 percent
in 1977, peaked at 19 percent in 1982, and dipped to 12 percent in
1990. Farmers, although few in real numbers, also demonstrated an
increasing percentage, from 1 percent in 1973 to 4 percent in 1982 and
1990.[61]

Recent immigration statistics bear out these shifts. Insook Han Park
and his colleagues conducted predeparture interviews with approximately one-tenth of the 1986 emigration adult cohort (1,834 people);
they also surveyed 549 Koreans in the United States who had their
status adjusted that year. Reflecting the combined (family) chain and
mobility aspects of the immigration, 74 percent of those surveyed
answered that their primary reason for first thinking about immigrating
was for family affiliation; others referred to education (8 percent) and
work or livelihood (8 percent) (Park et al. 1990, p. 69). Family reunion,
albeit inextricable from other motivations, is a potent factor in immigration. Eligible relatives who emigrate, however, increasingly constitute a minuscule percentage.[62] Instead, it is necessary to consider who
among this pool of eligible relatives chooses to come. Park and his
colleagues found that the vast majority, 73 percent, came from Seoul
and neighboring Kyŏnggi Province. This is double the 37 percent of
population concentration that these regions represent in South
Korea.[63] The mean years of education were 11.7 for those surveyed
in South Korea, and 13.2 for those who were naturalized by ad-
justing their status in the United States. Although these figures are
considerably higher than the South Korean mean, 9 years, this difference is in part accounted for by the younger age of the immigrant
population than the general South Korean population (pp. 32–35).
Excluding immediate relatives who have a lower educational mean,
there are few significant differences among the various family and
occupational preference immigrants, except for the fifth preference—

brothers and sisters of U.S. citizens—whose education levels are slightly lower.

In the 1986 survey, 33 percent were engaged in professional and managerial work, a vast overrepresentation compared with the 8 percent engaged in such occupations in South Korea (Park et al. 1990, pp. 46–48). Occupational preference immigrants were more professional (49 percent), followed by a considerable drop for immediate relatives (15 percent), and a slight drop for family preference immigrants (10 percent) (p. 49). Park and his colleagues conclude that "Korean immigrants entering under family provisions . . . represent a diverse range of skills, including white-collar, blue-collar, technical, and service occupations" (pp. 49–50). This 1986 cohort group indeed confirms the increasing diversity of the immigrant population. With regard to class identification, 52 percent of the immigrants considered themselves upper (5 percent), upper middle (30 percent), or middle class (17 percent); 47 percent identify themselves as lower middle (28 percent) or lower (19 percent) class (p. 58).

Overall, 1970s immigrants were considerably better educated and well off compared with the South Korean population. Even in the 1970s, however, all classes were represented. In the course of the 1970s and 1980s, chain migration led in effect to more and more "poor cousins" who immigrated to the United States.

Resignifying South Korea and the United States

Many Korean Americans have suggested that the L.A. riots will come to mark a watershed in Korean immigration. Independent of the riots, however, South Korea–U.S. immigration has been decreasing since the late 1980s, and it may prove difficult to judge the independent effects of the riots. In 1992 fewer than 20,000 South Koreans emigrated to the United States, the lowest level since 1972 (Seo 1993, p. 14).

South Korean economic growth has delivered "the modern" to South Korea. The 1988 Seoul Olympics marked an important "arrival" for many South Koreans, who were keenly aware that the 1964 Tokyo Olympics symbolized Japan's global ascendance. For some, the Olympics signified a turning point for Korean American status in the United States. One older woman remarked that people used to ask her "Japanese? Chinese?" but, she smiled, "no more." Korean Americans were no longer just another Asian group, but "Koreans." The L.A. riots, however, add an ironic footnote to this equation as Korean Americans gained both fame and notoriety.

South Korea's growing prosperity and increasing political, social, and personal freedoms make many first-generation Korean Americans lament that they left. It becomes less and less clear that life in the United States ensures upward mobility when the signs of modernity have become readily apparent in the homeland. One Korean American merchant described the odd crossroads of the Korean immigrant in the United States today: "While [South] Korea is old, but getting young, the United States is young, but getting old."

These shifts in consciousness create immigration anachronisms. Late 1980s immigrants set off for the United States in a different crucible, and often found their predecessors' images of the United States behind the times. One Korean American remarked that the Koreans in the United States have not kept apace of the popular politicization in South Korea of the 1980s. A student immigrant noted: "Their [older immigrants'] idea of Korean identity is entirely from the 1960s, unchanged. For example, they still have an incredible anti-Japanese consciousness. After the recent publicity of the *wianbu* [comfort women], many boycotted Japanese goods. They don't distinguish recent Japanese immigrants from old immigrants." A Korean American merchant spoke about the "time bubbles" of various cohorts of immigrants: "They are all trapped in the bubble of when they left Korea." Returning from a trip to South Korea recently, he took a cab and met up with a Korean American trapped in such a bubble: "He [the cab driver] came from Korea as a student and went to the Midwest. He hasn't been back for twenty years and all he could do was talk nonsense about military dictatorships and this and that. He seemed like a stranger to me." He went on to refer to the Rip Van Winkles in his midst. One 1984 immigrant was surprised to find himself surrounded by people *still* talking about *ppalgaengi* (Reds, or "Commies") in the 1980 Kwangju Uprising, a civilian challenge to an undemocratic regime that was brutally suppressed.

If South Korea has changed, so has the meaning of success. Few Korean American triumphs can begin to approximate the lavish lifestyle of some in Seoul. Unearned income, particularly from land speculation, has created a class of nouveau riche whose members flaunt their wealth. Class distinction in Seoul is made particularly visible by the spatial segregation of the classes and by conspicuous patterns of consumption (D. Hong 1992). One student immigrant describes Seoul's privileged class: "They just sit back, not needing to work, and get treated well. They receive all sorts of services—chauffeurs and so on. They can order people around. For the same amount of wealth they get much more than they could dream of in the United States." A 1970s immigrant noted the changes in marriage preference that accompanied these shifts: "Until the [1988 Seoul] Olympics, every Korean mother seemed to want to marry off her eligible daughter to me because I had an American citizenship. After 1988, I noticed that fewer and fewer were willing to let their daughter settle in America."[64] Another immigrant remarked: "We used to visit Korea and hold our heads high; people were jealous. Now we go and they tease us." We frequently encountered the comment: "They think of us as kŏji [beggars] when we visit Korea." A swap meet guard, a Korean American Vietnam veteran, put it matter-of-factly: "Everyone would go back to Korea if they could; there is no immigration now; if someone talks about immigrating now in Korea they would be slapped across the face."

What makes the South Korean ascendance all the more remarkable is that many Korean Americans can point to the amazing successes of their South Korean counterparts, enriched by unearned income and political favor, who lead lives of luxury and comfort, while they themselves struggle to maintain squarely middle-class lives in the United States. Second-generation Korean American youths tire of the never-ending laments of their fathers that, had they stayed in South Korea, they would have become rich, a company president, a high government official, or a Seoul National University professor. The turns of fortune that affect the economic and status dispersal of any cohort of people—high school chums, business associates, neighbors, relatives, and so on—are more pronounced and more poignant in South Korea because of the rapid economic and social change over the last thirty years. And these class dispersals are palpable because sibling groups are often scattered across the class spectrum as marriage has largely determined women's social mobility. A second-generation Korean American said that while his uncle stayed in South Korea and purchased a plot of land south of the Han river—which by the 1980s had become fabulously valuable—his father had wagered on a plot close to the Los Angeles airport. His uncle is a very rich man in Seoul; his father a mere wage earner in the United States.

The rapid flow of information communicated personally and through the media to South Korea, replete with the blemishes and economic downswings of the United States, has tarnished the American dream. Stories of young people with college degrees who cannot find jobs, youth gangs, urban violence, racial tension, and most recently the L.A. riots have become commonplace narratives about the United States in South Korea. *Western Avenue*, a South Korean film that premiered in April 1993, depicts the lives of one entrepreneurial immigrant family and their losses in the L.A. riots and portrays the underside of the United States. The daughter, a theater student at Yale, ends up in a drug den. The film turns from this portrayal of moral turpitude to the trials of her immigrant parents as the daughter returns to Los Angeles to help out in their grocery store. The film climaxes with the riots, when the father, guarding his store, accidentally murders his son. The daughter's new love interest, the African American son of a long-term employee at her father's store, is killed by African Americans chiding him for coming to the rescue of Korean Americans.

One 1970s immigrant noted that until the early 1980s, when she returned to Seoul her friends and relatives were envious of her material possessions and the charmed life in America. Yet by the late 1980s, she was shocked that a salesperson in a small Seoul store offered her a great discount on a dress she wanted to buy: "He told me that he had a sister who emigrated to America and what horrible trials they had to go through. So he said: 'I know the kind of troubles you face in America so I want to sell the dress at cost. It's the least I can do for people like you who have suffered so much.'"

Anti-emigration sentiments are not entirely new to the 1980s, of course. Images of immigrants who desert the nation and rob it of its material and human assets are long-standing. A second-generation Korean American recalls being taunted by poor residents in Seoul for being a "traitor": "When they [poor urbanites] found out that we were Korean Americans, they started yelling at us. A drunk man in fact tried to slug one of my friends. They said that we had betrayed the homeland. Of course, we didn't decide to emigrate; our parents did." But the 1980s added new and deeper meaning to these sentiments. A young Korean American who left behind a sister who had been imprisoned in antigovernment labor struggles suffered enormous inner turmoil knowing that her sibling was deeply disappointed that she had decided to forsake the political and social struggles of South Korea. Elaine Kim recorded the life story of her half-sister in South Korea, who denigrates emigration to the United States:

> We are Koreans and we want to remain Koreans. My second son says that he'd rather live in the filthiest and poorest Korean place than in the most luxurious American place, just because he wants to live in his own country. Even though we aren't as comfortable, we like living in our own country. There's no place like your own country. During the past ten or fifteen years, many people have been leaving for the United States and Canada. . . . They sneak money out with them so they can start businesses, make money, and live out their dream of being like kings and queens in foreign countries. Sometimes these days, people in Korea criticize those who leave for America, saying they have deserted their motherland, taking all their wealth with them and leaving the problems for someone else to solve. (E. H. Kim 1989, p. 91)

The purported danger, depression, and disappointment of American life, however, are but part of the changed image of the United States in South Korea. Also important is the rapid escalation of anti-Americanism in South Korea of the 1980s. The roots of anti-Americanism are diverse, including radical political ideologies, economic nationalism, and nativistic cultural consciousness (Cho 1989; Choi 1989; Choi, Kim, and Cho 1991; Clark 1991). The 1980s was a decade of escalating popular political struggle; South Koreans went to the streets for political democracy, improved wages and work conditions, relief for farmers and the urban poor, freedom of the press, and reunification. By the end of the decade South Korea was transformed: the unthinkable was published in commercially circulated books and the unimaginable was voiced in private and in public. One Korean American woman comments: "It is best to think of each year in Korea as a decade; the changes are so great." Like much else, the United States too has been re-imagined.

Central to the changed popular image of the United States is the 1980 Kwangju Uprising, the civil insurrection against the ascendancy of military general *Chun* Doo Hwan to the South Korean presidency that resulted in an estimated two thousand deaths (Clark 1988). Because the South Korean military has been officially under the operational control of the U.S. military since 1950, many South Koreans insist that the commander of the United States military troops in South Korea approved the suppression of the uprising. The suppression was hushed up in the early years of the decade, and official tolls conceded only two hundred deaths. Official silence, however, was but a veneer over a rumbling ground swell nurtured by underground videos taken by German, Japanese, and British cameras, by books and political pamphlets, and by the transnational lines of communication in which South Koreans learned of domestic developments from their relatives and friends abroad and from American and Japanese television and radio.[65] By the end of the 1980s the government was forced to proclaim the "truth" of the Kwangju Uprising and to bring the by then former President Chun to trial. The United States was implicated in Kwangju many times over: its initial directives; a 1981 White House invitation extended to President Chun and continued U.S. support of his regime; and subsequent diplomatic decisions that demonstrated little understanding of the changing political tides in South Korea, such as the Bush appointment of a career CIA man, Donald Gregg, as ambassador.[66]

Kwangju was paradigmatic of a broad constellation of criticisms of the United States that crystallized over the decade. The 1980s were dotted with public protests against the United States, including several sieges of the U.S. Cultural Center and the Embassy. What started as policy-specific criticisms "began to acquire a coherent conceptual and theoretical structure, transforming anti-American *sentiments* into anti-American *movements*" (Choi 1989, p. 4). Anti-American movements criticized the dependent nature of South Korea's capitalist development and blamed the United States in part for the North-South division. Many South Koreans, even those of the moderate middle class, began to question long-standing positive images of the United States. The consensus on U.S. troops and nuclear weapons on South Korean soil and on U.S. support for Korean reunification faltered, and the muffled reporting on the crimes of U.S. military troops in South Korea came to light (Choi 1989, p. 7). While President Roh urged the U.S. Congress in 1989 to continue its military support—"imagine, if you will, hostile and combat-ready forces positioned as close to this capitol as Dulles Airport" (ibid.)—at home many opposed the extent and nature of the U.S. military presence and became convinced that reunification would only be realized after the American troops withdrew.[67] The Korean American writer Theresa Hak Kyung Cha's description of a return visit to South Korea after a long absence offers a sharp critique: "Our destination is fixed on the perpetual motion of search. Fixed in its perpetual exile. Here at my return in eighteen years, the war is not ended. We fight the same war. We are inside the same struggle seeking the same destination. We are severed in Two by an abstract enemy an invisible enemy under the title of liberators who have conveniently named the severance, Civil War. Cold War. Stalemate" (1982, p. 81). Here the United States is implicated as an accomplice in the division.

Contemporary South Korean cultural movements have also refashioned both South Korea and the United States. For example, visceral anti-Americanism emerges in the nativist cultural movements that reject U.S. cultural imperialism: American consumer goods, aesthetics, standards of beauty, Hollywood, and so on. By the end of the 1980s, the once ubiquitous English phrases on T-shirts were joined by han'gŭl (Korean alphabet) maxims and indigenous images, including Korean masks and dancers. These are, however, still minority movements;[68] Seoul's celebration of global consumer capitalism is readily apparent. Nevertheless, music clubs, dance troops, and art groups have turned inward, researching indigenous Korean music, dance, drama, and artistic expression.[69]

These South Korean cultural struggles are waged in Los Angeles as well. Through 1992 the most prominent façade of the Korean Federation Hall, identified as Koreatown's primary landmark, was a gigantic mural of a Korean mask dancer (J. W. Lee 1986, p. 36). We can imagine the effects of rapid cultural resignification in South Korea on the meanings attached to such an image; for those who left South Korea in the 1980s or who kept abreast of South Korean cultural politics, this enormous landmark was perhaps transformed from a mere marker of "traditional" Korean culture to a symbol of protest. We were surprised when we returned to Los Angeles in the early days of 1993 to find a new mural: a scene of farmers' music and dance. Indeed, by the late 1980s, farmers' music and dance had become powerful expressions of social dissent in South Korea.[70] An array of meanings envelop this Los Angeles mural as well.

The transnational diaspora situates Korean Americans in a historically deep and geographically wide displacement. Twentieth-century Korean history—colonialism, war, and their legacies, including national division, military authoritarian political regimes, and class polarization—is an inextricable part of the structure and meaning of immigration. In South Korea and the United States, immigrants are continuously being imbued with new meanings and metaphors. Shifts in South Korean ideologies and social structure, including meanings attached to the United States and increased class differentiation, are changing the face and extent of immigration. We observed earlier that riot responses must be understood in this crucible. Diaspora communities take form and transform amid these changes—changes of structure as well as of meaning. There is no pat answer to the question "Why did you immigrate?" Nor do immigrants arrive merely as vessels ready to assimilate, to imbibe a new culture. The gaze homeward is colored by ever-changing contexts. Nostalgia is only one face of a heterogeneous relationship to the homeland, and identities are constantly in flux.

4

Mapping the Korean Diaspora in Los Angeles

Koreatown, Los Angeles, is a major symbolic destination of Korean immigration to the United States. The portable homelands that immigrants carry in their minds have been materially re-created near downtown Los Angeles. Newcomers find that Koreatown in Los Angeles is in part a simulacrum of Seoul in Southern California, a Korea away from Korea: *han'gŭl* (Korean alphabet) signs line the streets, advertising Korean bookstores, restaurants, and shops in all directions. Koreatown, moreover, uncannily reproduces life in South Korea. Entering a *tabang* (café), we encounter unmistakably Korean furniture and decoration in a dimly lit room. Wafts of smoke float above businessmen conferring over low tables; a "no smoking" section remains a foreign concept. Puffing *p'alp'al* ("88," commemorating the Seoul Olympics) cigarettes, men exchange opinions, their white socks visible between their dark suits and their leather shoes. Female office workers huddle together, identified by polyester uniforms or tailored dresses. Waitresses take orders languorously and then bang saucers and dishes on the table; there are no seconds on coffee here. Exits entail cash payment; credit cards have yet to colonize all of Koreatown. Cultural certitudes crumble as we wonder whether this is South Korea or the United States.

Koreatown in Los Angeles, where Korean Americans across the labor and class spectrum gather, is a daily carnival of the display of Korean American difference: a parade of clothing tastes, automobile purchasing power, regional patois, and competing standards and expressions of "Koreanness." Yet what is a vibrant Korean American city

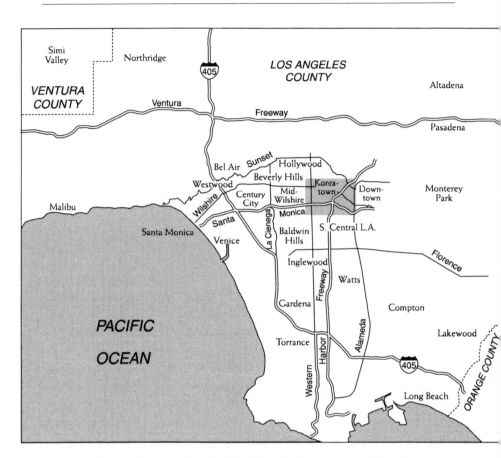

Map 1   The greater Los Angeles area (for shaded area, see Map 2)

by day turns into a quiet and primarily Latino town by night. Only a
tenth of Koreatown residents are Korean Americans (Yu 1990a, p. 3).

"White" Los Angeles

Los Angeles is geographically ambiguous and amorphous; there is no
unity of place or people. Famous locales—Beverly Hills, Santa Monica,
or Compton—constitute independent municipalities. The County of
Los Angeles, 465 square miles, contains the City of Los Angeles and
over eighty other cities. People from the counties of Los Angeles,
Orange, Riverside, San Bernardino, and Ventura—including 150 municipalities and over 14 million people—can all claim to be from Los

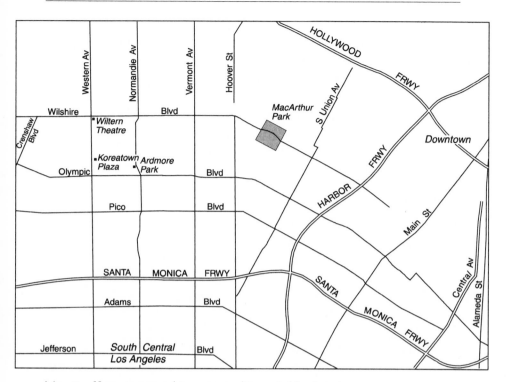

Map 2   Koreatown and its surrounding neighborhoods

Angeles. The intractability of Los Angeles invites extended metaphors and exorbitant claims. "Southland" to its residents, "La-La Land" to its detractors, Los Angeles is at once "the ultimate city of our age" (Rand 1967, p. 3) and the "most insulted city in the world."[1] Beyond the artificial oasis in a desert lies a mirage: Los Angeles as the final frontier of the American dream. Where the physical frontier of the American dream ends, there its fantasy life prospers. In the capitalist dream, however, begins the racial nightmare. Los Angeles's utopian characterizations are duly matched by its tragic and brutal history.[2]

Los Angeles's early history unfolded slowly. After its European discovery in 1542 and its founding in 1781, its population was only 139 in 1800.[3] Even after the post-1848 U.S.-Mexican War annexation of western and southwestern North America, Los Angeles remained a small town. Only with railway linkage to the eastern United States in the 1870s did Los Angeles begin to transform from the "Queen of the Cow Counties" (Caughey and Caughey 1976, p. xiii) into a terminus of westward expansion for landlocked European Americans. The process entailed the extirpation of Native Americans, the exploitation of Mexican and Chinese labor, and the establishment of a "white republic."[4]

The modern history of Los Angeles, as Carey McWilliams (1973, chap. 12) famously observed, cannot be told apart from a series of booms. Aided by citrus and oil, the city expanded continuously from the late nineteenth century. The completion of the aqueduct system connecting the verdant Owens Valley to arid Los Angeles (memorably fictionalized in Roman Polanski's film *Chinatown*) and the consolidation of the very source of American mythology (the Hollywood film industry) marked Los Angeles's coming of age in the early twentieth century.[5]

From the efflorescence of agriculture (oranges, for example) and other primary sector goods (oil, above all) at the turn of the century to the growth of manufacturing and service sectors by 1940, city boosters were critical in Los Angeles's seemingly endless booms.[6] Successive generations of boosters and capitalists, especially real estate speculators, constituted the ruling elite of Los Angeles. Its core was the Otis-Chandler dynasty and the *Los Angeles Times*.[7] For the first half of the twentieth century, local power elites rebuffed challenges from labor unions and progressives, and maintained racial exclusivity.[8] In the process, a relatively liberal and tolerant leadership transmogrified into a hard-line reactionary and racist stratum. We can glean the politics of white L.A. conservatives from two Southern Californian presidents, Richard Nixon and Ronald Reagan (whose presidential library is located in Simi Valley, the site of the Rodney King trial). It was only with the rise of Jewish Westside liberals in the 1950s that the WASP dominance of Los Angeles began to crumble (Davis 1990, pp. 101–128).

In the first half of the twentieth century, the vast majority of immigrants to Los Angeles, not just captains of industry and politics, championed white dominance. Bolstered by boosters and booms, Los Angeles promised prosperity especially to midwesterners smitten by its charmed life (Gregory 1989, pp. 42–52). Blessed by the nearly endless economic growth, arriviste Angelenos settled into a place where unbounded ambitions and desires might actually come to pass. Between 1890 and 1930, the population of Los Angeles exploded from 50,000 to 1.2 million (Fogelson 1967, p. 77). The "Great Migration" brought not destitute but relatively prosperous midwesterners (pp. 72–73). In 1930, 37 percent of L.A. residents were midwesterners, while southerners and easterners made up 13 percent each (p. 81). Further, though not rabidly racist by the standards of the time, many of them—like their descendants who joined the "white flight" of the 1980s and 1990s—sought racial and class homogeneity (p. 192).

Nowhere was homogeneity more striking than in residential patterns. What attracted midwesterners and other "native" immigrants, after all, was not only the warm climate and employment but also the possibility of home ownership. Suburbanization—made possible at first by the extensive public railway system and later by automobiles and freeways—extended the democratization of residential property (Bottles 1987, chap. 8; Brodsly 1981, chap. 3). By the 1940s, Los Angeles had become "the first modern widely decentralized industrial city in America."[9]

The curious mix of midwestern rusticity and Californian modernity was overlaid by racial homogeneity. Even new immigrant workers in the early twentieth century, including those from Mexico and Asia, did not vitiate the whiteness of Los Angeles; they were systematically segregated and sequestered into ethnic enclaves.[10] Incorporation and home-owners' associations were two of the primary mechanisms of exclusion.

The politics of incorporation proved to be a powerful bulwark in maintaining the class and racial exclusivity of L.A. neighborhoods. The incorporation of cities and municipalities enabled residents or businesses to achieve autonomy from public governance (Hoch 1984; Logan and Molotch 1987, pp. 181–187). Consider the history of Pasadena: "The excessively severe winter of 1873–74 convinced a number of middle class residents of Indianapolis, many of whom suffered from chronic ailments, that they had better emigrate to Southern California. . . . In 1875, when the community acquired a post office, it called itself Pasadena" (Starr 1973, p. 201). White middle-class Indianapolis was literally re-created in Pasadena, maintaining its racial and class composition. Beverly Hills, to cite another example, was essentially created by one company in 1906 (Banham 1971, p. 147). A city within the City of Los Angeles was thereby able to sustain its exclusivity. Where incorporation failed, homeowners' associations took over. Restrictive covenants, generated by grassroots racism, excluded nonwhite Angelenos from white neighborhoods. In the 1920s, for example, African Americans and Asian Americans could not purchase 95 percent of the houses in Los Angeles (Davis 1990, p. 161).

The flip side of "white" exclusiveness is the ethnic enclave, which some people believe arises out of ethnic solidarity.[11] But the facile belief in ethnic solidarity or the insouciant charge of inscrutability masks the vigorous racist practices that kept ethnics away from white areas.[12] While some areas, such as the barrios or Little Tokyo, became primarily identified with an ethnic group, the most salient division was between "white" and "nonwhite" (Sánchez 1993, pp. 76–77). A consideration of the concentration of Mexican and Japanese Americans in the barrios and Little Tokyo during Los Angeles's rapid growth from 1870 to 1930 is relevant to our examination of the Korean American experience.[13]

Mexican Americans have encountered systematic discrimination and exclusion from the powerful Anglo population at least since the annexation of California to the United States in 1848.[14] By the 1880s, most Spanish-speaking people lived "within a well defined adobe enclave surrounded by wood-framed Anglo-American suburbs. To the Anglos the barrio seemed to be a sleepy Mexican village, quaintly placed in the middle of their booming frontier city. They did not see that it was partially the creation of their own economic and social prejudice" (Griswold del Castillo 1979, p. 174). When Mexican Americans sought employment and residence in more prosperous areas, they encountered resistance. Simultaneously, the expansion of Anglo business areas or residential neighborhoods destroyed the barrios and forced their inhabitants to seek new residential areas.[15] By 1920, 40 percent of the estimated 50,000 Mexicans in Los Angeles lived in the Central Plaza barrio (Camarillo 1979, p. 205).

The residential segregation of Mexican Americans virtually hid them from the Anglo population. Charles P. Bayer of the Los Angeles Chamber of Commerce stated in 1926: "We do not have a varied group of different kinds of nationalities in Southern California" (Rieff 1991, p. 71). Mexican Americans were widely believed to be in decline, much like Native Americans (Griswold del Castillo 1979, p. 174; Steinberg 1989, p. 22). When they were noticed, racist practice and discourse awaited them; a 1928 *Saturday Evening Post* article wrote of East Los Angeles: "In no part of Poland or of southeastern Europe have I seen a more ignorant or more destitute class of people than the Mexican peons who were packed into the shacks that have flowed over this former truck garden district and in a few years time have buried it in slums" (Jacobs and Landau 1971, p. 257). Probably the worst outbreak of racism was the 1943 Zoot-Suit Riot, in which "a mob of 3,000 hoodlums dragged Mexicans, Filipinos, and Negroes from motion-picture theaters and street cars, beat them on the streets and sidewalks, and, in many cases, stripped them of their clothing. During the rioting, policemen watched the violence, made no attempt to intervene" (McWilliams 1973, pp. 319–320; see also Mázon 1984). In the 1990s, Chicano political exclusion, residential segregation, and underemployment and unemployment are reminiscent of their forebears' plight more than a century ago.

Japanese Americans, who first arrived in significant numbers in the 1880s, just as Chinese immigration ceased, were widely regarded by the 1930s as the most successful minority group in Los Angeles.[16] Their numbers grew from 41 recorded in Los Angeles County in the first census report of Japanese Americans in 1893, to 35,390 by 1930 (Modell 1977, pp. 17–18). Despite being better treated than Mexicans or African Americans, Japanese Americans still encountered significant prejudice, prompting Carey McWilliams to dub the period from 1900 to 1941 the "California-Japanese War" (1944, chap. 2). Japanese Americans' successes in agriculture, for example, generated white hostility and resulted in the 1923 Alien Land Law, which forbade non-U.S. citizens to own land. The legislation drove many first-generation Japanese Americans away from agriculture.[17] Japanese and other Asian immigrants could not become naturalized U.S. citizens until the 1952 McCarran-Walter Act.

Not surprisingly, Japanese American residences were concentrated in a few areas, most notably Little Tokyo. Contiguous to Chinatown and African American districts, Little Tokyo was one of the poorest areas of Los Angeles in the 1930s. In spite of its name, Little Tokyo was multiethnic, with substantial populations of European Americans as well as African Americans and Latinos.[18] Japanese American efforts to move into "white" areas generated neighborhood resistance, often leading to a covenant to exclude nonwhite people (Modell 1977, p. 60). A 1923 letter to the *Hollywood Citizen* exclaimed: "This is not a question of racial equality. It is simply the incompatibility of the white and the yellow races. We cannot mingle, socially, industrially, economically, or politically. Once a Jap always a Jap" (Modell 1977, p. 63). In such a racist climate, the terms of the 1924 Immigration Exclusion Act, which virtually ended Asian immigration to the United States, are no surprise.

The culmination of anti–Japanese American sentiments and movements was the internment initiated by Executive Order 9066 in 1942. Over 110,000 Japanese Americans, many of them U.S. citizens, were forcefully evicted from their residences and interned in various camps (Daniels 1962; Uchida 1982; Irons 1983, Okubo 1983). In this internment, ethnic segregation reached its modern American apogee.

"White" Los Angeles was thus a consequence of a century of racist exclusion. In the early history of Los Angeles, ethnic concentration stemmed more from white racism than from ethnic solidarity.

Economic Restructuring and Class Divisions

In the post–World War II period, the legal foundations of educational, employment, and residential segregation crumbled. The 1964 Civil Rights Act and the 1965 Voting Rights Act destroyed the legal and formal foundation of systemic ethnic discrimination and segregation in the United States. The Open Housing Act of 1968 rendered residential discrimination illegal. In Los Angeles of the 1990s, although financial constraints perpetuate exclusive enclaves of a rich, largely European American population, outright ethnic segregation is thwarted by the insistent reality of the multiethnic metropolis. What remain more resilient are class divisions. Beverly Hills residents, for example, can count on the real estate market, where a "shack" may cost half a million dollars, to prevent any influx of individuals unlike themselves; most people simply cannot afford to live in Beverly Hills.

The changing economy shaped Los Angeles's ethnic and class geography. In the 1970s, the U.S. economy deindustrialized, entailing capital flight from and plant closings in the traditional industrial centers.[19] Global competition pressured profit-driven U.S. industries to lower operating costs or relocate overseas to exploit cheap, nonunionized labor. In the aggregate, however, Southern California's industrial growth continued. The geographer Edward Soja writes: "Since the late 1960s, [Los Angeles] has experienced a concentration of industry, employment growth, and financial investment that may be unparalleled in any advanced industrial country."[20] From 1970 to 1985, although manufacturing declined 1.7 percent in the United States, it increased 24.2 percent in Southern California (Scott and Paul 1991, p. 191; see also Soja 1989, p. 192), making Los Angeles the largest manufacturing center in the United States by 1984 (Castells 1989, p. 218).

Aggregate statistics, however, hide important trends. In reality, as in the rest of the country, traditional manufacturing industries, including steel and automobiles, declined; by the late 1970s, Los Angeles faced a series of plant closings. Although Los Angeles had been the second-largest center for auto assemblies and rubber manufacturing in the 1970s, these industries had virtually vanished by the mid-1980s. Factory closures devastated the industrial heartland of Los Angeles, particularly South East Los Angeles. New high-tech industries, such as computers and biomedical products, established themselves in other parts of Southern California, primarily Orange County (Light 1988, pp. 63–64). While Fortune 500 plants were relocating to the Sunbelt or the Third World, new industries invigorated the Southern Californian economy.

New immigrants, primarily from Central America and Asia, have provided a large pool of low-wage, nonunionized labor. Low-tech industries in Los Angeles, such as the garment industry, which employed 65,000 in 1972 but over 100,000 by 1992, have been lowering wages to compete with cheap labor overseas (Cole 1992, p. 64). In addition to working at low wages, immigrant workers, unlike many "native" workers, have not been unionized. Power considerations thus join the short-term economic calculus in employers' systematic preference for immigrant workers, primarily Latinos, over "native" workers, including African Americans.[21] The deindustrialization of traditional industries went hand in hand with widespread deunionization; in the course of the 1980s, unionization rates of manufacturing workers fell from 30 percent to 23 percent in Los Angeles County and from 26.4 percent to 10.5 percent in Orange County (Castells 1989, p. 219). Both low-tech and high-tech industries have relied on cheap immigrant labor, which remains largely nonunionized and effectively controlled by management.[22]

The rise of Asian economies has heightened the importance of Los Angeles as a major node of the world economy. Asian, including South Korean, capital has looked to Los Angeles both as a place for speculative investment and as a foothold in the North American economy. Growing protectionist threats from the United States have also goaded Asian corporations to establish plants in the United States. Poor areas with new immigrants offer a rich repository of workers. The passivity and low wages of immigrant workers in the United States render them attractive for corporations facing militant workers in, for example, South Korea (Cho 1985). Financial speculation also provides stimulus for real estate development. Asian capitalists have often used existing ethnic enclaves as launching points; Little Tokyo attracts Japanese speculative capital, just as Koreatown attracts South Korean capital (Davis 1992b, pp. 27–29).

The L.A. economy in the 1990s is a bewildering composite: international finance, high-tech industries such as semiconductors, low-tech industries such as garments, and still significant entertainment, tourism, and service sectors. Los Angeles follows a powerful trend in the United States: the formation of a "dual city," marked on the one hand by professionals linked to the global capitalist economy, and on the other hand by manual and menial workers who serve them (Castells 1989, pp. 224–228; Reich 1991, p. 269; Sassen 1991, pp. 317–319).

In the 1990s, residential segregation is founded more on economics than on ethnicity in and of itself. Class divisions affect residential patterns. Privileged neighborhoods have seceded from the city as class divides have widened. The growing fear of crime has fueled attempts to insulate rich neighborhoods from the incursion of "undesirable" Angelenos. At its most extreme, neighborhoods have established gates to prevent nonresidents from driving on "their" streets. In 1993, nearly 150 neighborhoods sought to gate their streets.[23] While rich neighborhoods attempt to keep nonresidents away, the police and other security forces seek to "contain" poor people (Davis 1992e, pp. 160–167). The privatization of the public reaches its extreme in Los Angeles's myriad enclaves, reminiscent of Michael Frayn's dystopic world in his novel *A Very Private Life*.[24] Los Angeles resembles Third World capitals, where the rich–poor divide is literally unfathomable.[25]

Simultaneously, previously ethnic enclaves have often become multiethnic and impoverished. The rapid influx of Mexicans and Central Americans willing to work in low-tech and service jobs has transformed traditional working-class neighborhoods, such as South East Los Angeles: once a predominantly European American working-class area, it is primarily a Latino neighborhood in the 1990s. Similar trends exist in South Central Los Angeles and Koreatown, as we shall see.

The economic basis of residential segregation does not preclude racism. Both incorporation and homeowners' associations continued to be powerful forces in the postwar period (Davis 1990, pp. 165–169). Gary Miller comments that the newly incorporated "[city] guarantees that those population groups who demand welfare-type benefits will not be able to live within local boundaries" (1981, p. 98). Further, the suburban tax revolt of the late 1970s mobilized predominantly European American suburbanites to protect their capital gains and to resist inner-city residents and their demands (Lo 1990, chap. 7). Suburban incorporation and homeowners' associations in the 1950s often expressed white racism, and we may detect—through code words and symbols—the racist underpinning of the 1970s suburban tax revolts. In addition, informal discrimination has persisted throughout the postwar period. Mary Paik Lee, an early Korean immigrant in Southern California, recalls: "In the 1950s, most of the 'For Whites Only' signs on public restrooms, swimming pools, and so forth, were removed. But although there were no signs on barber shops, theaters, and churches, Orientals were told at the door that they were not welcome" (1990, p. 105). Three decades later, Mayor Barry Hatch of Monterey Park stated: "[A] billion Chinese . . . are looking for a soft place to land. There's nowhere else but here. The whole valley is what they want" (Davis 1990, pp. 207–208). Physical violence and egregious verbal abuse persist in the 1990s.

Yet it would be misleading to see only continuities. The civil rights movements destroyed the legal foundations of residential segregation. We are also likely to hear vehement denial from most European American suburbanites that they harbor racist sentiments (Sniderman and Piazza 1993). There is, however, the growing significance of class in determining the ethnic geography of Los Angeles in particular and the United States in general. Increasingly, class divides are more powerful than ethnicity in determining residential patterns (White, Biddlecom, and Guo 1993).

In the mid-1990s, Los Angeles is a city racked by economic inequality and ethnic divisions (UCLA Ethnic Studies Centers 1987). Driving on Wilshire Boulevard, an L.A. artery, from the ocean inland, one travels from rich to poor neighborhoods, encountering myriad linguistic and ethnic communities. The upside and the downside of the United States pose themselves in stark simplicity: while the rich live in sumptuous quarters and drive around in elegant cars, the poor work for substandard wages and move in decrepit jalopies. From the rich sequestered in their protected areas to the poor in their enclaves, one encounters both the opulent First World and the diverse Third World.

Let us now turn to South Central Los Angeles and Koreatown—the primary sites of the L.A. riots—as case studies of the class and ethnic divides of Los Angeles.

The Transformation of South Central Los Angeles

Despite South Central Los Angeles's notoriety, the political scientist Cynthia Hamilton notes, it "is simply home and neighborhood: many neighborhoods centering around churches and schools" (1992, p. 1). The *City Times*—a weekly—was started by the *Los Angeles Times* in the fall of 1992, after the riots, in part to demonstrate that beyond crime and drugs in Los Angeles's inner city exists neighborhood life.[26] In reports on the L.A. riots, however, South Central Los Angeles became synonymous with poverty, decay, and the urban underclass. The tension between Hamilton's description of solid neighborhoods and media reports on urban decay can in part be resolved by noting the changing contours of South Central Los Angeles. Originally a working-class neighborhood, South Central Los Angeles has suffered from deindustrialization and the exodus of working-class and middle-class African Americans. Since the 1970s, the influx of low-tech industries in nearby areas has increased the number of Latinos, particularly Central American immigrants. South Central Los Angeles has become increasingly multiethnic and poor.

Los Angeles's relationship with African Americans has been checkered (Glasgow 1980; Wheeler 1993). Although "white" Los Angeles sympathized with the Confederacy, midwestern immigrants, many of them Republicans and hence antislavery, made Los Angeles more tolerant of African Americans in the early twentieth century.[27] The Central Avenue area became a center not only of African American culture but of African American business by 1910.[28] Yet segregation was, as we have seen, the rule by the early twentieth century. In 1922 a Santa Monica newspaper admonished African Americans: "We don't want you here; now and forever, this is to be a white man's town" (Fogelson 1967, p. 200). In the 1920s, the potential African American political dominance of Watts, to the east of South Central, resulted in its annexation to "white" Los Angeles.[29]

African Americans gradually migrated southward and westward with the encroachment of European Americans (McWilliams 1973, p. 325). As with the barrio, African American residential settlement followed the dictates of white settlement. The African American population became concentrated in Watts and South Central Los Angeles in the 1940s in conjunction with the growing migration of African Americans to Los Angeles. The wartime industrial boom increased the number of

African Americans from about 64,000 in 1940 to 171,000 in 1950, while the overall population of Los Angeles rose by a third, from about 1.5 million to 2 million (Collins 1980, p. 41; see also Nash 1985, pp. 92–97). African American residences became concentrated roughly ten miles south of downtown for several reasons: the need to house newly arrived African Americans, the white desire to develop the downtown area without an African American presence, and the area's proximity to new factories in South East Los Angeles. South Central Los Angeles was divided by a "Cotton Curtain" that ran along Alameda Avenue, separating the African American from the European American working class. In 1950, 78 percent of African Americans in Los Angeles lived in Watts or South Central (White 1991, p. 510). Another area of concentration was Little Tokyo, which African Americans moved into and renamed Bronzeville after Japanese Americans were interned during World War II (McWilliams 1973, p. 325; Davis 1992c, p. 56).

The industrial boom of Los Angeles—powered by heavy industries located in South East Los Angeles—sustained South Central's economy in the 1950s and 1960s. Since the 1960s, however, two factors have devastated Watts and South Central Los Angeles. First, Watts's importance in urban and interurban transportation declined by the early 1960s as freeways replaced railways. Watts had been "a key junction and interchange between the long distance truck routes, the interurbans and the street railways," such that "it is doubtful if any part of Greater Los Angeles, even downtown, was so well connected to so many places" (Banham 1971, p. 173). But the freeways almost inevitably "left Watts always on one side. Whatever else has ailed Watts . . . its isolation from transportation contributes to every one of its misfortunes" (ibid.; see also Glasgow 1980, pp. 37–42). Second, deindustrialization wreaked havoc on African American workers, particularly in South Central Los Angeles. Between 1978 and 1982, ten of the twelve largest nonaerospace factories closed down, putting 50,000 blue-collar workers out of work (Davis 1992b, pp. 30–31).

African American workers suffered disproportionately from deindustrialization. Edward Soja writes: "In the decade and a half following the [Watts] insurrection, the predominantly Black area of South-Central Los Angeles lost 40,000 in population, the labour force was reduced by 20,000, and annual median family income fell to $5900—$2500 below the city median for the Black population in the 1970s."[30] Except for the college-educated, most African Americans living in South Central Los

Angeles were shut out of well-paying jobs in the service and high-tech industries. Simultaneously, they faced competition from new Latino and, to a lesser extent, Asian immigrants in low-wage jobs in low-tech industries and the service sector. Most critically, new immigrants were willing to work for less money and fewer benefits. Unionized jobs in the service sector, such as hotel work, previously dominated by African Americans, became nonunionized jobs held by Latino workers, as wages fell precipitously (Soja 1989, pp. 206–208; Davis 1992b, p. 32).

In addition to the loss of industrial and service sector jobs, the economy of South Central suffered from the exodus of middle-class African Americans. The gradual withering of outright residential segregation, along with the enrichment of some African Americans, enabled middle-class and professional African Americans to live in "better" neighborhoods (Farley 1991, p. 293; Massey and Denton 1993, pp. 67–74). South Central Los Angeles thereby lost some of its potential leaders (West 1993, pp. 35–37).

Since the 1970s, Latinos, particularly from Central America, have moved into South Central Los Angeles. The proliferation of low-tech industries in South East Los Angeles and the demand for low-wage service jobs greatly accelerated the immigration from Mexico and the rest of Central America. The drastic shift in ethnic composition is unmistakable. Consider Watts: 82.0 percent of its residents were African Americans in 1980; by 1990, the figure had declined to 58.7 percent. As many African Americans left the area, Latinos entered: their proportion increased from 17.7 percent in 1980 to 45.2 percent in 1990 (Barringer 1992b, p. A12). South Los Angeles was 83 percent African American in 1963; by 1990 it had become only 44.8 percent African American. In the same period, the poverty rate increased from 27 percent to over 30 percent.[31]

South Central Los Angeles in the mid-1990s ranks with the South Bronx in New York City and the South Side of Chicago as a symbol of urban decay. Yet despite plant closings, infrastructural decline, and overall impoverishment, South Central Los Angeles is not simply an agglomeration of boarded-up buildings and pot hole–strewn streets. It remains, as Cynthia Hamilton stated and several Korean Americans told us, a place for "home and neighborhood." Nevertheless its nefarious representation in the dominant Anglo press—an image supported by widely publicized poverty and crime—effaces the humanity of South Central Los Angeles. The extensive media coverage of the area during the L.A. riots offered many Southern California residents their first glimpse of the "inner city" in their midst and confirmed many of their worst suspicions about its violent nature (Davis 1992d, p. 57).

Multiethnic Koreatown

The explosive growth of Koreatown in Los Angeles occurred in the 1970s; Koreatown is a product of the post-1965 immigration (Kim and Wong 1977, p. 230). Although Koreatown is an indisputable economic and cultural center for Korean Americans of Southern California, the Korean veneer camouflages both the multiethnic composition of Koreatown and the class divisions among Korean Americans.

Los Angeles has been a center for Korean Americans in the continental United States since the early twentieth century. In the 1910s, an estimated 40 to 50 Korean Americans resided in Los Angeles (Yim 1984, p. 520). Although there was no Koreatown there at that time, Korean American residences were concentrated on Macy and Alameda Streets and in the Bunker Hill area in the 1910s, and in the area defined by Vermont, Western, Adams, and Slauson avenues in the late 1930s (Givens 1939, p. 22; Yim 1984, p. 521). By the 1930s, with roughly 650 Koreans, Los Angeles could "be considered the 'capital' of Korea in the United States."[32] The Korean Presbyterian Church erected its own building in 1938, which is still in use, at 1374 West Jefferson Boulevard, while the Korea National Association building was at 1368 West Jefferson Boulevard. This area, roughly two miles south of the current Koreatown, was then the center of Korean American activities (Yu 1985, pp. 34–36).

The virtual standstill in the Korean American population until the end of World War II and the slow growth until the late 1960s meant that as late as 1970, there were only 8,900 Korean Americans in Los Angeles County, accounting for roughly 13 percent of all Korean Americans nationwide. After Hawaii became the fiftieth state in 1959, some Korean Americans moved to Los Angeles; they were concentrated in the same area as in the 1930s, enclosed by Pico Boulevard, Hoover Street, Santa Barbara (now Martin Luther King Jr.) Boulevard, and Western Avenue (K. Lee 1969, p. 61). A Korean American businessman who came to Los Angeles for the first time in 1964 recalled the sight of illegal Korean immigrants who had arrived via Saigon, mess kits dangling from their belts, using outdoor public faucets to brush their teeth and wash their faces. Their collective image was negative. A 1972 report, for example, painted a bleak picture of Korean Americans in Los Angeles: "Their rudimentary agrarian background has not equipped them with the skills essential to making their way in their sophisticated new world" (Kwon 1972, p. 17). In the early 1970s, we find none of the accolades that were to stereotype Korean Americans in the 1980s.

The symbolic beginning of contemporary Koreatown in Los Angeles was the opening of the Olympic Market in 1971. Coming to Los Angeles via West Germany, where he worked as a miner, Hi Duk Lee bought the Olympic Market at 3122 West Olympic Boulevard, which attracted many Korean Americans throughout the region (Choy 1979, pp. 225–226; Holley 1985, p. 1; Yu 1985, p. 36). John H. Lee reminisces: "My memories of Koreatown go back to the early '70s, when I was a child. . . . We lived in San Diego, but periodically, religiously, [my mother] took my brothers and me on a two-hour drive north to visit relatives and to shop at a little market. . . . For years, Olympic Market was the best, if not only, place to buy Korean. My mother knew it, as did thousands of Southern California Korean-Americans" (1992, p. 157). Korean American businesses clustered around the food emporium. "A Korean bookstore, photo shop and barber moved into the same building, which Lee purchased in 1974. A second Korean grocery store came in across the street, and a Korean-owned bank building went up nearby" (Holley 1985, p. 1). From a few shops in the early 1970s, Korean American–owned businesses expanded in various directions. By the mid-1970s, the area was replete with such businesses and dotted with Korean-language signs. The Korean Americans who clustered there were generally new arrivals, not old-timers moving in from elsewhere in Los Angeles. "The area generally recognized as the area of Korean American concentration fans out about four blocks on either side of Olympic Blvd., between Hoover and Crenshaw Blvd." (Sunoo 1974, p. 7). Before 1970 Korean American concentration was south of Pico Blvd.; it shifted northward thereafter.

By the mid-1970s, Koreatown—or Korean Town as it was called then—was a recognizable entity. In 1974, for example, the first Korean festival was held (Choy 1979, p. 273). Nonetheless, the population remained predominantly non–Korean American. The 1970 census showed only 1,706 "Koreans" in the area, constituting about 2.0 percent of the total population. The largest group was "white" at 31.4 percent, followed by "blacks" at 28.2 percent, "Spanish surnames" at 15.9 percent, and "Asians" at 14.5 percent (J. W. Lee 1986, p. 24). In David Kim's study of Los Angeles Korean Americans, 76 percent of Korean Americans surveyed had come to the area in the last three years (1975, pp. 50–53). Of the 278 Korean American businesses in the area, 93 percent employed fewer than 10 people, and 68 percent had assets less than $50,000. The Korean American community was represented by younger people (between twenty-five and forty-four years of age), who accounted for 76 percent of the working-age population. An astonishing 83 percent of the men in the twenty-five to forty-four age group had college degrees. Of the men with college degrees, 51 percent were employed as operatives or craft workers, with only 7 percent in professional jobs. These settlers of Koreatown in the early 1970s were representative of the Korean immigrants to other parts of the United States. Won Moo Hurh, Hei Chu Kim, and Kwang Chung Kim characterize Korean Americans in Chicago in the late 1970s: "The Korean immigrants are relatively young (median age 36), most of them are married, highly educated (few years of college or more), and have been residing in Chicago less than six years (mean 4.47 years)" (1979, p. 91).

Koreatown grew uninterruptedly through the 1970s as the center of Korean American business and culture in Southern California. In addition to Korean American small businesses, South Korean money flowed into Koreatown. In particular, wealthy Koreans in South Korea and Japan sought an economic haven in the United States. Bong-youn Choy writes about the early 1970s: "Some [Korean American] businessmen profited from dubious political connections within South Korean ruling circles. A few wealthy Korean residents in Japan also entered the United States . . . to avoid unfavorable pressures from the Japanese government and business world. . . . Such businessmen . . . came to the United States because they felt it was a safe place in which to enjoy a luxurious life" (1979, p. 133). In addition to individual investors, South Korean banks and corporations established offices in Koreatown to gain a foothold in the United States where they could draw on Korean American employees.[33] This transnational business investment contributed to Koreatown's growth.

In 1980 "Koreatown" was officially designated by the City of Los

Angeles. While Los Angeles County accounted for only about 13 percent of the total Korean American population in the United States in 1970, the ratio rose to 17 percent by 1980 and to 20 percent in 1990 (including Orange County).[34] In the early 1990s, Koreatown was often described, in *Time* and elsewhere, as "prosperous" (Ellis 1992, p. 29). The predominance of Korean Americans and the surface opulence, however, are misleading.

Although devoid of a center, Koreatown is recognizable by its Korean-language signboards, South Korean and Korean American business establishments, and some Korean-style buildings with blue roof tiles. According to a 1986 study, however, more than half the Korean Americans surveyed could not name a recognizable characteristic of Koreatown. Koreatown was, in other words, "illegible."[35] This is symptomatic of the minority presence of Korean Americans in Koreatown, despite its Korean façade. The "illegibility" is not confined to Korean Americans. In spite of its size and proximity to downtown, Koreatown remains a foreign territory for many Angelenos.[36]

The fundamental fact of Koreatown for the larger public seems to be its hermetic character. None of our non–Korean American friends in Los Angeles had really been to Koreatown; some were even afraid of going there. A mid-Wilshire couple, living perhaps a ten-minute drive away from Koreatown, had never more than driven through it.[37] This is nothing new: a 1983 *Time* magazine article reports, "Stockbroker Jay Marshall, who lives in the upscale Westwood section, did not know until last week that there was an enclave of 150,000 Koreans downtown" (Andersen 1983, p. 19). The neglect of Koreatown by white L.A. residents can also be gauged by their general unfamiliarity with Korean cuisine. While Thai or Indian cuisine has enthusiastic followings, Korean restaurants appear to attract mainly South Korean visitors and Korean Americans. A 1993 restaurant review records others' responses: " 'I've never been to a Korean restaurant,' said the first person I took to dinner at [a Korean restaurant]. 'I've never been to a Korean restaurant,' said the second person. . . . 'I've never been to a Korean restaurant,' said the third, the fourth and the fifth."[38] Over many meals in Korean restaurants in Koreatown, we saw fewer European Americans than in some Korean restaurants in downtown Seoul.

Indeed, Koreatown appears to evoke horror for some European Americans; driving through Koreatown before the riots, the L.A. novelist Carolyn See writes:

[T]here's not an English sign to be found. Here, all is neon signs and minimalls and businessmen and women in high heels and shirtwaist dresses, and I'm wondering, why, when the U.N. supposedly fought the Korean War, did the *U.S.* end up with all the Koreans? Because, outside of kimchi [*kimch'i;* a spicy Korean staple], I just don't like Koreans. They seem to me to be the white Protestants of the Orient: all their Korean Airlines ads are just big lies—when you fly coach on that airline it's somewhere down below a zoo and into the prison-camp category. They are bad business as far as I'm concerned, but at least I'm making good time driving this stretch because if you caused or participated in a traffic jam in Korea-Town they'd haul you out of your car, take you into a freshly swept and whitewashed alley, put you into a tear gas canister, and sell your car for a tidy profit, but not before they detailed it carefully, and I don't like their roof tiles either! (1992, p. 102)

See's soliloquy encapsulates many stereotypes about Korean Americans —hard-working, gruff, enterprising, cunning, and so on. Moreover, she weaves seamlessly between South Korea and Koreatown, USA; the evocation of tear gas canisters recalls the U.S. media coverage of student demonstrations in the late 1980s South Korea. The widely disseminated image of fire and looting only reinforced many individuals' determination to avoid Koreatown.

It is not, however, only non–Korean Americans who neglect, or even dread, Koreatown. Several Korean American suburbanites claimed that they no longer went to Koreatown because it was "dangerous." The resistance of suburban Korean Americans to Koreatown has been devastating for many Koreatown businesses that cater to them. An owner of a restaurant that serves primarily wealthy Korean Americans told us that her business had been "terrible" since the riots. A self-professed "insider" said: "Korean tourists don't come to Koreatown anymore." A middle-aged Korean American woman told us: "My suburban [Korean American] friends don't even want to come to Koreatown to eat lunch; they would rather eat Western food [*yangsik*] in the suburbs than come into Koreatown." To be sure, she herself lived in posh Bel Air—at a thirty-minute drive, a safe distance from the cacophony of Koreatown.

What keeps suburbanites, whether European American or Korean American, away from Koreatown is its reputation as a "bad" neighborhood—an impression solidified by the riots. A young Korean American activist told us: "Koreatown has the highest crime rate in all of Los Angeles." We were repeatedly told to avoid Koreatown at night. The seemingly prosperous Koreatown masks pockets of palpable poverty. There are homeless people and panhandlers. One interviewee noted in horror that there were even Korean American beggars in Koreatown. The median household income of Koreatown residents is roughly half of the California average, and even lower than that of South Central Los Angeles (Senate Office of Research 1992, p. 2).

Koreatown is also multiethnic. By night, Korean Americans are virtually absent. Even during the day, smaller streets feature Korean signs alternating with Spanish signs. Next to a Korean herbal medicine shop, for example, stands a Salvadoran *pupusería* (restaurant), while a sign for a Korean *dentista* advertising *"se habla español"* is next to a *sundubujip* (Korean tofu stew restaurant). In 1990, 40 percent of Koreatown-area business was Korean American owned (Yu 1990a, p. 4). Four types of establishments exist. First, there are hotels, restaurants, and shops that cater primarily to South Korean businesspeople and tourists. Second, Korean Americans are the main customers at various shops and services ranging from Korean food stores to acupuncturists. Like the mother from San Diego who frequented the Olympic Market, there are many Korean Americans throughout Southern California and beyond who look to Koreatown as not only a symbolic but also a consumption center. The third type serves mainly Latino clients. They may be further subdivided on the basis of national origin: there are, for example, Guatemalan restaurants selling national newspapers and goods. Finally, there are multiethnic establishments, ranging from small supermarkets to "American" restaurants such as Denny's.

Beyond the Korean façade, Latinos are ubiquitous in Koreatown. Hardly an establishment exists without a few Latino employees. Peering into many kitchens of Korean restaurants, we discovered not only Latino dishwashers but Latino cooks. That many Latinos speak smatterings of Korean contributes to the seeming incongruity. In many Korean American stores and services, ranging from stereo stores to law offices, there are Spanish-language signs to attract Latino clientele. Along with suburban Korean Americans, Latino residents constitute a large group of customers. A Korean American graduate student, who studies Latin American politics, quipped: "Before I used to worry that I had never been to the countries I studied. But living in Los Angeles, I can rightly say that I am in the Third World."[39] The multiethnic composition of Koreatown—particularly the Latino majority—accounts in part for the large number of Latino looters during the riots. The census figures are telling. Korean Americans constitute only a tenth of the Koreatown population. Of the 1990 population of 61,000, 68 percent were Latinos and 26 percent Asian Americans (Yu 1993, p. 157).

Many Korean Americans, keenly aware of the undesirability of living in Koreatown, have sought suburban homes. As was true for African Americans, the decline in residential segregation after the civil rights legislation of the mid-1960s and the gradual enrichment of some Korean Americans led to their exodus from city centers.[40] Suburbanization continued even after the explosive growth of Koreatown in the 1970s. David Kim wrote as early as 1975: "American-born and not-so-recent immigrants who have better financial status are living more in the outer rings of the city and the suburbs" (1975, p. 50). A 1979 newspaper article reported: "Many second-generation Koreans or those who immigrated long ago have moved out to expensive residential neighborhoods. Brokers could cite dozens of families who have bought property in Bel Air, Beverly Hills, Holmby Hills and other exclusive areas."[41] In a 1986 study, over half of the Koreans surveyed said that they would rather not live in Koreatown. The most popular "first impression" of Koreatown was one of "disorder" (J. W. Lee 1986, p. 24). Jerry C. Yu of the Korean American Coalition summarized: "As soon as people can afford it, they move out of Koreatown. . . . Who would want to live here? We have the highest crime rate and the worst public education" (Schoenberger 1992, p. A20). Poverty, not ethnic solidarity, keeps Korean Americans in Koreatown. Korean Americans who remain in Koreatown, then, are generally poor or elderly (Yu 1990a, p. 44). While only 16 percent of Korean Americans in Koreatown own a home, the figure rises to 61 percent for those living elsewhere.[42]

Korean Americans live all over Southern California. The number of Korean Americans living in the generally affluent South Bay, for example, roughly doubled between 1980 and 1990. Although the majority live in middle-class Gardena and Torrance, Korean Americans are increasingly moving to wealthier suburbs (Millican 1992, p. B3). Because there are already two thousand Korean American–owned businesses in the South Bay, Ik Soo Kim told the Los Angeles Times: "I don't have any reason to go to Koreatown these days" (Millican 1992, p. B3).

The desire to live in solidly middle-class neighborhoods such as Torrance and Gardena, or in wealthier areas in the peninsula, is no surprise. Wealthy Korean Americans have fled to outlying suburbs and even to rich enclaves such as Beverly Hills. Ethnic enclaves are, as we have seen, not based simply on ethnic solidarity. Without strict residential segregation—which has been eroding in the post–World War II period—ethnic residential concentration dissipates. Following the flight of Korean Americans to various suburbs are Korean American businesses, and even South Korean businesses have migrated to the suburbs (G. W. Park 1988, pp. 59–60).

Korean American suburbanization recapitulates the dream of home ownership that brought midwesterners as well as African Americans to Southern California. Los Angeles suburbs, with detached houses surrounded by ample yards, are a compelling fixture of the American dream (Wright 1981). For immigrants with school-age children, a good school system is also extremely important. As we discussed in Chapter 3, a crucial concern for many Korean immigrants is their children's mobility. A middle-aged professional told us with some satisfaction that he had bought a house in one of the richest suburbs with an excellent school system. He added that there were very few minorities in the neighborhood, "proving" its desirability and exclusiveness.[43] Although social critics often decry suburban isolation and lack of community, Korean American suburbanites we interviewed were less troubled by the absence of community life. They prided themselves on their large houses, unimaginable had they stayed in Seoul. Many Korean Americans prefer isolation to the web of complicated and demanding human relationships associated with the South Korea they left behind. The pursuit of modernity and mobility, as we have seen, propelled Korean immigrants to leave their homeland. Indeed, the desire to be left alone often discourages ethnic solidarity. It is the source of the often-voiced criticism of "Americanized" Korean Americans (Choy 1979, p. 222).

Nonetheless, Koreatown remains important for many Korean Americans. As the demand for Korean-language professional services has increased, many Korean-speaking professionals, ranging from accountants and architects to lawyers and medical doctors, have set up offices in Koreatown. Beyond the economic, however, Koreatown remains symbolically important. One professional we interviewed said that his "mission" before he returns to Korea is "to make Koreatown better, like

Japanese Town and Chinatown, where everyone, not just Koreans, can come, eat, and shop." Furthermore, a Korean American pastor observes: "As Christian Korean Americans living in Los Angeles, our Jerusalem is Koreatown" (Kang 1993, p. 26). The Christian metaphor highlights Koreatown not only as the spiritual center for Korean Americans but also as a place where Korean Americans need to empathize with and proselytize the multiethnic poor. The symbolic significance of Koreatown explains in part the emotional devastation many Korean Americans, the vast majority of them living outside of Southern California, felt as they watched the fires on television during the riots. Elaine Kim, lamenting the destruction of Koreatown, writes: "Los Angeles Koreatown has been important to me. . . . For me, knowing that Los Angeles Koreatown existed made a difference . . . and I liked to think of it as a kind of 'home' " (1993a, p. 216).

Yet Korean American solidarity remains more rhetoric than reality. Koreatown lacks an ethnic residential community or a central political organization. There is a widespread perception of a leadership gap among Korean Americans in Los Angeles (H. S. Lee 1978). No major neighborhood associations exist. Even though over 80 percent of Korean American adults in Southern California read at least one Korean-language newspaper, newspapers have provided little local coverage of Korean American news (S. H. Lee 1988, pp. 106–111). Although there are five hundred Korean American churches in Los Angeles, they are divided along denominational lines, and are rife with institutional and ideological rivalries (Shin and Park 1988). Voluntary associations, albeit numerous, are small and revolve around particularistic ties, such as alumni and professional associations.[44] Finally, probably the most inclusive organization, the Korea Federation (Haninhoe), has been racked by bitter personal feuds, and many Korean Americans perceive it as being too attached to the South Korean government. Its inability during and after the riots to represent or unify the Korean American community has further diminished its legitimacy. It should be noted, however, that existing, as well as new, organizations have become increasingly active since the riots.

In sum, although Koreatown in the mid-1990s serves as the economic and cultural center of Korean Americans in Southern California, affluent Korean Americans have fled to the suburbs. The 1992 riots further loosened Korean American suburbanites' tenuous ties to Koreatown. Ethnic solidarity, in other words, is giving way to class polarization. In broad outline, the drama is being repeated in Korean American communities in other major U.S. cities. We can broadly generalize it as the fate of many ethnic enclaves in the United States: those who prosper exit, while the poor remain.

Class Distinction and Ethnic Solidarity

As Koreatown, Los Angeles, reproduces the material signs and consumer culture of Seoul, it also reproduces its visceral class distinctions. In our discussions with Korean Americans, we found a complex field of cross-cutting sentiments, identities, and politics. And nothing was more variously articulated than the question of class.

Our discussion with one Korean American woman revealed class diversity and class discrimination. She explained that while there were "lower-class" immigrants in the United States, she had never known any. But several minutes later in our conversation she suddenly exclaimed, "Wait, I remember, there are some," and continued, "my father's driver immigrated in the 1970s and really struggled. His mother opened a liquor store. Another of his relatives went to Brazil. Immigration seems to be about many of *those people* [*kŭrŏn saramdŭl*]. . . . Oh yeah, and I have relatives—they were poor in Korea—and they sent their daughter to immigrate and get married; things are getting a bit better for her." This woman's narrative—the awkward surprise in remembering that her father's hired hands were among the lower-class immigrants, and the surprise again that such immigrants even number among her own relatives—reveals the class cartography, its odd distances and denials, that is reproduced in the United States.

Mainstream media discussions have largely neglected class distinctions among Korean Americans. The media failure to appreciate the tremendous income and educational inequality among Korean Americans is in part due to the much-vaunted Korean American entrepreneurial success. As we will discuss in more detail in Chapter 5, the dominant perspective projected a particular role for Korean Americans: that of the hard-working immigrant entrepreneur. Yet this conflation is a particular instance of the more general American reticence to talk about class. It is a symptomatic expression of the ideology of the American dream, which we will explore in more detail in Chapter 6. Finally, there is little doubt that the strength of nationalism has led most Korean Americans to homogenize themselves as "Koreans," especially when talking to non–Korean Americans.

In discussing class differences, we do not mean to subvert the concerted efforts—both before and after the riots, discursive and organizational—to promote ethnic solidarity, but instead to highlight a crucial fault line of the transnational Korean diaspora. Korean Americans often describe immigration waves according to class character. They characterize, for example, their immigration cohort as having had a harder time than the next, or say that the immigrant "level" (class character) has been going down over time. Regardless of their year of arrival, many insist that the immigrants who have arrived after them are more fortunate, both for the paths that have been trod before them and for the spoils of recent South Korean prosperity that they bring with them. Indeed, South Korea's GNP growth, wage hikes, and official relaxation of rules regarding the amount of currency that can be taken out of the country have made it possible for immigrants to bring larger sums with them. The new wealth that older immigrants mention suggests money that has been tainted by the power elite in South Korea. One 1960s immigrant recalls: "My parents often speculated about all the new rich Koreans who came to America. I remember hearing about ties to President Park, KCIA [the Korean Central Intelligence Agency], and so on, and how the uneducated could be so rich."

Let us first listen to a middle-aged woman who regards herself as a paradigmatic hard-working and successful immigrant. In her spacious living room, Im spoke about the "swap meet problem." Referring to the women who tend the stalls, she said: "You know, they have no education; they are like the women you would meet at Namdaemun in Korea." Namdaemun, a sprawling outdoor market in Seoul, seems to stretch endlessly in a sea of haggling, quick transactions, regional patois, and city grime; there is nothing refined about the market. Im's description of the swap meet proprietors as nothing more than Namdaemun shopkeepers in an indoor, U.S. setting is a quick shorthand of distinction—noting that she belongs to an entirely different class of people. In South Korea the distance between outdoor markets such as Namdaemun and fancy department stores is enormous; items fulfilling the same function can be found at prices that are 100-fold higher at department stores. Similarly, in Koreatown in Los Angeles, the difference between the specialty shops catering to suburban Korean Americans and the swap meets for the local multiethnic clientele is like night and day. She continued: "Only 10 percent of them [swap meet stall owners] are OK. They don't behave well. I can't stand dealing with them so I don't go to swap meets." In past forays to swap meets she was appalled at the racist comments "such women" would make aloud in Korean. "I would hear them say 'hey you black thing, come here.' How terrible it would be if they [African Americans] knew how they were being spoken about."

Im did not reserve her critique to these "lower-class" immigrants, but went on to discuss "the problem of new immigrants"—another group, she explains, that has generated anti–Korean American sentiment and activities.

> The new immigrants—the rich ones—drive around in [Mercedes] Benz; earlier immigrants don't do this. Of course this angers the blacks; those people aren't contributing anything to the community. People like me who have worked really hard to finally be able to afford a house and live somewhat well, hate people like that who are just capitalizing on the incredible strength of the *won* [South Korean currency]. I mean just imagine that by today the submarine rides at an amusement park in Cheju Island [an island off the South Korean southernmost coast that is a frequent honeymoon and vacation spot] are $250! You can't even compare that to Disneyland. Things have changed so much, it is unbelievable. The newcomers laugh at Koreans like me who have worked so hard.

Sensing herself to be the object of class scorn and an anachronism as a result of the recent South Korean economic boon, she thus abhors the nouveau riche who flaunt their wealth in unflattering ways, which she feels reflects poorly on all Korean Americans. "The truly rich who come and can afford to purchase whole buildings just sit back smugly and sleep their days away." Im meets such women at the community pool, where the children in the after-school swimming program are over 80 percent Korean American. She complains that some mothers just lie down on the benches in the locker room meant for children to use: "They completely forget that there are non-Koreans there as well. Korea is like that—people who live well don't care about anyone else. These women live as if they were in Korea." The earlier immigrants, she remarks, were "better"—better educated and well mannered—"we made efforts to fit in." Her characterizations of people in other classes leave her suspended between low-class racists and high-class snobs.

Another woman spoke of "the problem of Koreans who arrived in the 1980s with piles of money": "They whiz about in their fancy cars, playing golf all day long. It's a huge problem." One former nurse who came via West Germany and opened a store in South Central Los Angeles three years ago complained that the 1980s immigrants have "an entirely different concept of money; it is a 'heaven and earth' difference. Their ways of thinking, their lifestyles, are completely different. They come and, boom, purchase a house immediately. Of course there are some newcomers who have known hard times and have no learning."

Class differences—usually described as "levels" or by educational attainment—are ubiquitous markers differentiating Korean Americans. A social service counselor explained the gulf between the owners of swap meet stalls and liquor stores, and between the nature and meaning of their riot losses. Beyond the scope of their businesses, the counselor suggests that class background in South Korea is crucial.

Swap meet stall owners haven't been in the United States very long. They can't speak English. What they lost didn't have so much value, so they can start up again. They are—well, I don't mean this in the bad sense—low class. Many of the liquor store owners were rich in Korea and sold lots of land to get capital to emigrate and start a business. They had lots to lose [in the riots]. They really can see how much better they would have been if they had never left [South Korea]. Everyday they put their lives on the line [to go to work]. Yes, their returns were big, but they never take even a day off.

In the same way that Im delineated class-inscribed occupations such as swap meet stall ownership, others suggested class divisions between Korean Americans in Koreatown and South Central Los Angeles. Yang explains that there are two kinds of immigrants, "high and low." A shopkeeper, he is an active participant in his college alumni association in Los Angeles. When we asked him if he might suggest any friends for us to speak with, he confidently told us that there would be no reason to, because all of the alumni of his prestigious alma mater think the same way and would say the same things. He continued:

The lower-class immigrants really know how to work hard and make money, and since they are uneducated they are the ones who don't speak English. After a while the "high ones" want to make that kind of money also. . . . It is the less educated ones who are in South Central, and many of them are from the Chŏlla provinces. People from the Chŏllas are survivors and they are good at making money—probably many of them were victimized in the riots.

Yang conceded that after some years—as educated Korean Americans join "lower" Korean Americans in small businesses, and as the children of "lower" immigrants succeed—the differences become blurred: "It gets all mixed up." Similarly, Whang, a suburban Korean American who lives off of inherited wealth, remarked that "educated or not, after several years in South Central Los Angeles, everyone becomes the same; educated people forget their education." Because he has never run a small business in South Central or anywhere else, those who end up in South Central blur into an undefined mass. The perspective of those who labor in South Central, however, suggests a rather different scenario.

The problem of class tensions manifested itself starkly in the struggles over money collected in South Korea and in the United States for the riot victims. Our intention here is not to review their labyrinthine struggles, but instead to discuss the struggles over the money as a window on class fissures among Korean Americans. One Korean American activist observed: "The riots and the disbursement problem distinguished economic strata among the owners."

Opinions clashed over how the money should be spent. Some felt strongly that a mere division and disbursement would be myopic and that, instead, the funds should be set aside for facilities for the Korean American community. One highly paid professional felt that the money should be used to make a commemorative building or statue; he castigated the short-sighted victims for selfishly thinking about their own minuscule needs. Another suggested that the funds should be used to prevent such riots from happening again. The distribution problem took on enormous symbolic value. Mental health counselors said that many riot victims were traumatized over it. Several counselors reported that for some victims the loss of this money, albeit a pittance in comparison with business losses, loomed larger than their initial loss.

Workers—unemployed after their employers' shops had been burned or looted—were outraged that none of the funds would reach them, saying that they were hurt more than the owners. For some Korean Americans, the situation pitted the individual greed of the victims against the collective good. Others, however, suggested that this was a case of upper-class Koreans promoting their cosmopolitan values while victims languished.

Overshadowed by successful self-made entrepreneurs, working-class and unemployed Korean Americans felt consistently neglected by the media and by the Korean American community. Shin, organizing to ensure that some of the collected money would reach the employees, explained that in "capitalist, socialist, and communist countries alike, it is absurd for employees not to be compensated." He noted that the disbursement issue was not about money but about power in the Korean American community. Repeatedly speaking of the *puja* (rich people) and "rich men" (in English), he was furious with the formal victims' associations that excluded people like him. When he went to Radio Korea: "They didn't want to hear from us. So we asked, 'Why don't you want to report on us? What are you, the victims' association [made up of owners] radio?' " While he refused to beg rich Korean Americans for the money, he was stunned that the money wouldn't come to people like him with "fierce hurt, mentally and otherwise."

There is something wrong: Radio Korea, the newspapers, the consulate, the certified public accountants. It is a "ridiculous" story; we need to announce it to the public. People [Korean Americans] need to be *kyemong* [enlightened; he asks us what the English word is]; who are we supposed to sue? The victims' association? The consulate? What is the matter with the Korean community? All these people have such high education, such high positions. I am truly embarrassed for them. I didn't even go to college. . . . There should be an FBI investigation [of these Korean American groups] to find out how the money has been spent and where the interest has gone. They should get the maximum punishment *regardless of their social status*. They should go to jail.

Folding down his lip to show us a huge canker sore from the stress and explaining that he has no money or access to medical services, Shin told us that many of the so-called victims were even making money off of the riots, grossly overreporting their losses, and that they knew nothing of the lives and plight of employees.

> This kind of thing [leaving employees out] can't be. Rich Koreans don't know anything. . . . You know I'm a church leader, an "evangelist" [he says in English]. The church just preaches about love: "If we had more love everything would be OK, blah, blah, blah, that our people [minjok] must have more love." But people with more money look down on us—that cannot be.

Another worker, Pae, complained that the leadership class or chidogŭp "knows nothing about the practical lives [sil saenghwal] of the lower class [hach'ŭng]." Again and again he talked about the "real lives" of "working people." Pae, who was seeing a counselor because of his "emotional suffering," had had most of his belongings "taken" and said that the bills were piling up. He explained that for a few hours after therapy he felt fine, but that he quickly began to feel crazy again.

> It is not that I want to fight against people who ignore us [rich Korean Americans]. . . . I feel embarrassed in front of my three children. I can't tell them that our Korean community is rotten. The leaders only know their own lives. This is unheard of—in any or all other ethnic communities the employees would be taken care of first—so why isn't this the case for Koreans? The owners [of stores] can only think about financial matters, but I am talking about bodily, psychological, and daily-life victimization. They lived well, their refrigerators are full; we only shop once a week. They are people "who have [own] [innŭn saram]," while we are people who live week to week. They always have something to eat; we live hand-to-mouth.

In spite of these comments on the chasm between the haves and have-nots, Pae insisted that the gap between the rich and the poor (pinbu ch'ai) is more severe in South Korea. Because the United States is a "credit society," at least you can live "as if" you are rich, he explained: "If I wanted to drive a fancy car I could—so America isn't as severe." He explained that very few laborers, about twenty-five, were gathered that day, although there were some six hundred who had lost their jobs. Many unemployed workers shunned the public meetings because "they are embarrassed to be workers, to appear in front of other Koreans as laborers. . . . Koreans always want to be the boss." Like many others he criticized the recent rich immigrants who brought in hundreds of thousands of dollars and purchased lavish homes without struggling "even a bit."

As Pae suggests, the desire for material plenty can be fulfilled by relying on credit cards. Class differences vanish—only to reappear with a vengeance in the form of debt-ridden futures. Several Korean Americans suggested that many Korean Americans live above their means and flaunt their wealth. Kim, a social worker, complained that people regard California Korean Americans as superficial and materialistic, but he conceded: "Many people live in cheap apartments ($300 a month), but drive Mercedes, wear Rolex watches, and play golf even though they can't really afford it. If you go to Koreatown restaurants you'll see these middle-aged guys hanging out after golf, showing off to each other." One rich woman suggested that Korean immigrants have become extravagant since they came to the United States. Her husband dismissed this notion out of hand: "No way, it's our [Koreans'] basic nature [ponjil]. The only difference here [in the United States] is that people have more money, so it's more obvious." What lies behind conspicuous consumption is the desire for material goods—which we examined in Chapter 3—and the desire to erase, at least on the surface, class differences.

The desire for mobility manifests itself in the difficulty of labor organizing.[45] A Korean American woman activist told us that labor organizing is extremely difficult because "Koreans look down on labor itself and thus on labor organizing as well." The combined legacies of Confucianism and of more recent labor exploitation under patriarchal capitalism in South Korea have succeeded in ideologically and economically devaluing manual labor; remarkable in South Korea is an almost universal desire to educate one's children to ensure their passage into the ranks of mental laborers. Perhaps the realities of blue-collar employment take on added symbolic meaning, suspended in the mobility dreams that collectively encompass the immigration itself.

Class tensions were also evident in social service organizations and emergency counseling offices that emerged after the riots. Irreconcilable sentiments surfaced in the interstices between organizations' political platforms and the political and personal demands of the riot victims. "Victim work," tending to the victims' emergency needs as they worked their way through the U.S. bureaucracy, represented a new, and sometimes very different, direction for some social service and political groups. For agencies formerly focused on Koreatown lower-income youth, for groups catering to the situation of laborers, or again for agencies catering to the mental health needs of the community, this work put them in contact with a much broader range of Korean Americans. Kwon, a social service worker, worried: "Nowadays [after the riots] everybody is only talking about 'race relations' and other preexisting programs seem to be going down. I think there is too much focus on race. We need to remember other problems, including drugs, AIDS, and family problems." Kwon continued that he has a "difficult time working with riot victims. . . . I wonder if we should be working with them—maybe we should stick with what we know best [working with youths]." Kwon, who identified himself as "Korean" although he grew up in the United States, was torn between the needs of "desperately poor" Korean Americans and the political requirements for collective action.

One social service worker explained: "How were we to turn our backs on people who had lost everything? What does it matter if they used to have ten employees?" Another social service worker laughed about having had to write numerous payment deferral letters—a service intended for those with poor language skills—for a victim with ten credit cards. Most remarkable among the deferral letters was the one to the *Wall Street Journal.* One young person with an official position in one of the trade organizations—introduced as "highly educated, single and an observant Christian" in the organization's bulletin—stated that he felt at odds with the emotional response of the merchants, who were inclined to protest rather than "lobbying through the state's proper channels."

Some spokespersons even found themselves in the awkward position of presenting positions that they could not identify with. Angela Oh commented: "The sentiments I am expressing are sentiments I know exist in the Korean-American community. I don't necessarily always agree with the stuff I am communicating to the public, but I feel I have a responsibility to do that" (Hicks, Villaraigosa, and Oh 1992, p. 46). In an interview, she elaborated: "I know I'm not a representative of the majority of the Korean community in Los Angeles. I think I give voice to their anguish. . . . But I'm not a merchant. I've never run a shop. Nobody in my family runs a shop. They're all factory workers."[46]

A lengthy discussion with Chon, a Korean American woman deeply concerned with the plight of Korean American laborers, similarly demonstrates the awkward play of class and ethnicity via the riots. An organizer in the South Korean labor movement before immigration, she explained that while Korean American shopkeepers in the United States were in fact "cheap labor"—whole families work absurdly long hours for minimum returns[47]—her true commitment was to workers. She acknowledged the complexity of such political work because "labor organizing can be counter-productive to community development and solidarity." She wavered: "Of course our focus is on the employees, but you need to be able to see it as a whole; if you break it down by employer/employee you end up dividing the community." For many community service workers and activists, these issues are particularly complex because of the difficulties in translating political agendas from South Korea to the United States. For Chon, the politics of labor organizing in South Korea translate with great difficulty in the United States, where all Korean American labor is minority work, where there is a politics of minority solidarity. She ended our discussion on yet another note at the crossroads of ethnicity and class: the great difficulty of organizing unions among Korean Americans who work for Korean American-owned companies.

Riot responses thus unleashed a wide spectrum of Korean American differences. Whether expressed as the time of arrival in the United States, educational and status backgrounds in South Korea, or newfound successes or failures in the United States, class cleavages defy any simple generalization about Korean Americans.

Class differences take on new meanings as they are resituated in the multiethnic United States. We recognized this in a discussion among four women, who were tending swap meet stalls. One of the women said that she knew of "no woman in Koreatown who hasn't been mugged," noting, "life is so much 'higher' [class] in Korea." By now (the 1990s), "even the [South Korean] women who come through international marriages [that is, military wives] are 'high level'—rich and educated." To mention that by now "even" military wives are well off and educated was her way of suggesting the changed meaning, or even the absurdity, of immigration for Koreans, her way of underscoring the chaos and blight she found in the United States. From here the four women talked about the abominable "education level" in the United States: "They [customers, mostly Latino] don't know right from

wrong—their 'level' [class] is extremely low." Their discussion moved
from the impossibility of returning to South Korea, to the danger of
inner-city life in a poor multiethnic neighborhood [Koreatown], to the
upward mobility of military wives, and finally to their lower-class,
uneducated customers. Although they represent the lower reaches of
the Korean American community, they point to the generally "low-
class life" in the United States and particularly the "low level of their
customers." In turn, while they are proud of South Korean prosperity
and "high levels"—that nowadays even military wives are rich and
educated—they realize that they have been shut out of this prosperity:
they cannot go back. Their discussions thus reveal a complex transnational play of class and status.

5

Korean American Entrepreneurship

We have stressed the heterogeneity of Korean Americans in Los Angeles. In the vast majority of media accounts, however, the figure of the Korean entrepreneur—a model minority seeking to achieve the American dream—came to stand for L.A. Korean Americans. In the next chapter, we will criticize this conflation and scrutinize its underlying ideological assumptions. In this chapter, we will analyze Korean American entrepreneurship.[1]

In most media accounts, Korean American entrepreneurial success is articulated as a function of cultural characteristics, such as hard work, frugality, family and ethnic solidarity, and so on. This essentialized ethnic portrait, however, is deceiving. The ability of Korean Americans to open small businesses depends on a confluence of factors that cannot be reduced to the ethnic or cultural characteristics of Korean Americans. It is necessary to transcend ethnic essentialism and consider the class-based resources of, as well as the opportunity structure facing, Korean Americans. Such a perspective also illuminates why Korean Americans, and not African Americans, tend to open shops in South Central Los Angeles.

Four Portraits in Search of a Stereotype

The following thumbnail sketches of four Korean immigrants who arrived in the United States in the mid- to late 1970s underscore not only their diversity but also their divergent fortunes.[2]

Lim, whom we encountered in Chapter 2, arrived in Los Angeles in the mid-1970s. In South Korea, he had amassed a vast fortune. Using his connections in the South Korean political and business world and his facility with English and Japanese to deal with U.S. and Japanese companies, he had enough money by the late 1970s to buy homes in Los Angeles, Honolulu, and Tokyo in addition to his domicile in Seoul. His children were schooled in the United States, and he continues to live in Los Angeles part of the year. His favorite Korean restaurant is in Beverly Hills; even before the riots, he hardly ever went to Koreatown.

Park studied architecture at a prestigious South Korean university. Because his wife was a nurse, the couple received an occupational preference visa to emigrate to the United States in the late 1970s. Park landed a job with an American architectural firm where he stayed until 1990, when he decided to open an independent firm in Koreatown. He earned enough with his wife, who continued to work as a nurse in a large hospital, to own a spacious suburban home and maintain an upper-middle-class lifestyle. Although he had been satisfied with his initial job, he seized an opportunity to achieve autonomy by meeting a growing demand in the Korean American community. Because his office is now in Koreatown, he has become more interested in Korean American affairs, although he claims to know very little about Korean American businesses or about the Korean American community in Los Angeles. Yet he considers himself a "secondary victim" of the riots; in post-riot Koreatown, the optimism to build has waned. At the time of our interview, his uncle's family was staying at his home. They were en route to Seoul from their "failed" attempts at immigrant life in Argentina and in the United States. The uncle said: "It was bad in Argentina but it looks worse here."

After graduating from Seoul National University, Yun came to the United States in the late 1970s intending to earn higher degrees in mathematics. He abandoned his plan for graduate study, however, because he needed to earn a living to support his wife and child. "I'm a failure of sorts," he said as we talked in his living room in a posh suburb. He joined one of his relatives in running a small store selling trinkets. "It is very embarrassing but there is an expression here: 'What you do depends on who picks you up at the airport.' I, too, just followed my relative into the same business." Drawing on personal and family savings and encouraged by his friends, he opened his own store and was then able to sell it and become a wholesaler by the late 1980s.

We met Pae at a rally of workers seeking compensation for riot-related damage. He initially arrived in Houston in the late 1970s and found work at a Korean restaurant: "There were relatively few Koreans in Houston at the time, so they were happy to hire me." Eventually, he made his way to Los Angeles and worked at a variety of jobs. He opened a stall in an outdoor swap meet but abandoned it when it failed to generate adequate income. Unable to amass enough capital to open his own store, he worked as a manager of a Korean American liquor store in South Central, overseeing African American and Latino workers. After the store was destroyed during the L.A. riots, he became unemployed and worries whether his family will be able to sustain itself.

Korean Americans as Horatio Algers

The complexities and nuances evident even in our compressed portraits have been lacking, however, in most media reports. The dominant media portrait has insisted that Korean American self-made entrepreneurs personify the American dream. *Time* magazine wrote in 1985: "Like previous generations of immigrants many Asians seek to realize their personal American dream not just by finding a good job but by starting their own business, the ultimate statement of independence" (Doerner 1985, pp. 43–44). Even among Asian Americans, according to the author, "the entrepreneurial impulse runs strongest among Koreans" (p. 44). Korean Americans seem to embody the entrepreneurial spirit. From greengrocers in New York to dry cleaners in Los Angeles, many local industries are nearly monopolized by Korean Americans. Survey figures attest to Korean American entrepreneurial success. While 7.4 percent of European Americans are self-employed, the figure is 16.5 percent for Korean Americans (Hacker 1992, p. 109). In Los Angeles in 1989, according to Eui-Young Yu's survey, close to 40 percent of employed Korean American men owned their own business (1990a, pp. 12–13). Forty-four percent of them had household incomes of over $50,000.

Furthermore, Korean American merchants often trumpet their own success. Peter Kim, a bakery shop owner in Gardena, told the *Los Angeles Times*: "Most Koreans would rather be self-employed than work for someone else. They're hard-working people, [with] high goals, and very competitive on the average" (Millican 1992, p. B7). Yet, when probed, the stories of people like Kim become more complicated; he was a veterinarian in South Korea. To understand the experience of Kim and others, we must first ask what we mean by entrepreneurship, both in economic theory and in American folklore.

In *The Theory of Economic Development,* Joseph Schumpeter delineates the entrepreneur as an innovative force in the capitalist economy. In the masculine imagery of a risk taker and innovator, the entrepreneur represents the anarchic force that sweeps away the debris of the old order and fosters economic development. This creative destroyer fuels the constant innovation that is the hallmark of the capitalist economy. Joseph Schumpeter wrote that it is "the carrying out of new combinations that constitutes the entrepreneur," thereby "breaking up old, and creating new, tradition." The entrepreneur possesses "the dream and the will to forward a private kingdom" (1934, pp. 75, 92, 93). The entrepreneur is the heroic figure of capitalism.

The self-made entrepreneur is also an iconic figure in the American cultural landscape. As heroes of laissez-faire capitalism, entrepreneurs such as Henry Ford and John Rockefeller express Americans' deepest yearnings for material success. Through inspiration and hard work, the entrepreneur becomes rich and also enriches the larger society. This version of the American dream—the self-made entrepreneur—is also central in South Korea's recent celebration of capitalism.

In addition, some Americans consider small business owners to be pillars of the community. In this vision, Main Street entrepreneurs and the local Chamber of Commerce are the bedrock of small town life; business owners not only provide goods and services but also contribute to the welfare of the community.

Korean American merchants in Koreatown or South Central Los Angeles, however, deviate from both the academic and the popular portrayal of the self-made entrepreneur. Ford was a key architect of the automobile industry and Rockefeller amassed colossal fortunes; Korean American entrepreneurs, by contrast, are petty merchants, who run small corner markets, dry cleaners, or liquor stores. Although these occupations are valuable, there should be no illusions about their grandeur. Neither do Korean American entrepreneurs make innovations that spur economic growth nor do they, by and large, amass a fortune or make a major contribution to society. Has a family with a shop of its own, working seven days a week and making $50,000 a year, achieved the American dream? Is this the entrepreneur celebrated by Schumpeter or American folklore? Yun and his colleagues are not the pillars of the communities in which they set up shops. Most Korean American merchants in South Central Los Angeles do not even live in the vicinity of their businesses.

The social origins of the Korean diaspora, especially for the predominantly college-educated immigrants of the 1970s, suggest that most Korean immigrants had something beyond petty retailing or service in mind when they embarked on their journey to the United States. Entrepreneurship was not glorified in the South Korea of the 1950s and 1960s when most 1970s immigrants were growing up. Educational success leading to a career in the government or in academia—in part a legacy of Confucian Korea—remained the desiderata (Eckert 1990; Eckert et al. 1990, chap. 10). Commercial pursuits, especially shopkeeping, were less prestigious, if not frowned upon. To be sure, South Korea's rapid economic growth fueled popular desires for material success, which have been manifested in the Korean immigrants who seek a fortune in the United States. Simultaneously, as the news of successful Korean immigrant entrepreneurs spread in the 1970s, more Korean immigrants arrived intending to open their own business. Yet for many 1970s immigrants, small business was not their primary goal in the United States.

As we noted earlier, many 1970s immigrants had graduated from college, including extremely prestigious universities such as Seoul National University (SNU), Yun's alma mater. SNU is far more prestigious in South Korea than, say, Harvard is in the United States; while up to a fourth of those admitted turn down Harvard admission, those who decline SNU amount to no more than a handful. Lim, our millionaire entrepreneur, points out that a South Korean in the 1990s would choose SNU over Harvard because the SNU degree and alumni networks would permit entry into the South Korean power elite (Hattori 1992, pp. 203–205, 226–228, 231–233). For an SNU graduate to "make it" as a greengrocer or a dry cleaner in the United States is akin to an elite U.S. university graduate's succeeding as a convenience store owner in opulent Japan. Yun's declaration of his "failure" stems at least in part from the enormous promise and ambition he has as an SNU graduate. His financial success is, after all, modest for a potential member of the national elite. A son of an early 1970s immigrant told us: "It was painful for my father to get the news from [South] Korea about new cabinet appointments; very often, one of his former subordinates or a college classmate, people my father considered inferior, would become a minister of education or whatever." There were reasons, however, as we have seen, why so many potential national elites were willing to emigrate to the United States: the promise of modernity in the United States and the experience of blocked mobility in South Korea.

A more appropriate question for college-educated Korean immigrants is: why are they willing to become merchants? Professional careers do not guarantee wealth or happiness, of course, but a disproportionate percentage of U.S. university graduates pursue careers in medicine, law, management, finance, and perhaps even academia. South Korean college graduates in the 1990s seek a similar array of occupations. Korean immigrants have been, at least in intention, no different. Park was able to realize his training as an architect in a U.S. firm. Other Korean immigrants, especially those who have earned their degrees in the United States, also become professionals, whether medical doctors or college professors (I. Kim 1981, chap. 5). Still others, like the millionaire Lim, would never deign to operate shops in Koreatown or South Central Los Angeles. Just as entrepreneurship has not been the royal road for most college-educated Korean Americans, people with accumulated capital do not open small businesses. They are more likely to invest in stocks and bonds or speculate in real estate. The economic behavior of rich European Americans and rich Korean Americans is similar. An older Korean American man told us: "Although brains can't make money, money can hire brains. It's always best to have money." As he implies, rich Korean Americans transcend linguistic and other barriers and are able to act like any other transnational capitalists.

In the ideology of the American dream, Korean American entrepreneurship is something to be celebrated. Yet this interpretation misses a prior and more pressing question: why would an elite seek entrepreneurship in a poor, inner-city neighborhood? Consider a college-educated European American: would she invest money and risk her life by opening a liquor store or a dry cleaners in a poor minority neighborhood? Wouldn't she rather pursue a professional career? If she were to go into business, wouldn't she open a business in Beverly Hills or Santa Monica rather than in Watts or Compton? The incongruous image of a college-educated European American opening a shop in a poor inner-city neighborhood should make us question the idea that

Korean Americans are somehow naturally inclined toward opening and running small businesses. The reality of Korean American entrepreneurship does not necessarily accord with the American dream; as a Korean American professional put it: "Why would you want to chase after pennies?" Why then do people like Yun, a Seoul National University graduate, decide to become small business owners?

Yun's experience suggests that many well-educated Koreans are unable to pursue professional careers in the United States. There are systematic barriers to converting their South Korean credentials into U.S. careers. College degrees or professional credentials are often not transferable across countries. What meaning does an SNU degree hold for most Americans? A dry cleaner's daughter told us: "I was shocked when I visited Seoul one summer to realize what it meant to be a Seoul National University graduate. Because so many of my father's friends had gone there, I thought it didn't mean much, although my parents had always been so proud of my father's alma mater. Now I feel that I understand my father's frustration and sacrifice better." In Marie G. Lee's novel *Finding My Voice*, the protagonist, a high school student, discovers that her father had attended SNU, "the very best school in Korea." Her father tells her: "Many of my classmates have gone on to become big people in . . . Korea. Yet over here, all people cared about was that my degree was not American. . . . So now . . . you and your sister can do more than I or your mother ever could: you will graduate with degrees from Harvard, and nobody can say anything to you, because everyone knows Harvard."[3]

Accompanying the institutional barriers are linguistic limitations. Many immigrants do not speak English well enough to attain a professional position. Although they could undoubtedly learn on the job, getting a job depends on their prior facility with English. No one we interviewed could think of a first-generation Korean American working for a major U.S. corporation. The language barrier is consistently cited by Korean immigrants as the most serious problem in their life in the United States.[4] While Park, the architect who worked in a U.S. firm for a decade, is able to articulate his thoughts in adequate English, the same feat is beyond Yun's capacity. This is hardly a reflection on Yun: nobody doubts his intelligence, but his English conversation skills have never developed beyond the minimum necessary to undertake business transactions. One Korean American woman, who writes that her father "is truly one of the most brilliant people I know," observes: "He does not speak English well at all. He has a very strong Korean accent. Ever since I was a little girl, I have seen how people treated him because of that. They treat him as if he is an idiot. They would raise their voices, thinking that would help him understand them better" (J. F. Lee 1992, p. 28). Another immigrant notes: "Sometimes I knock on doors to get business, and people look at me like I am a savage because I don't speak English right" (Trachtenberg 1986, p. 70). One of our interviewees, a graduate of prestigious Yonsei University's commerce department, possessed a knowledge of the international economy and its impact on Los Angeles that was as compelling and cogent as any that we had read. Yet his analytical prowess and economic erudition had been invested in his South Central Los Angeles store for the past twenty years. Although eloquent in Korean, he spoke English only haltingly.

Obstacles to white-collar and professional jobs are common for many immigrants. The case of Korean immigrants reveals the power of structural constraints; many 1970s Korean immigrants failed to obtain desirable jobs despite high educational credentials.[5] For Yun, even with his stellar (South Korean) academic credentials, English-speaking employment was out of the question. In 1973 only a third of the South Korean–educated nurses in Los Angeles held state licenses, while six hundred Korean American physicians in Southern California could not practice medicine (Choy 1979, pp. 227, 250). One immigrant told Bong-youn Choy in the 1970s: "We never expected to lose our profession when we immigrated to this beautiful and wealthy country. Today, most of us find ourselves in a job which is inconsistent with our qualifications and experience. We are living on starvation wages" (1979, p. 250). In the 1970s, there was little demand for Korean-speaking employees in law firms or corporations because South Korea was a peripheral economy. In addition, there was virtually no need for Korean-speaking professionals to serve the community. It is not surprising that Park had no intention of opening an architectural firm for Korean Americans when he first arrived in the United States.

Quite often, the boundary between racial discrimination and linguistic and institutional barriers is ambiguous. Accented, albeit adequate, English may contribute to examination failures, unsuccessful job interviews, or unemployment. Low regard for South Korean college degrees deprives Korean immigrants of licenses or jobs. The U.S. Commission on Civil Rights noted in 1975: "These professionals are encouraged to immigrate—given preference by our immigration laws. . . . Yet . . .

these same men and women are often told that their educational credentials are inadequate, their experience inapplicable, and their certification not recognized" (1975, p. iii). One witness "told the Advisory Committee that he had served the Korean Field Army as chief surgeon and was decorated in 1952 with a bronze star by President Harry Truman for his services to the U.S. Army . . . and has received only excuses as to why he cannot practice medicine in California . . ." (p. 28).

Personal experiences of discrimination goad many Korean immigrants to urge their children to pursue technical careers—fields in which subjective criteria are minimized. One second-generation professional told us: "My father insisted that I become a doctor because there would be less discrimination than in other jobs. In corporate jobs, he thought that white people would discriminate against me and block my promotion" (cf. Cha 1975, p. 23; Hurh 1977, p. 34).

The difficulty of attaining a professional career for first-generation Korean immigrants contributes to the high regard for professionals. Many Korean Americans we encountered, from college graduates to high school dropouts, expressed their earlier desire for an academic career. One entrepreneur, who had just sold his pizza shop, was delighted to have time to compose poetry and paint.

What awaited many well-educated 1970s Korean immigrants were not brilliant careers as professionals but, rather, manual and menial jobs requiring little English.[6] As a result, their income was low; in the early 1970s, the average median income of college-educated Koreans was below the median income of all households in Los Angeles and Long Beach (D. S. Kim 1975, p. 54). The general pattern continued in the 1980s.[7] One of our interviewees told us: "So what if you're college educated? No matter how well they may read English, English conversation is out of the question for many [Korean immigrants]. No one—I don't know of any—works for an American company." The status inconsistency is well captured by a Korean American pastor: "He [a typical Korean American] is a trained engineer, but he can't get that job. Where is his English? What is *for* him? Maybe only to be janitor in a building, *custodian!* And I am speaking of very proud man. In Korea he *is* someone; in America, where he go to *be* someone . . . here he is *nobody*" (Raban 1991, p. 268). In this regard, Yun is a paradigmatic example.

Intense disappointment has been a common experience for Korean immigrants. "Many Koreans soon find themselves in dead-end, low-paying secondary labor market jobs, or worse, no jobs at all. In the face of their high aspirations, Koreans become intensely dissatisfied and frustrated and search eagerly for other avenues of mobility" (D. S. Kim and Wong 1977, p. 232). According to Won Moo Hurh and Kwang Chung Kim, immigrants experience in their first two years the "early exigency stage," a period of intense deprivation and disappointment, although they gain stability after five to six years (1990, p. 468). There is, then, an inconsistency between immigrants' (South Korean educational or occupational) status and their employment in the United States (Barringer, Gardner, and Levin 1993, pp. 227, 266–267).

For most 1970s immigrants, manual jobs were necessary for sheer survival. Partially due to the language barrier, many relied on personal contacts to find employment and worked for Korean American employers (K. C. Kim, Kim, and Hurh 1981, pp. 228–229). Manual jobs also awaited later immigrants. For example, in a study of Korean American garment workers: "All cited the language barrier as the most influential factor in their choice of jobs." Not surprisingly, working conditions of Korean American workers are often poor. "The workers were paid by piece rate, and none received paid vacations, overtime pay, unemployment benefits, sick leave, or bonuses" (R. Kim et al. 1992, p. 75). Employed in nonunionized sectors as seamstresses, custodians, domestic workers, guards, and restaurant workers, many find themselves in low-paying, dead-end jobs. A young college graduate was shocked on his first day as a labor organizer to face a middle-aged woman who had just been fired from her restaurant job after she had fainted. "The boss put her in a cab and fired her. She worked something like 70 hours a week with no days off."

Between the unattainable professional career and futureless manual work lies the promise of self-employment. In a self-owned business, linguistic limitations are less of a liability (Yu 1982b, p. 69; Hurh and Kim 1984, p. 115). Self-employment is, in other words, an adaptive response to the credential and linguistic constraints that Korean Americans face.[8] Small businesses offer a promise of financial success and an escape from manual work. Examples of success naturally breed imitators among people who are facing similar structural constraints. Yun's decision to follow his relative is, as he suggested, more the rule than the exception among Korean Americans. In general, as we shall see, Korean Americans have invested in enterprises with relatively low start-up capital, usually in retail or in service businesses, and low technological or cultural requirements.

Nonetheless, the experience of structural barriers—whether purely linguistic problems or more insidious racial discrimination—is not the sole determinant of Korean Americans' economic decision making. Korean immigrant entrepreneurship is not only a reflexive response to the instrumental or structural dictates of U.S. capital.[9] Making the best of individually immutable conditions, Korean Americans seek a pragmatic solution (Min 1988a, p. 125). Their dream of mobility is deferred to the next generation.

Korean immigrant entrepreneurship should thus be seen as a concatenation of conscious decisions, albeit made under strong structural constraints. The decision to start a small business represents a calculated intergenerational mobility strategy—the strategic adaptation of the dreams of modernity and mobility. Like many petite bourgeoisie in contemporary capitalist societies, the stratum of small business people is transitional, not hereditary (Bechhofer and Elliott 1981b; Bertaux and Bertaux-Wiame 1981). Many Korean American shopkeepers balk at the prospect of their children's succeeding them in their businesses or opening small retail stores of their own; the first generation's desire for the second generation is for them to achieve prestigious and remunerative careers.[10]

The desire to pursue self-employment is more pronounced among later immigrants. Encouraged by their compatriots' successes and striving for a fortune, many 1980s Korean immigrants expected to become entrepreneurs. Manual jobs for them are planned means to accumulate sufficient capital—if they did not have adequate capital at the time of emigration. In Park and his colleagues' 1986 predeparture survey, over 70 percent of the men expected to go into business in the United States (1990, p. 86). In particular, 85 percent of the fifth preference immigrants—siblings and their children—intended to start a business (p. 53). Furthermore, many immigrants had some experience in running a small business in South Korea; according to In-Jin Yoon's survey, one-fourth stated that running a small business had been their main occupation in South Korea.[11]

Many post-1980 immigrants, who include an increasing number of less-educated and poorer South Koreans, have not fared so well. One labor organizer told us: "As the community stabilizes, a labor class will emerge. People will realize that they will not become shop owners.

There will also be more people who try to become merchants and fail, falling flat on their face and back into the working class." These would-be entrepreneurs encounter a more competitive environment. Both Koreatown and South Central Los Angeles are nearly saturated with Korean American businesses. Liquor stores for sale in South Central Los Angeles command premium prices because of their proven profitability. Although some immigrants come with enough capital— made possible by liberal capital export laws in South Korea and the general enrichment of South Korea—many others come with little money. Class divisions remain salient.

Many Korean Americans have little prospect of starting a small business. As the chain migration of the 1980s continues into the 1990s, more and more Korean immigrants are bereft of either educational credentials or capital. Lim, the millionaire entrepreneur, commented: "There will always be Korean immigrants because there will always be those who fail in Korea—it's the nature of capitalism." Korean Americans facing blocked mobility in South Korea find in the United States a situation that is probably no more hopeful than what they left behind.

Of the four Korean immigrants we encountered earlier, Kim and Park had no need or desire to establish a small business. Yun followed his relative into a small business as he jettisoned his academic ambition. Pae, however, experienced a setback as a swap meet stall owner and failed to become a self-made entrepreneur. Between the millionaire Lim and unemployed Pae lies a gulf that impedes ethnic solidarity and complicates any facile generations about Korean Americans. The simple equation of Korean Americans with entrepreneurship is thus problematic. The self-made entrepreneur is not inevitably the ideal of the Korean immigrants, especially of the 1970s. Not all Korean Americans, moreover, succeed. It is crucial to understand the constraints and opportunities facing Korean Americans.

The Sources of Korean American Entrepreneurship

Many media accounts stress the ethnic resources and cultural characteristics of Korean Americans to explain their entrepreneurial success. Hard work, frugality, and family solidarity are undoubtedly important. They are not cultural characteristics unique to Korean Americans, however; indeed, they are common among successful middle-class people of all countries. Furthermore, there are at least three other resources that are indisputably important for small retail and service businesses: labor, money, and networks.[12]

The self-imposed super-exploitation of one's own and others' labor is critical in the day-to-day operation of small enterprises (Light and Bonacich 1988, chap. 14). Long work days, with no days off, are often the fate of small business owners.[13] Both retail stores and service outlets need to be open long hours in order to enhance business; they also require low labor costs to eke out a profit. Because the enterprises that Korean Americans tend to be engaged in have generally low profit margins, the mandate of keeping labor costs down is essential. John Y. Lee's 1983 study found that many Korean American businesses, such as dry cleaners, are more profitable than their American counterparts primarily because of their lower operating costs.[14]

The enterprise of running a small retail store or a service outlet is similar to the economy of peasantry, in which self-exploitation is critical to subsist and prosper (Chayanov 1986, pp. 73–76). In the early 1980s, 32 percent of Korean American small businesses had no employees (Oh 1985, p. 183). The rapacious demand generated by small business operation relies on free family labor, especially that of spouses, grown children, and elderly parents or relatives. For many Korean American women, the United States introduced the world of non-household work. Some scholars suggest that the authoritarian and patriarchal family structure facilitates the mobilization of family labor (Hong 1982a, p. 129; Hurh and Kim 1984, pp. 127–128). Yet the extent of patriarchal authoritarianism should not be exaggerated; the new cultural milieu and the dual-working situation temper male power (K. Park 1990b, p. 18; cf. Paik 1991). Many of our interviewees were wife-husband teams in a variety of venues—operating a dry cleaners, running a small store, or working as acupuncturists.

Family labor is often not enough. Korean American entrepreneurs seek Korean immigrant employees as well as non-Korean labor (Shin and Han 1990, p. 55). The growth of a business requires more labor power, yet it often coincides with the aging of children who become less available to work as they get older. The demand that exceeds the availability of family labor can be satisfied by fellow Korean American workers. The growing influx of Korean immigrants provides a pool of cheap labor. Korean American shop owners can communicate with their compatriot immigrant workers, who are in turn often willing to work at low wages. In this way Pae, when he first arrived in the United

States, simply went to Korean American stores and restaurants to seek employment (Light and Bonacich 1988, pp. 185–190).

Yet the relationships between Korean American owners and their co-ethnic employees often become tense (Kim and Hurh 1985, p. 107). Bonds of language and ethnicity do not preclude Korean American employers from exploiting their compatriots (Bonacich, Light, and Wong 1977, p. 56; I. Kim 1981, p. 112; Light and Bonacich 1988, p. 176). Ethnic solidarity, in other words, generates ethnic rivalry. New employees, moreover, often work at low wages in order to learn "trade secrets." One dry cleaner told us: "It is hard to hire Koreans because they often want to work just long enough, six months or one year, to get the necessary information and try to start their own business." The claims of ethnic solidarity and economic rivalry are often in conflict, and economic considerations appear to be more powerful (I. Kim 1981, p. 115; Min 1988a, p. 45; Yoon 1990, pp. 304–305).

The desire to protect trade secrets and to squelch potential business competitors leads some Korean American merchants to shun Korean American workers. Latinos, moreover, tend to work for even lower wages and are therefore all the more attractive. Pae, for example, managed the store for the Korean American owner, but the other employees were African Americans and Latinos. In Los Angeles, recent Latino immigrants are consistently the lowest-paid workers and are also considered hard working. One former nurse, whose South Central shop was destroyed during the L.A. riots, told us: "Mexicans [all Latinos, not just Mexican Americans, are called 'Mexicans' by most Korean Americans] are good because they work hard for low pay. You can pay them as low as $20 a day and they still work hard. Blacks, on the other hand, don't work that hard even if you pay them $50 a day." Most non–Korean American employees in Korean American enterprises are Latinos (Hess 1990, p. 98). Cheap Latino labor leads Korean American shop owners to hire fewer African Americans; this employment preference, as we saw in Chapter 4, is shared by non-Korean American employers.

In addition to labor, capital—money and credit—is critical in any fledgling enterprise. Most Korean Americans rely on personal savings and loans from family members, relatives, and friends. To a lesser extent, some use formal channels, such as loans from U.S. or South Korean banks, and informal sources, such as rotating credit associations (kye). In the 1980s, as immigrants increasingly came with the intention of starting a business and as the South Korean capital export laws became more liberal, more Korean immigrants carried capital from South Korea.

Korean American merchants in Koreatown and South Central Los Angeles generally do not—because they cannot—embark on enterprises with high capital requirements, such as large retail outlets or manufacturing concerns. Ease of entry is crucial (Hess 1990, pp. 82–83). In spite of low capital requirements for starting the typical Korean American enterprise, most Korean Americans rely on informal and formal loans to go into business. A 1983 study observes that most Korean American businesses "carry a high debt/equity ratio, indicating a low degree of protection provided by the business owner for the creditors" (J. Y. Lee 1983, p. 37). Some businesses are small indeed: swap meet stall owners merely rent their space and their whole inventory may amount to only a few thousand dollars.

Numerous studies of Korean American entrepreneurship agree on the importance of personal and family savings, usually ranging from 60 percent to 80 percent of the start-up cost.[15] For pre-1980 immigrants, facing an extremely stringent South Korean government ban on capital export, personal and family savings were especially critical. Although we heard some stories of smuggling money from South Korea into the United States—one man told us of rolling hundred-dollar bills in cigarette wrappers—most immigrants could not rely heavily on South Korean capital (H. C. Kim 1977b, p. 104; I. Kim 1981, pp. 64–69). Many of them, after all, came to the United States intending to seek employment, not to start a business. South Korea in the 1970s was also a poor country, with a per capita GNP of under $1,000 (by 1990, the figure had risen to $5,400). Very few, therefore, had large savings to start major business ventures in the United States. Except for a handful of wealthy immigrants, like Lim, part of the very rationale of immigration was that they were not "making it" in South Korea.

Formal channels, such as South Korean or U.S. banks, and informal means, such as kye, are less important. Kye, or rotating credit associations, function like banks in that they collect savings from and disburse credit to members. In South Korea, farmers and urbanites use kye to raise funds for significant life course events, such as weddings or funeral ceremonies. For immigrants to the United States, there was a dearth of South Korean banks in the 1970s, while U.S. bank loans were difficult to obtain. In their place, kye were widely regarded to be a crucial source of venture capital for Korean Americans; *Forbes*, for example, wrote: "*Kyes*, prevalent in South Korea, are being used in America to finance thousands of small, Korean-owned businesses" (Schifrin 1988, p. 92). Rotating credit associations, then, appeared to be a quintessential ethnic or cultural resource for Korean Americans.

In general, however, the media emphasis on rotating credit associations for Korean American entrepreneurs seems exaggerated.[16] The vast majority of Korean immigrants invest what money they have for their own businesses, above all, and for close kin and possibly friends. In this regard, the nature of chain migration and the significance of kinship are crucial for many immigrant entrepreneurs. The support from relatives, as Yun's experience suggests, is critical not only in determining the particular lines of business later immigrants enter but also in providing crucial start-up capital and business information (Shin and Han 1990, p. 51). We should overstate neither the extent of ethnic trust and solidarity nor the significance of individualism and self-interest.

Many post-1980s immigrants expected to open businesses in the United States and therefore relied more heavily on formal and informal means to raise capital, especially on savings in South Korea and loans from South Korean sources. Twenty percent of respondents to a 1986 survey indicated that they had enough capital to start a business at the time of their departure for the United States. Thirty-one percent expected to rely on their savings in the United States, while nearly 75 percent expected to combine their savings with bank loans (Park et al. 1990, p. 91). Although many of them entered the same lines of business as the 1970s immigrants, the profitability of dry cleaning or liquor stores drove the costs of entry higher (J. Y. Lee 1983, p. 38; see also I. Kim 1981, pp. 121–143).

Finally, in addition to labor and capital, network resources are important. Network, or social, resources include the knowledge of local business, which ranges from familiarity with suppliers and wholesalers to understanding customer needs and wants. Business expertise, like investment capital, is often acquired through strong ties, such as close relatives.

Network resources include transnational ties to the homeland. Many Korean American businesses began as import-export concerns, which relied on homeland connections to start a retail or wholesale outlet in the United States. Illsoo Kim has extensively documented the importance of South Korean exports, such as wigs, for Korean American merchants in New York in the 1970s (I. Kim 1981, pp. 121–143). Relying on a captive market, early entrepreneurs broke into the U.S. market by selling South Korean products.[17] In 1986, for example, South Korean import concerns were the largest group of Korean American–owned enterprises in Southern California (Min 1988b, p. 155; Oh 1988, pp. 180–181). Yet as labor costs have risen in South Korea, the competitive edge has shifted to other ethnic entrepreneurs with ties to China and Southeast Asian countries. This worries Yun the wholesaler, who relies on cheap South Korean products; he faces stiff competition from other Asian American merchants, who similarly rely on their homelands' cheaper production.

The significance of family and kinship ties begins with the immigration process, as we saw in Chapter 3 (Kim and Hurh 1991, pp. 119–120; see also Choldin 1973). Furthermore, as with capital formation, family members and kin contribute disproportionately to launching businesses. Many Korean Americans, including Yun, learned their business from their relatives. Kinship ties may resolve the problem of trust that arises when dealing with co-ethnics. Nevertheless, serious conflicts do occur among close kin and even family members and at times sever ties.

Informal ties are often important in disseminating business-related knowledge. Because most 1970s Korean immigrants lacked experience in running a small business, they often began by working for non-Korean employers. As Korean American businesses became established, the owners' relatives and friends acquired business know-how through them. Even the simple news of a successful line of business can spread rapidly through informal channels; Illsoo Kim writes of New York Korean American greengrocers in the early 1970s: "News of their success quickly spread throughout the Korean community in the area, and new immigrants from South Korea quickly followed them into the business" (1981, p. 113). Ethnic media, which reach South Korea, also play a crucial role for potential and actual Korean immigrants (pp. 59–60).

Informal ties are complemented by formal business or industry associations. The existence of informal ties and formal associations creates a facilitative environment and infrastructure for Korean immigrant businesses such as grocery and liquor stores. Although crucial business information travels primarily between family members and friends,[18]

Korean American churches, along with alumni and other voluntary associations, provide important nodes of information exchange (Light and Bonacich 1988, pp. 192–193; Min 1988b, p. 162).

Ethnic ties often contribute to business success (Portes and Zhou 1992, p. 492). Ethnic solidarity arises not merely from Korean Americans' cultural propensity or ethnic loyalty but because of their economic relations (Min 1991a, pp. 225–226; cf. Bonacich and Modell 1980, pp. 256–257). A significant concentration of co-ethnics, as occurs in Los Angeles, generates niches for ethnic professionals and businesses, ranging from Korean-speaking lawyers to Korean food stores and restaurants. As many as 30 percent of Korean American enterprises cater to fellow Korean American consumers (Min 1988b, pp. 155–156). Park is a good example of someone who turned to the Korean American community as the demand for Korean-speaking architects increased with the enrichment of the community. The ability to monopolize the captive linguistic market is crucial for the subsidiary growth of professional and service work in the ethnic community (D. O. Lee 1992, pp. 264, 272). Nonetheless, monopoly erodes over time; ethnic solidarity is transient. As Eui-Young Yu found out in his 1989 consumer preference survey: "Korean shoppers patronize Korean markets because Korean ethnic foods and groceries are not available in other markets. Otherwise, they would appear to prefer non-Korean markets" (1990a, p. 106). Korean Americans are not committed to ethnic solidarity when they spend money.

What facilitates intra-linguistic ties may hinder extra-linguistic relations. Although ethnic-based retail or industry associations facilitate individual Korean American businesses, they contribute to a continuing reliance on Korean language and ethnic ties that impedes the development of other interethnic relations. Yun told us: "[Korean Americans] do business with things—and cash—we don't get into the service industries [i.e., deal with people]." Consequently, Korean Americans pursue enterprises requiring little customer interaction, such as dry cleaning, or running a gas station.

In summary, many Korean Americans opened shops because they were shut out of white-collar jobs and found small businesses to be more desirable than manual labor, while others, especially in the 1980s, came to the United States planning to open shops because their prospects in South Korea were limited. For many first-generation immigrants, small businesses offered an opportunity for decent profit, given the available resources and existing constraints. Although dry cleaners or liquor shops were sold at inflated prices, later immigrants also wielded more financial resources. Korean American families, moreover, were able to draw on family labor. The large number of Korean immigrants provided an encouraging business environment and cheap labor.

Korean American sources of entrepreneurship thus cannot be reduced to ethnic or cultural characteristics. The dependence on cheap labor, capital, and network resources, moreover, ensures that small businesses remain a transient phenomenon. The particular concatenation of resources is unstable; having more capital may propel one into Lim's world of millionaires, while financial hardship may force one to be part of Pae's world of wage workers or even the unemployed. More crucially, immigrant entrepreneurship does not reproduce itself over generations. Although a career option common to many immigrants, it is usually not passed down from generation to generation. The entrepreneurial ethos is not designed to be heritable; the whole rationale of the enterprise is for the second generation to achieve mainstream success and therefore upward mobility.

Korean American Businesses in South Central Los Angeles

Why do Korean American merchants set up shops in poor neighborhoods? Pyong Gap Min (1988a, p. 45), drawing on his thorough study of Korean American small businesses in Atlanta, argues that "in spite of the risk of armed robberies, Korean immigrants in Atlanta prefer a grocery store located in a black residential area to the one located in a white residential area because the former is known to be more lucrative." In contrast, Kyeyoung Park (1991, p. 181) suggests another reason: "Although Korean businessmen can make more money in a white neighborhood, they prefer the friendliness of Hispanics and blacks. In other words, they do not feel the same warmth from white customers. Another rationale is their explanation that Hispanics and blacks are easy to deal with as customers. That is, they do not take much time to buy goods and are not difficult to please. They complain less than white customers." Neither explanation is sufficient in and of itself. It is unclear why merchants wouldn't make more money in more affluent neighborhoods. Just as profit-driven as the next small businessperson, they are not necessarily motivated by a desire for friendly encounters.

It is the opportunity structure facing Korean American merchants that in large part explains the Korean American entrepreneurial concentration in poor inner-city neighborhoods.

Affluent areas are dominated by large chains—able to offer goods at lower prices—and specialty shops—where customer interactions and good service are essential. In such locations Korean American merchants face initially insurmountable obstacles. A housewife who had opened a store selling party dresses mainly for Latinos told us: "It takes a long time to set things up in a white neighborhood; they are really picky. They won't take something with a lipstick mark or any problem. You have to serve them perfectly. Win their trust, and only then will things go OK. With blacks and Hispanics, and Koreans too, if it's not perfect people just say 'it's OK.' " A jewelry merchant, mimicking a pair of scissors cutting with his middle and index fingers, said: "With Koreans, you sell the merchandise and it's over. With white customers, the deal never ends. They expect to be able to bring it back, have it repaired." A swap meet stall owner remarked: "Every Korean would like to go and work in a white neighborhood, but the barriers are too great—the wall—whites simply ignore us, won't let us in." Most Korean Americans lack the financial and cultural capital necessary for success in affluent areas with demanding European American customers.[19]

In contrast, poor areas offer Korean American merchants little competition. Moreover, poor African American and Latino customers are less demanding than upper-middle-class customers. Ethnic enclaves in Los Angeles, in other words, provided a suitable niche for Korean American merchants in the 1970s and 1980s. After the 1965 Watts upheaval, many Jewish and Italian American merchants moved their shops out of the area. Although these entrepreneurs had been shut out of affluent areas before the 1960s, many of them possessed enough financial and cultural capital to operate in richer areas by the time of their exodus. Furthermore, as Jewish and Italian American merchants were retiring, their children, schooled in the United States, found jobs in the mainline corporate sector and the professions rather than in their parents' stores. Simultaneously, as smaller merchants were leaving poor areas, many supermarket and retail chains were shutting their operations in South Central Los Angeles. The ghetto outlets were generally less profitable than other profit centers. Less disposable income, petty crime (especially shoplifting), and rising labor costs made poor areas appear unattractive to corporate decision makers.[20] Moreover, the city government did little to encourage—and, in fact, often discouraged— opening stores in South Central: "The [Community Redevelopment Agency] has played a Mephistophelean role in fomenting disinvestment in South Central L.A. Its sole project in the ghetto, a small shopping complex near Watts's 1965 'Charcoal Alley,' languished through fifteen years of 'planning.' More insidiously, the CRA helped destroy the leading retail district in the black community, the Crenshaw Shopping Center, by providing redevelopment subsidies to the wealthy promoters of the Fox Hills Plaza on the ghetto's periphery" (Davis 1992b, p. 31).

Although small merchants and larger chains left South Central Los Angeles throughout the 1960s, residents and their demands remained. Their poverty did not mean that they did not spend money. One Korean American woman told us: "White people don't realize that poor people—blacks and Mexicans—have money. They have cash and they buy things."[21] After the 1992 L.A. riots, Vons Supermarket estimated that about 1.2 million people in South Central Los Angeles lacked access to a supermarket (Sims 1994, p. C3). In the absence of other accessible stores, the residents constituted a captive market; in the case of Watts and South Central Los Angeles, this has been accentuated by their relative isolation. Many poor people have no ready access to automobiles, while public transportation has remained underdeveloped in Los Angeles. For many poor African Americans and Latinos, supermarkets or discount stores are not readily accessible. Furthermore, they depend heavily on cash transactions and credit from merchants (Wong 1977, p. 445).

There are two primary institutions through which Korean American enterprises have filled the niche vacated by supermarkets and retail chains in South Central Los Angeles: liquor stores and swap meets. Although designated as "liquor stores," most of them serve a variety of functions, ranging from selling groceries to offering services such as check cashing. Their role as a neighborhood supermarket hence makes the label "liquor store" inappropriate and incurs the wrath of Korean American merchants. As already noted, such stores are profitable; as one female store owner told us: "The reason people go into South Central is because of money. You can make a lot of money there." Another interviewee said: "After Watts [the 1965 Rebellion], desperate [Korean] immigrants went into those stores. They would sit in there all day long—click, clack, click, clack—at their cash registers, going absolutely bonkers. But they were making lots of money. This appealed to all sorts, but particularly to those who had failed once in Korea." Although requiring high capital investment and personal risk, liquor stores virtually guarantee returns on investment (Lacey 1992; Light and Bonacich 1988, pp. 227–242). It is therefore not simply a matter of ethnic solidarity that prompts Korean American merchants to buy these stores, even at steep premiums.[22] What may seem like a foolhardy venture from the outside turns out to be a calculated risk for Korean Americans intent on quick and reliable returns. This gamble is necessitated by the constraints they face—the near impossibility of a professional career or white-collar work, and the daunting difficulties in opening a store in an affluent neighborhood. The enormous investment in acquiring liquor stores, moreover, explains the devastation that the merchants experienced after the L.A. riots. A lifetime's saving was wiped out in an evening. Jin Lee told the Los Angeles Times: "Who wants to go back [to South Central Los Angeles] unless they're crazy. The reason we'd have to is because that's where our assets are, that's all we have" (McMillan 1992d, p. B3).

In the mid-1980s, Korean Americans started swap meets, which simulate open-air markets in South Korea. Swap meets function as department stores in South Central Los Angeles, offering a wide range of consumer goods ranging from clothes to jewelry. Asian, particularly South Korean, imports have been crucial for swap meet growth (E. Chang 1990, p. 150). By converting empty warehouses into rows of stalls, swap meets gather petty retailers. Most warehouses are owned by non–Korean Americans, who lease them on a long-term basis to Korean Americans, who in turn rent stalls to both Korean American and non–Korean American retailers. A Korean American woman told us: "Most owners have no idea how much money is being made in their warehouses. They don't understand how it works." Swap meet stalls are also run by members of other ethnic groups, such as Arab Americans and Latinos. Because of the stalls' low overhead, merchandise can be sold at lower prices. In an intensely competitive environment—one swap meet will have a number of stores selling the same goods— competitive prices, not the quality of service, are the key to success.[23]

Korean American merchants have thus filled the gap created by the impoverishment of South Central Los Angeles and the flight of large retail outlets. While some businesspeople may be attracted by a "friendly" clientele or believe that African American neighborhoods are more lucrative, formal barriers of capital and competition, as well as informal barriers of cultural capital, are more important. Korean American merchants' "preference" for African American neighborhoods represents their understanding of and response to structural constraints.

If we comprehend the trajectory of Korean American merchants, we are still left to wonder why African American merchants do not set up shops in South Central Los Angeles. As we saw in Chapter 4, those who are most able to do so have left the area, while those who lack the resources to launch a business remain: those who are poor and undereducated.

Many African Americans have moved to middle-class neighborhoods like Baldwin Hills, if not to predominantly European American enclaves. College-educated African Americans pursue careers in medicine, law, government, or business, not petty entrepreneurship. Leanita McClain writes: "Here's a discovery that too many people still find startling: when given equal opportunities at white-collar pencil pushing, blacks want the same things from life that everyone else wants. These include the proverbial dream house, two cars, an above-average school and a vacation for the kids at Disneyland. We may, in fact, want these things more than other Americans because most of us have been denied them so long" (1992, p. 120). It is a figment of ethnic romanticism to think that affluent, educated African Americans, even those who were born and grew up in the ghetto, would strive to return to the "community" and devote their lives to running a corner grocery store. Horatio Algers—whether African American, European American, or Asian American—do not return to the ghetto.

There are additional complications for would-be African American entrepreneurs in South Central Los Angeles. Consider the three factors of labor, capital, and network resources. As we have discussed, small enterprises require self-exploitation; wage costs must be kept at a minimum through the sacrifice of family members' labor. Why should an African American family devote family members' precious labor time to sustaining a corner shop when they can become gainfully employed in a variety of jobs with benefits? African Americans—as U.S. citizens fluent in English—are eligible for a wide range of government and private sector jobs. To the extent that a family has members willing to work hard, they can seek outside employment rather than working in a family enterprise.

There is also the problem of capital. Given the difficulties in borrowing from financial institutions, the lack of capital in the community (or ties to a homeland), and the profitability of illegal businesses, raising capital for a small business remains difficult for poor African Americans. Even if an individual can raise the necessary capital, there is no reason why she or he should set up shop in South Central Los Angeles. Lacking the Korean immigrant problem with language, African American shop owners face one less obstacle in opening shops in more affluent areas.

African Americans who remain in South Central Los Angeles also lack the network sources of Korean American success. There are few, if any, formal or informal associations of African American entrepreneurs in South Central Los Angeles. There are virtually no ties to homelands that would facilitate import-export businesses. Furthermore, the paucity of ethnic- or kinship-based lending institutions or supporting associations places would-be African American entrepreneurs at a disadvantage (Wong 1977, p. 456).

The structural prerequisites of Korean American entrepreneurship, then, are missing for African Americans in South Central Los Angeles. It is not that African Americans lack a cultural predisposition toward entrepreneurship; U.S.-educated Korean Americans do not open up shops in South Central Los Angeles, either. More critical than ethnicity or culture is the opportunity structure, which, for ambitious African Americans, points toward professional or bureaucratic careers—just as much as is the case for most European Americans and for Korean immigrants' children. Poor areas such as South Central Los Angeles are not attractive for the ambitious. Korean Americans have set up shops in South Central Los Angeles not only because they had the resources to do so but also because they have been forced to choose among limited options.

The significance of these factors—labor, capital, and network resources—can be highlighted by considering the difficulties of early Korean immigrants in Los Angeles in opening businesses. In the early part of the century: "Many Koreans took the first opportunity to go into business, no matter how small. . . . Many Korean small businesses exacted long hours of work from the owners and their families and yet yielded little income" (Yim 1984, p. 534; see also Givens 1939, p. 50). There were, however, no celebrations of Korean American entrepreneurial success. Even Syngman Rhee, who later became president of

South Korea, experienced a dismal failure in his 1924 attempt at entrepreneurship in Los Angeles (H. C. Kim 1977b, pp. 89–90; Choy 1979, pp. 129–133). Korean Americans before World War II faced enormous obstacles. Professional opportunities were virtually absent, while prejudice and discrimination circumscribed business opportunities (Givens 1939, pp. 48–50).

The difficulties of these early Korean American merchants cannot be ascribed to their poor work ethos or the unavailability of cheap labor. Rather, they operated in a much less favorable environment than have Korean American entrepreneurs in the 1970s and 1980s. Most crucially, the early Korean Americans lacked both capital and communal support.

Korean American Merchants and the Elusive American Dream

The celebration of Korean American success hides an ambiguous story. The original dreams of many 1970s immigrants are now long abandoned, while those of the 1980s immigrants face a less hospitable environment. Even for those who have amassed considerable fortunes, success has come at a cost. The original dream of Korean immigrants is fulfilled in the mainstream successes of their children, although, again, the triumph is not always as clear cut as it may seem from the outside.

We must remember that not all Korean Americans are shop owners. Not all—indeed, not many—are successful even by the standards of monetary remuneration. There are many Korean Americans who in the wildest stretch of imagination do not approximate the ideal of the model minority. They are as poor as they would be in South Korea, but are additionally plagued by displacement and disappointment. Many working people we interviewed repeatedly said: "We want to go back, I don't know why we came, but we can't because we don't have money or jobs." Although some have become professionals, like Park the architect, others, like Pae the unemployed worker, never accumulate enough capital to start their own store. Class polarization is a social fact of Korean American life in Los Angeles. According to Eui-Young Yu's 1989 survey, for example, over 26 percent of Korean American employed men were skilled or manual workers (1990a, pp. 13–14). Furthermore, according to the 1980s figures, Korean Americans account for the second-highest percentage of families below the poverty level among Asian American ethnic groups (Barringer and Cho 1989, p. 42). Herbert Barringer, Robert Gardner, and Michael Levin conclude that while some Korean Americans resemble "successful Chinese and Asian Indians," there are others who are in "the same situation as Vietnamese refugees" (1993, p. 316).

The undeniable success of many Korean American entrepreneurs must be viewed in the proper context. Many 1970s Korean immigrants came from the same social and educational background as South Korean government officials and businesspeople who catapulted the South Korean economy into one of the most dynamic in the world by the 1980s. It is not surprising that well-educated, highly motivated immigrants should do well, no matter where they land. Again, Yun is a striking case in point. A man of intelligence and drive, he could easily have become a top bureaucrat in the South Korean government, a high-ranking manager in a large corporation, or even a mathematics professor as he imagined himself when he came to the United States. That he should succeed in his business is no surprise.

The mobility strategy of Korean immigrants came, however, at a considerable cost. Status inconsistency between educational attainment and career became the norm (Jo 1992, pp. 406–407). What would otherwise have been brilliant careers in prestigious professions shattered against institutional and linguistic barriers. Korean Americans were forced by circumstances to choose careers—in retail or service—that would have been unthinkable had they remained in Korea. As the calculus of staying and going shifted for professional-class Koreans, there was increasing bitterness among many immigrants who regretted their earlier decisions to emigrate. For some, like Park, the growing affluence of Korean Americans encouraged him to abandon his mainstream career and seek his fortune in Koreatown. Many others, however, did not have the resources or capacity to shift their focus.

Indeed, rather than finding phenomenal success in the United States, the vast majority of Korean Americans lead lives of constant work and little luxury. Korean American entrepreneurs are not Fords and Rockefellers but small business owners who must endure long working weeks—"labor slaves," as the millenarian Korean American said in Chapter 2.

Contrary to the promise of modern gender relations, women in particular shoulder heavy burdens as wives and mothers, as factory laborers, and as usually undocumented laborers in family businesses.

Studies document their "second shift" at home after their workplace duties (cf. Hochschild 1989). Kwang Chung Kim and Won Moo Hurh's interviews with immigrant women in Los Angeles in 1979 demonstrate the "persistence of the traditional [Korean] family ideology among Korean immigrants" (1988, p. 162). Korean American women work more often in peripheral sectors of the economy and their wages for comparable work are lower than those of Korean American men (Barringer and Cho 1989, pp. 91–92). Like their male counterparts, they often hold jobs far below their education and skill levels. In addition, violence against them has been widely reported (Yim 1978).

Nonetheless, the strategy of professional-class immigrants has often been realized in their children's mobility. The educational and cultural capital that the immigrants themselves could not take advantage of in the United States had to be transmuted into cash by dint of their hard work. In turn, the number of Korean Americans increased at prestigious universities across the United States. Class reproduction occurred across the Pacific at the sacrifice of the first generation.

Younger immigrants of the so-called "1.5 generation" (Hurh 1990)— immigrants who came as children—also have their laments. A young Korean American dentist, for example, insists that she would have become a doctor had her family stayed in Korea. She also regrets that in South Korea she had been a good writer—she remembers writing Korean poems—while "now I feel like nothing," unable to write literary English or Korean.

Immigrant children, furthermore, face a world altogether different from that of their parents' dreams. Even children who are successful frequently turn out to be different from what their parents expect, often creating tragic rifts between generations. Some are barely able to communicate across linguistic and culture divides.[24] Angela Oh, the Korean American attorney who was widely regarded as the main voice of the community after the L.A. riots, observes: "In reality, I am probably every Korean mother's nightmare as a daughter. It's true: I'm thirty-six years old, not married, don't have kids who are going to take care of me when I get old and gray, with no husband in my life who's a doctor, lawyer or other professional who can take care of not only me but my parents when they get older" (Hicks, Villaraigosa, and Oh 1992, p. 46).

Many Korean American entrepreneurs' children grow up in households where parents are often absent. Chungmi Kim's "Living in Dreams" captures children's resentment (1982, p. 23):

Slaving themselves to their careers
they too lived in dreams.
"Some day we wanna buy a big house
and a fancy cadillac,"
said the man proudly grinning.
He was a janitor, his wife a nurse.
The children watched the house
killing time with toys and guns.

Kathy Kim's parents worked sixteen, seventeen hours a day, seven days a week, and commuted from suburban Fullerton to South Central Los Angeles. She said: "Family-wise, everything stopped with the store. I can't even remember the last time my family ate dinner together" (S. Kim 1993, pp. 6–7). Such sentiments are common among shopkeepers' children, whose American outlook questions both the ostensibly blind materialism of their parents and their neglect of family life and even their seeming lack of love. These second-generation Korean Americans' attitudes cast doubts on the uncritical celebration of Korean American entrepreneurship, even as first-generation parents see in "materialism" an expression of their love and deferred dreams for their children.

The transference of ambition from parents to children extracts a considerable toll. The repressed return with a vengeance in numerous instances of intergenerational conflict. Parental ambitions for their children, often elevated to the status of a *raison d'être* for immigration, weigh heavily on children's minds. Although some, like the protagonist in Marie G. Lee's novel *Finding My Voice* (1992), manage to enter prestigious colleges, many others do not achieve the model minority ideal. Juvenile delinquency was, for example, a major problem facing the Korean American community in the 1970s and 1980s.[25] Furthermore, some families suffer dysfunctions, often directly related to the perceived failures of immigrant life (Y. Song 1986, p. 189; see also M. Song 1993). The situation may not be so different from that of the earliest immigrants. In 1927, a second-generation Korean American said: "So far I have read very little about my parents' native land. I have never felt a sense of pride in knowing about my parents' native land but I have pity and sympathy for them" (Melendy 1977, pp. 144–145).

The American dream remains elusive for most Korean Americans, including those who have succeeded by conventional measures of success. Korean Americans may in fact be more like the real Horatio Alger—Horatio Alger, Jr., the author of the "Horatio Alger" novels: "Ironically, the writer most often credited with popularizing a rags-to-riches mythology failed to realize his own early promise and vaunted ambition. Much of his life reads like a case study in frustration" (Scharnhorst and Bales 1985, pp. xix). The uncritical celebration of Korean American entrepreneurial success or the faulty generalization that all Korean immigrants are successful obfuscates the problems facing Korean Americans.

6

American Ideologies on Trial

As the complex realities of the multiethnic L.A. riots came to the surface, the media fixated on the conflict between African Americans and Korean Americans.[1] Their mutual animosity became an article of faith. The *Los Angeles Business Journal* reported: "The feelings of many in the black community toward Koreans had become comparable to that of a vanquished populace to the occupying army" (McNelis-Ahern 1992, p. 4). Simultaneously, as Harold Meyerson explained: "Many within the Korean community conceal a raging anti-black animus behind a wafer-thin veneer of peace rhetoric" (1992, p. 2). The looming "race war" prompted Jeff Yang to observe: "The broadcast barrage turned the L.A. riots into a sensationalistic Tale of Two Tapes: Rodney King versus Soon Ja Du, the 'killer Korean shopkeeper'" (1992, p. 47). Instances of the "black-Korean conflict" beyond Los Angeles, ranging from episodes in Spike Lee's film *Do the Right Thing* to the well-publicized boycott of a Korean American grocer in Flatbush, New York, suggested that it might be a nationwide phenomenon.

Here we criticize the "black-Korean conflict" frame of the L.A. riots and examine its ideological context. We realize that challenging its explanatory power or noting its ideological construction does not fully explain particular instances of African American–Korean American tension. The reality of individual anger and passionate prejudices held by some African Americans and Korean Americans toward each other cannot be denied. Nor do we wish to dismiss vitriolic expressions of dislike and distrust broadcast in the media simply as articulations of dominant ideologies. Nonetheless, we advance two interrelated arguments against the "black-Korean conflict." First, we argue that it reifies both African Americans and Korean Americans, and the instances of conflict between them. In other words, it homogenizes diverse peoples and phenomena and thus elides alternative interpretations. Second, and more important, we trace the ideological currents that bolster the "black-Korean conflict" as a depiction of the two groups as antipodal minorities: the Asian American model minority epitomized by Korean entrepreneurial success and the urban underclass represented by the impoverished African American community. These two portraits constitute flip sides of the same ideological coin, which presumes that the United States is an open society with no systematic barriers to success. The same constellation of factors—culture, attitudes, and family structure—is used to explain the success and failure of each group. We locate the sources of this ideology in the conservative climate of the 1980s in particular and in the idea of the American dream in general. The ideological construction and constitution of the "black-Korean conflict" should alert us to the dangers of emphasizing this interethnic conflict.

Korean Americans and African Americans on the "Black-Korean Conflict"

How do Korean Americans and African Americans make sense of the interethnic conflict? We should state at the outset that, although our discussion of Korean Americans relies on firsthand interviews, our analysis of African Americans depends on written sources, and therefore remains tentative.

Many Korean Americans hold unflattering stereotypes about African Americans. In seeking to understand this, we need to consider racial and ethnonationalist ideologies in South Korea. Some Korean Americans also accept conservative American ideologies, which render them susceptible to facile generalizations about African Americans. Yet Korean American racism is but one strand of a complex web of relationships with African Americans. Most Korean Americans, for example, even while acknowledging some racism toward or tension with African Americans, deny the significance of the "black-Korean conflict."

As in the case of Korean Americans, we also need to consider several factors in order to understand African American resistance to Korean

Americans. Beyond difficulties in dealing with Korean American merchants, African Americans' expectations of small business owners differ from those of Korean Americans. In addition, Korean Americans represent the dominant ideology that many African Americans reject. Further, Korean Americans are "outside merchants" who are playing roles in a history of African American oppression. At the same time, we should also recognize the diversity of African American opinions, even within South Central Los Angeles; many have come to terms with, even if they do not actively welcome, Korean American merchants.

The primary source of Korean American racism toward African Americans is the American racial ideology. The pervasive American cultural presence in South Korea has contributed to Korean immigrants' racial attitudes. South Koreans note the (informally) segregated restaurants, bars, and brothels, and the black-white geography of the U.S. military in South Korea: the heavy concentration of African American troops at the demilitarized zone, and the "whiter," easier assignments in Seoul (cf. Sturdevant and Stoltzfus 1993). Images are as complicated as they are racialized: African American–South Korean marriages present narratives of the South Korean bride who travels to the United States to meet both anti-Asian and anti–African American racism, and anti-Afroasian racism with the birth of her children. In the film *Deep Blue Night*, the Korean divorcee of an African American soldier remembers: "He would come home drunk and crying—putting on me the sorrow that was his as a black man." Beyond these stories, the American mass media have racialized South Korea through both South Korean television and American military television, AFKN; surprising numbers of South Koreans sit in their Seoul living rooms and watch an array of U.S. news and entertainment. One Korean American explains: "I had the idea that blacks were dirty and aggressive from American films and from our experience with black soldiers. My very first day in America, I was afraid to go outside because of the dangerous blacks."[2] Korean American racism thus rides on the coattails of American cultural dominance.

Furthermore, many Korean immigrants, bred on fervent nationalism in South Korea, are wont to see the social world in an ethnonationalistic frame. For some Korean American entrepreneurs, their daily troubles with shoplifting and violence lead to negative overgeneralizations about African Americans. Several children of Korean American entrepreneurs were critical of their shop-owner parents' stereotypes of others; they had learned to dismiss such views through their multiethnic school environment. Their parents generally encounter poor and uneducated customers; their ethnonationalist frame thereby falls prey to facile prejudices, which are supported by the prevailing media degradation of African Americans.

In a related vein, some Korean Americans accept a conservative understanding of African American poverty and blame what they perceive as African Americans' unwillingness to "try harder," as Korean Americans have.[3] Even Korean American merchants who explain African American poverty through structural factors still suggest that African Americans follow the Korean American example. Yoon, a swap meet stall owner, comments: "In the beginning, I clothed my own daughter with secondhand clothes I bought at outdoor swap meets. I think sometimes people don't understand how hard we struggle. [Such] lack of understanding causes conflict. . . . That's the tragedy of Korean-American immigrants" (Shiver 1992, p. A12). Many Korean American merchants, in other words, believe in the American dream.

To focus exclusively on Korean American prejudices or anger against African Americans distorts the complexities of Korean American reactions toward African Americans. Korean American merchants and employees who come into contact with African Americans remark on their lack of education and even laziness, but they also express complimentary opinions of their friendliness and strong communal ties. Although Korean Americans working in South Central Los Angeles speak of a poor neighborhood with serious problems, they do not project the infernal image of a war zone propagated in the mass media. These ambivalences and complexities are at the heart of Korean American encounters with African Americans in South Central Los Angeles.

Korean Americans are generally defensive about charges of Korean American racism. Many of our interviewees claimed extenuating circumstances. Language barriers, for example, often create misunderstandings. Responding to the charge of Korean American racism, a young Korean American told us: "But you must understand that Korean shopkeepers don't speak English well and often feel frustrated. When they can't express themselves, they sometimes blow up. And blacks and others see Korean racism when it is just a matter of accumulated frustration." Simple misunderstandings, in this view, are generated by interethnic encounters.

Other Korean Americans charge that they are unfairly portrayed by the media. One Korean American woman complained about the media coverage of the Soon Ja Du–Latasha Harlins incident: "Over and over all they showed was the orange juice, again and again just the orange juice [that was allegedly stolen by Harlins and the source of the ensuing scuffle that led to Du's killing of Harlins], nothing about how the girl grabbed her, and the hundreds of Koreans who have died." She continued that she could fully understand Du's rage, rage at young customers' cavalier attitude to older shopkeepers. She was happy about the Korean American protests at Channel 7—"people think lightly of Koreans, but finally they had to at least pretend to take us seriously." Several days after a single day when three Korean American shop owners had been murdered, one Korean American social service worker explained that riot victims were growing more and more angry at all the Latasha Harlins commotion: "Yes, her life was important, but what about the dozens of Korean merchants? What about their lives? Don't they matter?" Here they referred to the danger and even death that confront Korean American shopkeepers in South Central Los Angeles.

More crucially, however, almost all Korean Americans we interviewed challenged the "black-Korean conflict" as a major factor in the L.A. riots. The L.A. riots and their media representations were inseparable for many Korean Americans. They objected to offensive media representations, ranging from the striking image of gun-toting vigilantes to the pathetic figure of non-fluent Korean American merchants on talk shows. The "black-Korean conflict" media portrait incurred the intense wrath of some Korean Americans. Angi Chon, an owner of a South Central L.A. gas station, said: " 'Koreans and blacks kill each other over a little argument about shoplifting' is the way it gets out on TV. . . . Just like the animals, they think. And because of the language problem, usually there is no one who can say otherwise" (J. H. Lee 1993, p. 25).

While the stories and tenor of objections varied, all the Korean Americans we interviewed converged in their conviction that the "black-Korean conflict" was not at the root of the riots. One former South Korean Marine stated flatly: "This [the L.A. riots] has *nothing* to do with the Korean-black conflict [*hanbŭk kaltŭng*]; there is no such thing." Almost everyone, moreover, tackled the question of causes of the L.A. riots, whether we asked or not. For the most part, ascertaining the causes was at once a response to the media and the point of departure for dismantling the "black-Korean conflict" frame. Some Korean Americans, especially college-educated shop owners, invoked the political economic structure of the United States to explain what had happened. Although these structural stories took a variety of idiomatic forms, they all sought to undercut the media prism. These structural explanations were offered as if to say: "Don't people know what is going on in this country?" Many were punctuated with: "We live and work here; we know what is going on." Several Korean American merchants spoke of African American history not as a strange or distant story but as one they knew, in some cases through decades of contact.[4]

Large portions of Korean-language newspapers were devoted to the American coverage. On several occasions Korean Americans demonstrated at local television and newspaper companies. Angela Oh's appearance on *Nightline* was made possible after a sustained protest by Korean Americans in response to a show on the "black-Korean conflict" in which no Korean Americans were present (Korea Times 1992, p. 7; see also K. Y. Lee 1992, p. 6). Yet Oh was still subject to a media frame at cross purposes with her message. Before the camera turned to her, a voice-over surveyed the riot destruction, saying, "Korean American businesses were targeted for annihilation because of high animosity by African Americans." She describes how she was often pigeon-holed in the media: "The producer will call you up and say, we are going to talk about where we go from here, and they interview you and do this whole little prep, and when you go to the station—and this literally happened to me on a national network station—the issue becomes 'black-Korean conflict,' the reason for the riots in L.A." (Hicks, Villaraigosa, and Oh 1992, p. 47).

Many Korean Americans dismissed the "black-Korean conflict" not only as a media fabrication but also as an attempt to engender intra-minority conflict. Kyung Kyu Lim of the Korean Resource Center argued that the media aims to "divide and conquer" minority groups, and that it anesthetizes Americans to accept this racialized vision:

They then attributed the "Black-Korean conflict" as the underlying factor of the violence. To justify their point, images of crying Korean merchants damning the looters, and angry African-American bystanders asserting that Koreans received what they deserved flooded the media. Unfortunately, people's sense of judgment became anesthetized after a while so that many accepted race conflict between Korean and African Americans as a motivating factor for the violence. (1992, p. 25)

Similarly, Roy Hong of Korean Immigrant Workers Advocates suggested that the mainstream media manufactured the "black-Korean conflict." Media attention to the arrival of South Korean officials, for example, created a chimera—the seeming political favoring of Korean Americans: "I believe the South Korean government's involvement doesn't help us in any way. But when these people come the mayor greets them, gives them the key to the city and so on, and the Black and Latino communities understandably feel something is going on. Well, all the sucker got is a key!" (Hong 1992, p. 11). The city authorities and the mass media are thus complicit in paying special attention to the Korean American victims, thereby making them appear "favored": "The politicians are again exploiting the Koreans by appearing to favor us."[5]

In this vein, some working-class Korean Americans stressed their solidarity with African Americans. Their voices fracture assumptions about ethnic homogeneity. One unemployed worker asked for our notebook and jotted down a map. Drawing a series of wavy lines for the major East-West streets that traverse Koreatown and South Central Los Angeles, he explained: "Blacks are being squeezed out by Koreans and Hispanics." He repeated several times: "Blacks did well; they had to do something or they were going to disappear—that is my interpretation." Having worked side by side with African Americans for many years, he was angry that in the government and other disbursements African Americans had been excluded. Another worker suggested:

> Blacks felt ignored. It was mob psychology. Blacks are better than we Koreans—they are pure. Of course with numbers [in groups] it is a different story. You have to look at their long history of being put down, hundreds of years—they have been put down by every single ethnic group. Fifty years ago they rose up, they rose up in the [1992] riots, and they will rise again in fifty years.

After this passionate exegesis on African American history—riots every fifty years—he continued that the greatest sadness for him in the riots was that a younger African American co-worker, who for years had called him "Daddy," left him at their place of employment, saying: "I'm not going to die here." That worker solidarity evaporated in the riot flames—that he was left alone in the store, unable to reach the absent Korean American owner residing in the suburbs—was deeply upsetting. He also wished that Korean American, Latino, and African American employees who had lost their jobs through the riots could fight together for government aid. As much as national and ethnic solidarity is "real" for him, interethnic class solidarity also remains a possibility.

Nonetheless African Americans' anger against Korean American merchants seemed widespread. Consider a voice from South Central Los Angeles reported in the *Los Angeles Times* after the riots. Johnnie Tillman-Blackston, an elderly African American woman, told the reporter: "The Koreans run the liquor store and don't let no black people work in there, and they treat black people like they're dogs" (Los Angeles Times 1992c, p. 8). After the Latasha Harlins murder, she stopped her grandchildren from buying at a nearby Korean American–owned store. In its extreme formulation, as in rapper Ice Cube's 1989 song "Black Korea," the anger against Korean Americans becomes a racist harangue.[6]

Beyond the anger generated by unpleasant encounters, the most persistent criticism levied against Korean American merchants in South Central Los Angeles was that they exploited the community—in other words, that they failed to use some of their profit for community betterment. As we have seen, mobility-oriented Korean Americans work to achieve their personal Americans dreams. The Korean American shop owners who offer compelling structural accounts to explain the riots do not propose structural solutions; for them, the object is to exit from poor areas and from petty entrepreneurship. They have come to make money in, not to change, the United States. They left South Korea, after all, to seek greater opportunities.

Quite simply, many Korean American merchants work within the dominant capitalist framework. In this line of reasoning, it would be a flight of ethnic romanticism to believe that African American merchants, should they replace Korean American merchants, would curb their profit motives or return their profit to the community. Ethnic altruism evaporates against the pressing demands that shape individual decisions and actions. The community in South Central Los Angeles, furthermore, is eroding because of larger socioeconomic forces, not Korean American merchants. In addition, Korean American "liquor store" merchants justify their businesses by pointing out that they serve as grocery stores and fulfill unmet needs of poor neighborhoods. This is, of course, true in the sense that one African American woman lamented after the riots: "My store, my store, what have they done to my store? . . . I stopped here everyday. These people were wonderful. Now there's no place to shop. I mean I need milk. I have two grandchildren to look after. Where am I gonna shop? The Valley?" (L.A. Weekly 1992, p. 37; see also Mydans and Marriott 1992). Korean American merchants in South Central Los Angeles, generally blind to the dysfunctions they may be causing, see themselves as serving a function. From their standpoint, it is a misplaced expectation to hope that they will act like good suburban retailers or have the common good as their primary goal. Korean American merchants did not come to the United States to improve the lot of poor African Americans or to reform the inner city.

For some African American activists, Korean Americans represent the model minority and thus personify a dominant American ideology that chastises African Americans. African Americans' refrain that Korean Americans come with capital from South Korea is an implicit critique of the American dream ideology that anyone can make it in the United States. Comparisons that contrast supposed Korean American success with a concomitant supposed African American failure in entrepreneurship are fraudulent because the preconditions of the two groups are different. In a sense, resistance to Korean American merchants is an implicit critique of the dominant American ideology.

Just as an influential black nationalist ideology stresses "community control," some African Americans' political efforts target the nearest group of "successful" newcomers. Numerous historical examples demonstrate that the "black-Korean conflict" is in fact only a contemporary manifestation of a long-standing pattern. It is possible to read U.S. history as a series of new immigrants benefiting from the systematic disadvantages facing African Americans: poor European immigrants in the eighteenth century and "white" working class in the nineteenth century gaining material and psychological advantages over their African American counterparts—slaves and serfs (Morgan 1975; Roediger 1991; see also Fuchs 1990). What emerges is the often-neglected history of slavery, Jim Crow, and persistent discrimination.

Consider the diverse ethnic groups in "conflict" with poor African American urbanites in the 1980s and 1990s. In Cleveland, there was the black-Palestinian conflict; in Philadelphia, the black-Laotian conflict; in

Washington, D.C., the black-Chinese conflict; in Miami, the black-Cuban conflict; and in Los Angeles, the black-Latino conflict (Jennings 1992a, p. 45; Portes and Stepick 1993, chap. 8; Fuchs 1990, pp. 330–335). In most large American cities with a significant population of poor African Americans, new immigrants fill the niche of petty entre-preneurs. The coming and going of ethnic groups, past and present, suggests that the source of tension is fundamentally economic and structural rather than ethnic and cultural. The interethnic conflict frame elides the more crucial structural context.

For some African Americans, the "black-Korean conflict," articulated as "outside merchants" against the impoverished community, is there-fore another page in the long history of African American struggles against oppression. Tony Martin, professor of Africana Studies at Wellesley College, writes: "Ethnic groups that have made it into the American Dream have traditionally stepped on the necks of African-American communities on their way up. Jews, Italians, Greeks, Chi-nese, Arabs and now East Indians and Koreans" (1993, p. 32). Manning Marable's characterization of the 1960s Watts is suggestive: "In Los Angeles' Black ghetto, Watts, the vulgarism employed by unemployed Black teenagers for teaching Jewish shopkeepers was 'pushing peanuts up Goldberg's nose.' Jews, and after 1945, Lebanese, Palestinians, Latin Americans and Chinese were often the symbolic targets of Black eco-nomic animosity, primarily because they were the most visible non-Black entrepreneurs in ghetto life" (1983, p. 150). In effect, Korean Americans in the 1990s play the role that European American "ethnic" merchants played in the 1960s.[7]

This distinction—between an interethnic conflict and a class con-flict—is not merely an academic matter; as E. Erick Schockman suggests, the media coverage of the "black-Korean conflict" contributed to African American hate crimes against Korean Americans (K. Y. Lee 1993, p. 1). Media images and ideological presumptions have an impact on social reality. Some African American activists make "scapegoats" of Korean Americans for the problems afflicting their community.

Yet there are other voices to be heard. The African American writer Charles Simmons, for example, wrote: "Although there is friction be-tween Black customers and Korean merchants, this issue was overstated by the media" (1993, p. 142). In a similar vein, gang member Nate II of the Watergate Crips said: "It's not a Korean/Black thing; the merchants were there, there were problems, but it's a diversion to get us not to think about the real problem, which is the oppressor, which is the major majority which are whites" (Elkholy and Nassef 1992, p. 8). In a 1993 *Los Angeles Times* survey, the most common answer to the question—"Is there one specific group of Asians you think is particularly causing problems in Southern California these days . . .?"—was "no group" at 28 percent, followed by "all" at 26 percent, Korean Americans at 19 percent, and Vietnamese Americans at 12 percent (1993, p. 5). In the same survey, "whites" were regarded as more "prejudiced" than "Asians." Ellen Stewart, moreover, reported that the African Americans she surveyed were less prejudiced against Korean Americans after the riots than in the late 1980s (1993, pp. 33–35).

African Americans, even within the narrow area of South Central Los Angeles, express a diversity of opinions. Undoubtedly, a minority of African Americans, motivated by the Black Power ideology of community control, seeks to drive out Korean American merchants. Yet many others have made variable degrees of accommodation with Korean American merchants' presence in South Central Los Angeles. Just as some Korean American merchants contribute to community betterment, some African American customers welcome their presence. Otherwise, we cannot make sense of numerous instances of friendship and goodwill. Destroyed Korean American stores in South Central Los Angeles attracted sympathy from African American customers; when Chung Lee's store was burned down, a "Sorry Mr. Lee" sign came up after the riots (McMillan 1992a, p. B1).

Even the Soon Ja Du–Latasha Harlins incident cannot be subsumed under the "black-Korean conflict"; there is no clear-cut ethnic polarization. George, an African American resident of South Central Los Angeles, "felt sorry" for Du and told the writer John Edgar Wideman: "[She came] to this country speaking no English. Husband watching TV while she did all the work. She couldn't speak or read, held a list you'd hand her upside down. You had to point to what you wanted. Husband started running around with young black girls. Didn't recognize her when I stopped in one day. She came here a girl. Looked sixty in a couple of years" (Wideman 1992, p. 153). Or, as Du's African American neighbor said: "The girl's dead; the lady's on probation. Let it rest. Don't hurt other people because of it" (P. Morrison 1992, p. B3).

We do not deny that there are tensions between some Korean American merchants and some African American customers or that there are demagogues and xenophobes among both African Americans and Korean Americans. But the situation is not simple; the responses are not singular. There are Korean American merchants who work hard to better community life by holding neighborhood picnics, sponsoring sports teams, and offering scholarships. Nor should we ignore human bonds between Korean Americans and Africans Americans, even though some links, such as the worker's "paternal" relationship with an African American employee, burned in the riot flames.

As our discussion of the Korean diaspora—with its consciously mobility-oriented immigration—suggests, African Americans are incidental to Korean Americans' visions of life in the United States. In pursuit of their private American dreams, African Americans in South Central Los Angeles are temporary customers for most Korean Americans. That so many Korean Americans have sought their fortune in predominantly poor African American neighborhoods, including South Central Los Angeles, stems from structural factors. In turn, the ultimate goal of inner-city African American movements is to achieve some measure of collective control over their destiny. Above all, structural problems, including American apartheid, deindustrialization, and the shrinking welfare state, remain the most pressing forces confronting African Americans. To emphasize the "black-Korean conflict" only diverts our attention from more pressing problems. The interethnic conflict, outside of its historical and political economic context, misses the central problems facing both ethnic groups and South Central Los Angeles at large (Aubry 1993, pp. 155–156). The "black-Korean conflict," in spite of prejudices and tensions, is ultimately beside the point in the central concerns of most African Americans and Korean Americans.

The Reification of the Interethnic Conflict

Before we explore the ideological roots of the "black-Korean conflict," let us consider its descriptive and explanatory problems. The "black-Korean conflict" reifies both African Americans and Korean Americans and the conflict itself. In so doing, the interethnic conflict becomes a ready-made explanation for diverse phenomena and diverts our attention from other events and explanations.

The media disseminates ready-made stereotypes as truths about the two groups. All African Americans are not poor, nor do they constitute a homogeneous or cohesive group. Similarly, neither are all Korean

Americans shopkeepers nor do they constitute a unified community, even within the narrow perimeters of Koreatown. Multiethnic South Central Los Angeles and Koreatown belie simple ethnic generalizations. We must, therefore, beware of presuming widespread interethnic animosity from individual expressions of anger and prejudice by people in particular social positions.

Beyond promoting overgeneralizations concerning each group, the frame reifies the conflict itself. Uncritical acceptance of the frame leads to descriptive and explanatory errors. In narrating a set scenario depicting warring factions of Korean American merchants against African American residents, distinct events, with different causes and characteristics, become instantiations of the same conflict. In effect, the "black-Korean conflict" frame acts as an ex post facto explanation; disparate events are treated under the same rubric. Consider, for example, a 1990 boycott in New York. Although ostensibly a case of "black-Korean conflict," the reality in Brooklyn was not the same as that in South Central Los Angeles. The initial conflict arose between recent Haitian immigrants and a Korean American shopkeeper (Rieder 1990). Although long-term African American residents of South Central Los Angeles and recent Haitian immigrants in Brooklyn are both black within the American racial framework, it would be a mistake to consider them in the same category. In this regard, we should note that in Miami, for instance, people speak of the "black-Haitian conflict" (Portes and Stepick 1993, pp. 190–192).

The interethnic conflict frame leads to explanations, which, in keeping with the prior reifications of each group, locate the conflict's cause in each group's characteristics. Rather than focusing on the broader political economic context, the presumed interethnic conflict pits one homogenized group against another. Consider the hypothetical case of a Korean American shopkeeper who fires an African American employee. In the dominant media frame, the individual case may stimulate a narrative about the "black-Korean conflict" and explanations based on different interpersonal interaction styles or cultural characteristics. Yet the case may be nothing more than an employer laying off an employee—a product of capitalist social relations rather than interethnic conflict.

The presumed existence of the "black-Korean conflict" blinds us to a number of inconvenient facts. If there were seething hatred between the two groups, then one might have expected some instances of interethnic killing during the riots. Yet there were no such documented cases. More crucially, the ground zero of the 1992 upheaval was the verdict in the Rodney King beating. African Americans' anger was primarily directed against white racism and the attack on the "black body" (Turner 1993, pp. 207–208). Most immediate reactions as well as later reflections by African American writers rarely mentioned Korean Americans (Cleage 1993, pp. 123–127; Wiley 1993, pp. 82–91; Alan-Williams 1994, pp. 169–173). During the riots: "People took up chants proposing alternative targets. 'Beverly Hills!' shouted one cluster. 'Parker Center' (Los Angeles Police Department headquarters), yelled another" (Meyerson 1992, p. 2; see also Ward 1992). Pamela Franklin told the *New York Times*: "The looting and violence was the only way angry blacks in Los Angeles had left to express their bitterness to whites. She said the destruction should be carried to Beverly Hills" (Marriott 1992, p. A11). Rioters and looters were unable to go to Beverly Hills because of police protection and logistical difficulties, not lack of intention. Hence Korean Americans focused not on African American rioting or looting but, rather, on the state's abandonment of Koreatown and South Central Los Angeles during the riots.

The "black-Korean conflict" also averts our gaze from interethnic conflicts that have *prima facie* plausibility. African Americans and Latinos, especially recent Central American immigrants, compete for employment, housing, and political power. Thus one might expect a potent interethnic conflict between African Americans and Latinos—the so-called "Black-Brown conflict" (Oliver and Johnson 1984, pp. 75–84; Miles 1992; Skerry 1993, pp. 83–86). Korean Americans, in contrast, do not generally compete with African Americans, particularly in South Central Los Angeles, for manufacturing or service jobs. Very few Korean Americans live in South Central Los Angeles, and therefore they do not vie for existing housing stock or struggle over political power and representation.

Alternatively, we might have expected more media coverage of the "Korean-Latino conflict," especially given that so many Latinos work for Korean American businesses and industries. As we have noted, the majority of rioters and looters arrested were Latinos; recall the second-generation Korean American's shock over the looting in Koreatown carried out by his Latino neighbors and acquaintances.

Our intention is not to initiate discourses on the "black-Latino conflict" or the "Korean-Latino conflict" but to question the salience of the "black-Korean conflict." Indeed, we might ask why the media did not seize on the "Korean-white conflict," given that European Americans also looted Koreatown stores. The African American novelist Ishmael Reed queries: "Why doesn't the looting and burning of Korean stores by whites in Koreatown—which was witnessed by Pacifica Radio's Kwazi Nkrumah—indicate a bias of whites toward Koreans?" (1993, p. 44).

The Antipodal Minorities

Why should the "black-Korean conflict" emerge as a central phenomenon in the reporting on the 1992 L.A. riots? We argue that the "black-Korean conflict" is deeply rooted in American ideologies.

Media reports on the "black-Korean conflict" often highlight different customs and interpersonal interaction styles as the source of friction between Korean American merchants and African American customers (Stewart 1989, 1993; Cheng and Espiritu 1989, pp. 525–528). Korean American merchants are said to avoid eye contact, slam the change on the countertop, fail to make small talk, and, in general, refuse to assimilate to American cultural norms.[8] The journalist C. Connie Kang explains: "In the Confucian-steeped Korean culture, a smile is reserved for family members and close friends. . . . Expressions such as 'thank you' and 'excuse me' are used sparingly."[9] A source even more likely than Confucian legacies, however, is the experience of living in Seoul, which, as one of the world's most densely populated and rapidly urbanized cities, has not been congenial to refined manners. At worst, Korean American merchants are depicted as rude, racist, and rapacious. In turn, African American customers are said not to understand Korean cultural norms and to act in such a way as to offend Korean American merchants. H. Andrew Kim writes: "Blacks have little understanding of Korean merchants, who are in constant fear of being robbed or shot, while going through the massive readjustment to a strange culture, customs and language" (Korea Times 1992, p. 6).

The concept of culture generally denotes a constellation of attributes, transient and intransigent, that distinguishes one group from another—for example, the French from the German. Cultural characteristics may be easily transferable—a Korean may become inordinately fond of truffles, a French person may acquire a taste for *kimch'i*, a spicy Korean dish—or more intransigent: values and world views often do not translate or transplant well across cultures. Both the transient and the intransigent aspects of culture are used to characterize the conflict between African Americans and Korean Americans.

The focus on transient aspects of culture mandates cosmetic changes in order to achieve interethnic reconciliation. From this perspective, better understanding, promoted through mutual recognition and interethnic interaction, would solve the problem. The stress on transient cultural attributes leads the *New York Times* to celebrate New York's "admirable example" (that is, its lack of rioting and looting after the L.A. riots) as the result of the Human Rights Commission's providing "sensitivity training to Korean merchants and the black community on how to prevent tensions and what to do when problems occur."[10] Seminars, furthermore, teach Korean American merchants to "smile more frequently" and African American leaders are invited on tours of South Korea (D. Martin 1993). Though commendable, these steps provide superficial solutions. After all, smiling Korean American merchants and understanding African American customers leave both groups in the same place they were in to begin with: Korean Americans as merchants and African Americans as customers.

Many commentators therefore seek deeper causes of the conflict and argue that the two groups manifest contrasting values, attitudes, and behavior—intransigent cultural differences. Accounts emphasizing intransigent aspects of culture highlight Korean Americans' education, hard work, and family solidarity as corollaries of the Confucian ethos and their supposed corresponding absence among African Americans. These contrasting cultural constructs are used to explain the different success rates of Korean Americans and African Americans.

At the heart of the interethnic contrast lies the Korean American entrepreneur—independent and diligent—who embodies the promise of capitalism and the free enterprise system. The *Economist* writes: "The Koreans have a remarkable business bent. . . . They are also capitalists. In short, they are model American citizens" (Grimond 1982). Edward Norden waxes enthusiastic about a Korean American shop owner, Roy Kim: "Kim's story . . . was the usual one for [Korean Americans] who had set up in South-Central. He stepped off the plane with $100 in his pocket, and by mobilizing his family, joining a *kye* [rotating credit association], and working fifteen-hour days for fifteen years, put enough aside to buy a mortgaged house in the suburbs" (1992, p. 33).

In contrast to the entrepreneurial heroism of Korean Americans, African Americans cut a pathetic figure in this ideological fabric. Norden is indignant about an African American activist who faults the larger society: "So why not found bigger, stronger, more aggressive black banks with the black money out there, or the black version of the *kye*, the hybrid lottery and savings-and-loan scheme to which masses of KAs [Korean Americans] belong?... Or why not mobilize families ... to run mom-and-pop shops for fifteen hours a day in place of KAs [Korean Americans]?" (1992, p. 38). The contrast is drawn more starkly regarding their relationship to welfare. "It's rare for Korean immigrants to go on the dole, even in the beginning. For these people [after the riots] it was shameful to have to prove, in triplicate, not only that the livelihoods they had created had been destroyed, but that they had no savings, no insurance, and no close relatives working" (p. 35). Korean Americans, in this line of argument, are exemplary for not relying on welfare.[11]

According to these accounts, not only do Korean American merchants exhibit the virtues of rugged individualism and make a mockery of racism and welfare, but they rely on familial and communal resources. Jim Sleeper proclaims:

> Many of the Koreans get their business going because they have a sense of responsibility to each other. They pool their limited resources to "stake" one another—in a way we don't see happening even with these African Americans who make it out of the ghettos. . . . It's just so obvious that family units are critical to success. Inner-city black communities do not have the social structure to sustain the bonds of trust that are needed to "stake" one another and sustain that kind of family output.[12]

In these accounts, Korean Americans and African Americans are polar opposites.

The contrast is most insistently articulated by conservative commentators.

> [It] was permissible to explain black antagonism toward Koreans in Los Angeles in terms of "anger" over Soon Ja Du, the Korean shopkeeper who, having shot and killed a 15 year old black girl named Latasha Harlins who had assaulted her, was then released by a judge. But it was impermissible to note that 25 Korean merchants had been murdered in the ghetto in the last two years. It was permissible to mention that blacks were "frustrated" by

Korean economic success. It was impermissible to specify that this
rise was based on 14 hour work days, personal sacrifice often
approaching indenture, and family solidarity. (Heterodoxy 1992,
p. 10)

In lionizing the Korean American shopkeepers, the polemic simultaneously belittles African American charges of racism and discrimination: "The Koreans had given the lie to fantasies about racism and its
discontents on which black leadership has come to depend. . . . They
were a living refutation, right there in South Central Los Angeles, of
the notion that job equals chump, an argument against the narcotic of
self-pity and the whine of victimhood which has become the elevator
music of the ghetto."[13]

In these narratives, Korean American entrepreneurs personify the
values of individual responsibility and family solidarity, while African
Americans stand for welfare dependence and family dissolution.These
views appear to be widespread. Neil Saari wrote to *Time* that "the
intense attacks directed at the Koreans were unmistakably racist. Instead of burning them out, Los Angeles' African Americans would do
well to study and copy the Koreans' work ethic and family solidarity"
(1992, p. 10). Or, as one "white man" told the *Los Angeles Times:* "I'm so
goddamn mad. Let these people burn their own stuff down. If you don't
like the Koreans, why don't you go get your own grocery store, mister?" (Los Angeles Times 1992c, pt. iii, p. 6). Max Kerstein, publisher
of *Beverage Bulletin,* wrote: "It is a sad commentary when honest, hard-
working citizens of our city face criminals within our society bent on
destruction, injury, death and hate. Of all the people who suffered
those terrible losses [during the riots], the Korean community felt the
devastation and ruin more than anyone else" (1992, p. 18).

In summary, many accounts depict African Americans and Korean
Americans as antipodal minorities. The comparison highlights the contrasting portrait of each group in the 1980s: Korean Americans as a
model minority and African Americans as an urban underclass.

Korean Americans, the Model Minority

By the mid-1980s, many people were celebrating Korean Americans'
coming of age. They exemplified the model minority: hard working,
highly educated, and, above all, successful nonwhite Americans.

Nonetheless, the positive stereotype has not always reigned. Korean Americans—and Asian Americans in general—have historically been characterized as inscrutable and unassimilable. A 1983 *Time* article exclaims that "Los Angeles is being invaded" by immigrants "who cling to their ethnic identity, preserving their customs and language, nurturing old prejudices (the Japanese look down on Koreans), developing new ones (Koreans look down on blacks and Chicanos)."[14] Many assume irrevocable ties between Asian Americans and their Asian homelands; ignorance and prejudice about the homeland merely accentuate contempt for fellow Americans of Asian ancestry. Myung Mi Kim captures the pervasive ignorance about Korea in her poem "Into Such Assembly": "Do they have trees in Korea? / Do the children eat out of garbage cans?"[15] To the extent that an image existed of South Korea, it was largely as a poor Asian country, remembered primarily for the Korean War.[16]

By the time Korean immigration to the United States accelerated in the 1970s, some coverage became positive. A 1975 *Newsweek* article introduced Los Angeles's Koreatown as a place where "dozens of Asian visions of the American dream are being played out. . . . Koreatown does abound with Horatio Alger success stories" (Dotson 1975). By the time of the L.A. riots, Korean Americans had come to embody the American dream. In a 1992 front-page article entitled "American Dreams," the *Wall Street Journal* asks: "How do Korean-Americans do it?" The answer recalls the 1975 *Newsweek* article; Byung K. Kim and his family "achieved success the same way other Koreans have: hard work, financial support from fellow immigrants, free labor from family members and a cultural tradition of pride and self-reliance" (Yoshihashi and Lubman 1992, p. A1).

The ingredients of Korean American success touted in such reports were a constellation of cultural propensities. References to the Confucian ethos—hard work, stress on education, and strong family ties—became virtually unavoidable in discussing Korean Americans. In one of the earliest popular books on Korean Americans, published in 1977, Wayne Patterson and Hyung-Chan Kim explain the group's success by citing their hard work and their high educational attainment (p. 51). Luciano Mangiafico writes of "Korean immigrants' tenacity, distinct work ethic, commitment to educational achievement, and entrepreneurial spirit" (1988, p. 108).[17]

The celebration of the Korean American success story cannot be severed from the glorification of Asian Americans as the model minority in the 1980s.[18] In education, they were overachievers, overrepresented at leading universities such as MIT and Stanford. In business, their diligence blossomed in both high tech—computers and related fields—and low tech—small grocery stores and similar establishments. Even in literature, novelists such as Maxine Hong Kingston and Amy Tan became best-selling authors. Further, Asian Americans were, as *Business Week* announced in 1991, "a marketer's dream": "their high incomes, education, and rising numbers have companies scrambling to win them over" (Shao 1991, p. 54). There exists no better imprimatur of success in the consumerist United States.

In popular imagery, Asian American success was often coupled with the rise of Asian economies. By the late 1980s, the relative economic decline of the United States and the rapid ascent of Asian economies had become established wisdom. The link between Asian economic dynamism and Asian American success was direct for Lawrence Harrison, who stressed the common cultural origins of Asian and Asian American success: "The economic miracles of Taiwan, Korea, and Japan were made by people imbued with the Confucian values of work, education, and merit, and the Taoist value of frugality" (1992, p. 149). Referring to Asian Americans, he noted: "The experience of these 'Confucian-Americans' parallels the experience of their homelands." In this view, Confucian values and attitudes account for the model minority's success.

Perhaps the clearest indication that the model minority thesis is ideological, rather than an unproblematic reflection of social reality, is its fluctuation over time. Why did Asian Americans—who were widely depicted as difficult to assimilate as late as the early 1980s—suddenly come to embody the American dream? The popularity of the model minority thesis is due in part to its demonstration of the openness of the United States to minority advancement. It is not surprising that the thesis was born in the mid-1960s, during the height of civil rights movements, when African Americans and others openly charged that the United States was racist.[19] The model minority, by contrast, disproved the existence of American racism.

The model minority thesis distorts Asian American reality in several pernicious ways. First, it elides the considerable diversity among Asian Americans. Second, it underemphasizes the persistence of anti–Asian American racism. Finally, it implicitly criticizes other minorities who do not measure up to the rate-busting achievements of Asian immigrants.

It is difficult to generalize about a large group of people. There were, for example, over 700,000 Korean Americans in the United States in 1990, and over 7.2 million people of Asian descent. Cleavages of class, gender, and generation, not to mention disparate national origins and languages, elude facile generalizations. There are no clear-cut characteristics or essential features: some are fourth- or even fifth-generation immigrants, others have immigrated recently or are war refugees; some are Buddhist, others are Christian; some speak only English, others speak any number of literally hundreds of languages. Take educational achievement: in 1980, 51.9 percent of Asian Indians held college degrees, while the comparable figure was 2.9 percent for the Hmong from Southeast Asia. At the same time that the poverty rate among Laotians was 67.2 percent, it was only 4.2 percent for Japanese Americans. Although Korean Americans' median family income was slightly above the U.S. average, so was their proportion of persons below the poverty level.[20] Inequality and poverty remain serious problems for Asian Americans.[21] Although Japanese Americans rank the highest among all ethnic groups in terms of per capita income, many Asian Americans face problems in finding jobs and fail to earn wages commensurate with their educational level.[22]

More mundanely, little unity exists among Asian Americans. Conflict and even animosity plague different groups—oldtimers and new immigrants, Japanese Americans and Korean Americans, rich Korean Americans and poor Korean Americans, and so on.[23] These latent conflicts manifested themselves during and after the L.A. riots; some Asian Americans blamed Korean Americans for what took place. Roy Yokoyama, a retired Japanese American grocer, said: "I did business with nothing but blacks and I never had no problem. You think, gee, these Koreans must be doing something wrong."[24] Past and present conflicts refute the presumed solidarity among Asian Americans. Intra–Asian American difficulties are not new. Historically, for instance, the relationship between Japanese Americans and Korean Americans reflected the Japanese colonization of Korea from 1910 to 1945. When the war broke out between Japan and the United States in 1941: "Koreans in America were excited. 'Korea for Victory with America,' they shouted. The *Korean National Herald-Pacific Weekly* declared the 'fact' that 'every Korean born' was 'an enemy born for Japan.' "[25] The unity of Asian Americans is often based solely on the racist characterization that Asian Americans "look alike."[26] The widespread conflation of all Asian Americans is well captured by Susan Moffat (1992, p. A20): "At the same place where Reginald O. Denny was attacked, Takao Hirata, a Japanese-American born behind barbed wire in a World War II internment camp, was nearly killed by a mob shouting anti-*Korean* epithets. Other Asians across the city were attacked or threatened in the same manner" (see also Alan-Williams 1994).

The model minority portrait thus obfuscates the racism and discrimination that persist against Asian Americans in general and Korean Americans in particular. The Korean American poet Chungmi Kim writes: "To say that I've suffered from the discrimination in this society because of my yellow skin and my flat nose is simplistic but true. To say that I've suffered from a sense of alienation because of the discrimination is painful, but true" (1992, p. 28).[27] Ironically, the very perception of successful Asian Americans may breed resentment, ranging from European American students who complain of nerdy Asian American students to African Americans resentful of successful Asian Americans (Takagi 1992, pp. 60–61; Wellman 1993, pp. 235–236).

Racism against Asian Americans appears in a variety of guises. Some attempt to put Asian Americans in "their place" by not serving them promptly, while others harass them verbally; few Asian Americans have not heard the ugly cry: "Go back to where you came from."[28] Historically, nativist attacks on Asian Americans have been common; the worst blights include the 1882 Chinese Exclusion Act and the 1942 Japanese internment (see, respectively, Saxton 1971 and Irons 1983; see in general Higham 1955). Until the 1948 repeal of the Alien Land Law, non–U.S. born Asian immigrants could not own land in the United States, and until the 1952 McCarran-Walter Act, they could not be naturalized (Takaki 1989, pp. 41–43; see also Newman 1993, pp. 151–166). Recently, Asian American activists and scholars have criticized restrictive admissions for Asian American students at some prestigious universities and a "glass ceiling" for Asian American employees (Takagi 1992; U.S. Commission on Civil Rights 1992, pp. 131–136; Hsia 1988, pp. 146, 203). More ominous are the physical assaults on Asian Americans. Perhaps the most publicized incident was the 1982 baseball bat beating of Vincent Chin, a Chinese American man who was mistaken for a Japanese American by laid-off Detroit auto workers angry at the Japanese.[29] Their displaced anger reveals the conflation of all Asian Americans into a single group, and the irrevocable connections drawn to their homelands.

The straitjacket of the model minority imagery also flattens the individuality and humanity of a multitudinous group. Dan Kwong's monologue, written after the riots, satirizes the reigning stereotype, which projects quiet, rule-obeying, and smiling Asian Americans: "*Sorry!* Sorry, I forget—*I'm a member of the 'Model Minority'!* Shouldn't rock the boat! Don't wanna make any waves! Just shut up, be 'industrious and hardworking' so we can be held up to all those *other* minorities as a target—I mean, *an example*—of how well the American system works well for everyone, equally" (1992, p. 20). The image is an upgraded version of that of a smiling Chinese laundryman or a Japanese gardener. As a *maître d'* at a fancy California restaurant told a second-generation Korean American when she made several requests: "Why can't you act like an Oriental!"

Finally, as Dan Kwong suggests, the model minority thesis exists not simply to praise Asian Americans but to chide lazy and rebellious minorities. At times the invidious comparison is direct and straightforward. Lawrence Harrison observes: "The Chinese, the Japanese, and the Koreans who have migrated to the United States have injected a dose of the work ethic, excellence, and merit at a time when those values appear particularly beleaguered in the broader society. In contrast, the Mexicans who migrate to the United States bring with them a regressive culture that is disconcertingly persistent" (1992, p. 223). Harrison also argues that the "black ghetto problem is now principally a cultural one" and that the solution is to acculturate to the mainstream culture (p. 211).[30] In this line of reasoning, because cultural values determine the success of different ethnic groups, it is necessary to change the cultural values of unsuccessful ethnic groups. His analysis of the success of Asian Americans thus entails an explicit contrast with failed groups. Lurking behind the positive portrait of the model minority is its negation, the urban underclass.

The Urban Underclass: The Non-Model Minority

The concept of the "urban underclass" became popular in U.S. policy and media discourse in the 1980s. It stressed the cultural origins—expressed in attitudes and behaviors—of the persistence of poverty among inner-city residents, particularly African Americans. As a cultural explanation for the failures of African Americans, the underclass thesis constitutes the flip side of the model minority thesis.

A constant theme in media discussion of the 1980s was the intractability of African American poverty.[31] The underclass denoted a group of people beyond redemption. Yet despite the term's popularity in public policy discussions, exactly to whom it applied remained ambiguous. Note the *Economist's* description:

> When Americans talk about an "underclass" in their cities, they do not simply mean the poor; they mean poor but healthy young people who cannot or will not, but anyway do not, get a job. The images are vivid: an unmarried mother who lives off welfare cheques; a young man who drifts from girlfriend to girlfriend, selling drugs to get by. Estimates of the size of this underclass vary hugely from about 5% to 50% of all the poor—2m-15m people, of whom some two-thirds are black, a tenth Hispanic. (1991, p. 17)

As the ill-defined estimate—ranging from two million to fifteen million—suggests, identification of the underclass is not based on objective features, such as income level or occupational classification. Instead, what emerges most distinctly are images—many of them popularized by Ronald Reagan—of welfare queens and drug pushers in bombed-out ghettos where no European Americans dare tread (Katz 1989, p. 195).

Beyond its obvious reference to nonwhite poor urbanites, particularly African Americans, the underclass is usually defined by its behavior or culture.[32] Ken Auletta writes: "The underclass suffers from *behavioral* as well as income deficiencies. The underclass usually operates outside the generally accepted boundary of society. They are often set apart . . . by their 'deviant' or antisocial behavior, by their bad habits, not just by their poverty" (1982, p. 28).[33] As the reference to the culture of poverty suggests, the substantive underpinning of the underclass idea was not new to the 1980s. In the 1960s, the culture of poverty thesis was widely disseminated as an explanation of ghetto poverty. People with the culture of poverty, according to the anthropologist Oscar Lewis, were characterized by "lack of impulse control; strong present-time orientation, if relatively little ability to defer gratification and to plan for the future; sense of resignation and fatalism"

(1968, pp. 10–11; see also 1966, p. xlvi). What made it a culture was the durability of attitudes and behavior once they were impressed on individuals as children.[34]

The urban underclass thesis in the 1980s continued to stress defective culture and the disintegrating family as the causes of poverty. While the 1960s variety emphasized the *adaptive* nature of the culture and argued that economic aid alone would not alleviate poverty, these caveats and contexts were jettisoned from much of the 1980s discussion. Rather than understanding the culture of poverty as making the best of an intractable situation, conservative scholars and polemicists limned it as a semipermanent condition. Instead of calling for more than just economic aid to the ghetto, the 1980s discussion bypassed the earlier insights by suggesting that the government stop providing even economic aid. As we saw earlier in Harrison's comparison of Asian Americans and "ghetto blacks," the culture of the underclass was declared ill suited for economic success. Given that culture—understood as intransigent—was immune to quick change, there was consequently little to be done about urban poverty. In this line of reasoning, governmental and external efforts to eradicate poverty were doomed to fail.

The political and intellectual background of the urban underclass thesis is the conservative ascendancy in the 1980s, which in turn was sustained by a fear and loathing of the underclass (Ferguson and Rogers 1986; Edsall and Edsall 1991, pp. 232–244; Schaller 1992, p. 35). In particular, the Reagan and Bush administrations reneged on measures to ameliorate the lives of African Americans (Omi and Winant 1986, chap. 7). Perhaps the most notable intellectual rationale was put forward by Charles Murray in *Losing Ground:* "My conclusion is that social programs in a democratic society tend to produce net harm in dealing with the most difficult problems" (1984, p. 219). His main evidence was that "in the late sixties, still more in the seventies, the number of checks, the size of the checks, and the number of beneficiaries all increased. Yet, perversely, poverty chose those years to halt a decline that had been underway" (p. 58; see also Glazer 1988, chap. 1). Murray argued that social programs dedicated to alleviating or even eradicating poverty did more harm than good. Needless to say, his book became popular among conservatives and was used to justify the Reagan administration's effort to eviscerate welfare programs.

The underclass concept must be placed in the context of the broader political and economic forces that caused massive unemployment in the inner city, as William Julius Wilson has done in *The Truly Disadvantaged* (1987; see also Jencks and Peterson 1991). By ignoring these structural forces, the conservative articulation of the underclass argument is problematic (Steinberg 1989, chap. 4; Gans 1990; Reed 1990; Franklin 1991, pp. 89–116; Henry 1992; Katz 1993). As with the model minority thesis, the category homogenizes and reifies African Americans, and thereby perpetuates racist stereotypes. Furthermore, it erroneously characterizes various aspects of inner-city life. Finally, it serves as an ideological weapon against social programs that might alleviate some of the pressing problems facing the urban poor.

The term "underclass" evokes an array of distressing inner-city pathologies. Although some are careful not to racialize the category, many others collapse and, in effect, equate the underclass with African Americans. In projecting a "black" and bleak picture of urban poverty, they glide over many African Americans' undeniable mobility into professional and middle-class status (Davis and Watson 1982; see also Boston 1988, chap. 2; Jencks 1991, pp. 96–98). Although the persistence of racism against middle-class or upper-class African Americans should not be underestimated (Zweigenhaft and Domhoff 1991, chap. 7; Cose 1993), the racialized image perpetuates the conflation of race and class. In reality, class divisions among African Americans manifest themselves in a variety of ways, as they do for Korean Americans (Muwakkil 1993).

In projecting a horrific picture of urban decay and poverty, the urban underclass thesis transmogrifies a serious issue into a hopeless case. In the thesis's master narrative, gangs and pimps ravage the neighborhood, perpetuate a range of pathologies and perversions, and contribute to the decline of family and community. But this view is misleading. Although decade-long neglect and even older fiscal urban crises have transformed formerly thriving city centers into struggling urban enclaves, the social and moral order, along with kinship ties, remains resilient.[35] Denigration of African American family and culture is in part a contemporary manifestation of racism. Images of crack houses and drug pushers, for example, are associated with the urban underclass. Yet while serious drug problems exist among poor African Americans, they are by no means unique to this group.[36] Beyond its hypocrisy,[37] the Reagan administration's effort to incarcerate drug traders ignored the root problem of poverty among inner-city residents. Instead of creating jobs, the Reagan and Bush administrations transformed the United States into the nation with the highest percentage of its population jailed.[38]

The underclass is thus employed as an ideological construct (McKibbin 1990, pp. 192–193). Its portrait of life in the inner city expresses an *a priori* characterization of otherness. The conservative rendition of the underclass thesis ignores the *adaptive* nature and other, noncultural, causes of the poverty culture. The vision of the hapless and hopeless underclass is a convenient justification for government passivity. Rather than aiding exploration of the external contexts that have contributed to the internal causes of urban decay, the idea of the underclass contributed in part toward realizing its very premise. In contrast to Murray's contention that government spending has been increasing without alleviating poverty, welfare spending declined dramatically in the 1980s. As a result, poverty grew: 4.3 million more people joined the ranks of people below the poverty level between 1979 and 1989 (Barringer 1992a, p. A1; see also Braun 1991, pp. 179–197; Goldsmith and Blakely 1992). Shrinking welfare programs only ensured the persistence of attitudes and behaviors associated with the underclass.

The dwindling opportunity structure is critical to the perpetuation of poverty (Orfield and Ashkinaze 1991). The experience of Salvador Martinez, an eighteen-year-old "high school drop out from one of the poorest neighborhoods of Los Angeles," is not altogether atypical; "he has never held a steady job, and the more he looks for one the more he thinks he never will" (Mydans 1992a, p. A1). As the sociologist Elijah Anderson (1992) relates through the life story of a poor African American man, the attractions and the viability of the "street" economy—drug trade, above all—are obvious, while the possibility of a steady job in the "mainstream" economy is fleeting and difficult. "The oppositional culture is alluring in large part because the conventional culture is viewed as profoundly unreceptive by many blacks in the inner cities" (Anderson 1992, p. 33). Moreover, about 40 percent of full-time manufacturing workers earned less than the wage necessary to keep a family of four out of poverty (Schwarz and Volgy 1992, pp. 13–14). Consider that the minimum wage was $4.25 per hour in 1992. If we assume a forty-hour workweek, a worker would have made $8,840 per year before taxes, which is below the government poverty figure for a family of three. Walter, a Harlem teenager, told President Bush: " 'I'm not working for $125 for a whole week. At McDonald's? Flipping hamburgers?' Walter said indignantly. 'One hundred dollars a week? That ain't no money. I can make that in 15 minutes selling drugs' " (Mattera 1990, p. 150; see also Jennings 1992b). Given the lack of opportunities, the appeal of illegitimate businesses remains irresistible for some, while poverty forces others to adopt survival strategies, which appear as features of the poverty culture to unsympathetic observers. From residence to education to employment, poor African Americans in particular face discrimination and disadvantages (see, respectively, Massey and Denton 1993; Ogbu 1978, chap. 14; Kirschenman and Neckerman 1991). Before we "blame the victims," we must comprehend their constraints.

The American Dream: Capitalism, Race, and Community

The celebration of the model minority and the denigration of the urban underclass reflected and basked in the conservative climate of the 1980s, a decade of both greed and denial, during which the rich grew richer and the poor grew poorer (Mattera 1990). Kevin Phillips writes: "The 1980s were the triumph of upper America—an ostentatious celebration of wealth, the political ascendancy of the richest third of the population and a glorification of capitalism, free markets and finance" (1991, p. xvii). The unfettered pursuit of profit became fashionable; capitalist theologians such as George Gilder and Charles Murray celebrated the entrepreneurial spirit of U.S. capitalism and simultaneously absolved the system of any problems. Concomitant with the unleashing of the greed motive was the denial of its costs. As Haynes Johnson (1991) entitled his book on the Reagan years, the United States seemed to be "sleepwalking through history."[39] While the United States was gradually losing its claim as the premier economic power in the world, the momentary euphoria of the Gulf War victory symbolized, while the Rodney King beating epitomized the underside of, the decade of self-congratulation.[40]

It is in this context that we need to understand the popularity of the underclass thesis, as well as its foil, the successful model minority. The underlying message is that people succeed or fail in spite of external constraints and contexts. The self-evident successes of Asian Americans, in the absence of government support, supposedly controvert the claim that more welfare or antiracist remedies are necessary to alleviate inner-city poverty.

The categories of the model minority and the urban underclass became ubiquitous in the 1980s because of their affinity with the dominant ideological movement. Their popularity, however, is not a temporary aberration. Rather, the archaeology of the dominant ideological current in the United States suggests their venerable provenance—the ideal of the American dream. Its principal tenet is that the United States is essentially an open society in which everyone can achieve her or his dream. A corollary of the belief is a series of assumptions about the nature of the economy, race, and community in the United States.

From Alexis de Tocqueville to Robert Bellah, foreign visitors and domestic commentators have defined a constellation of Americans' widely shared beliefs in individualism, freedom, and equality. In *An American Dilemma*, published in 1944, Gunnar Myrdal outlined the main constituents of the "American Creed" as the belief in "the essential dignity of the individual human being, of the fundamental equality of all men, and of certain inalienable rights to freedom, justice, and a fair opportunity" (1962, p. 4). Published over forty years later, Bellah and his colleagues' *Habits of the Heart* also sounded similar themes: "Freedom is perhaps the most resonant, deeply held American value" (1985, p. 23). Whether called the American Creed or the American ethos, these themes—individual freedom and opportunity—broadly defined what the United States was about. Myrdal pointed out, moreover, that even African Americans suffering violent prejudice may nonetheless believe in "the entire American Creed of liberty, equality, justice, and fair opportunity for anybody" (1962, p. xiv). So too the poor and the unemployed hold tenaciously to the American dream ideology (Schlozman and Verba 1979, pp. 103–138, 346–351).

Needless to say, the keywords that express ideals over generations experience semantic shifts and offer interpretive latitudes. What one person understands by "freedom" may not be shared by another. The commitment to individual freedom and dignity led ineluctably to neither the emancipation of African American slaves nor the open immigration of Asians. Although the same ideal can be used in struggles against injustices, the broader point is that the substance of the American dream ideology is relatively indeterminate. As an ideology, it can be used to advocate, denounce, and justify a variety of concrete deeds and measures. Our intention is to delineate the constituent beliefs of the American dream—without its nuances, complexities, and conflicts—in order to illuminate the broader ideological crucible within which the model minority and the urban underclass are forged.[41]

The American dream denotes a belief in the United States as a land of opportunity in which no major obstacles exist to individual success. Unlike in the Old World or the Third World, individuals are liberated and unleashed from their pre-American fetters to pursue their vision of happiness.[42] Inequalities and divides of class, gender, and race are ultimately meaningless; rugged individualism reigns supreme in this social view. Put simply, people with talent and who work hard succeed, while others do not. Those who fail, then, have no one to blame but themselves.[43]

The American dream is an individualistic ideology. The projected economic order is *laissez-faire* capitalism, in which sovereign individuals compete with one another to pursue material gains. In this vision, the entrepreneur, relying essentially on ingenuity and hard work, represents the iconic figure of success.[44] In turn, social welfare programs are never legitimate except as expressions of collective "charity" to the "truly needy." Michael Katz comments in *The Undeserving Poor* (1989) that there is a long tradition of sequestering the comfortable middle-class "us" from the morally inferior and impoverished "them." The moral primacy of work and its flip side, the ethical castigation of the "lazy" poor, is a deeply ingrained Americanism, a civilization founded on the rejection of European aristocrats and the denigration of African slaves (Shklar 1991, chap. 2; see also Rodgers 1978). In this line of thought, people on welfare are, almost by definition, morally suspect; the very concept of social welfare carries a pejorative connotation. When the Reagan and Bush administrations castigated the moral standing of welfare recipients, they were expressing a conservative reading of the American dream ideology.[45] In 1987 Reagan said of welfare: "It is time to reform this outdated social dinosaur and finally break the poverty trap."[46]

The celebration of the individual often entails the neglect of collective and systematic constraints. Class is eschewed in public discourse.[47] Racism, sexism, or other forms of systematic discrimination neither explain nor justify existing inequalities. The refutation of racism constitutes, as we have suggested, one of the appeals of the model minority thesis.[48] One terminus of the denial of racism is universal "ethnicization." In effect, everyone becomes an "ethnic" in the United States. Richard Alba argues: "The thrust of European-American identity is to defend the individualistic view of the American system, because it portrays the system as open to those who are willing to work hard and pull themselves over barriers of poverty and discrimination" (1990, p. 317). Charges of racism lose force if all ethnicities are considered to have struggled their way toward equality and prosperity under the same conditions.[49]

Finally, the American dream offers a particular social vision (Baritz 1989). The outline of a good society is constituted by two pillars: the family as a "haven in a heartless world" and the community that upholds the individualist ethos. In this vision, "home" is the nurturing environment, while the larger "community" protects the "home." The family is a sacred institution in the ideal of the American dream. Essentially, the home is a "haven" where individuals are nourished and protected; it is an incubator and protector of individuality.[50] The community is inseparable from the family.[51] Reagan, for example, spoke of America's "bedrock, its communities where neighbors help one another" (Reich 1991, p. 277). In turn, the idealized environment of the ideal family in modern America is suburbia. "The central symbol of the nearly perfected America . . . was the suburban family. Suburbia meant more than physical comfort; it embodied a long-held American dream of a happy, secure family life" (Skolnick 1991, p. 2). "Bourgeois utopias" of American suburbia became the ideal community (Fishman 1987; see also Hayden 1984 and Jackson 1985). In contrast, urban life represents an undesirable ideal. The city, with its disorders and dangers, represents a demonized environment. In the cacophony and heterogeneity of city life, deviant social relations and institutions proliferate.[52] More prosaically, the city is where the "community," understood in all its suburban splendor, breaks down; in cities, strange languages, foods, and peoples coexist. The city is, moreover, racialized and poor. Instead of individual achievement, there is sloth and dependence (on government welfare); instead of family values, there is deviance; instead of suburban *communitas*, there is urban anomie; and, finally, instead of "real" Americans, there are minorities.[53] The city—particularly the inner city—is the racialized "other" of the American dream.

The American dream thus projects a vision of the United States where individual initiatives and efforts determine success and failure, racism is not a serious affliction, and the family and the community exist to nurture sovereign individuals.

The social reality of the contemporary United States contradicts the idealized vision of the American dream. The world of entrepreneurial capitalism, for example, occupies a relatively small, if surprisingly persistent, part of the contemporary United States economy. The global economy of the late twentieth century is dominated by large corporations and large governments. It is via corporations and professions, not classical entrepreneurship, that most Americans seek material comfort in affluent suburbs. The free market ideology, however, celebrates nineteenth-century entrepreneurial capitalism, while ignoring the reality of twentieth-century corporate capitalism.[54] To be sure, instances of individual success continue to exist, but it would be egregious to deny the predominance of large corporations in the contemporary economy.

The individualism articulated in the American dream downplays systemic barriers to individual success, such as racism. Such a view misses not only racism's historical ferocity against African Americans—Jim Crow laws that rendered them virtually an "untouchable" caste into the 1960s in some regions of the United States—but also its contemporary, albeit weakening, force.[55]

The ideal of the nuclear family, similarly, diverges from the reality of most U.S. households. Many people of all ethnicities live in a variety of "nontraditional" households.[56] In addition, a generation of women's movements and feminist writings have noted the dysfunctions of the patriarchal nuclear family (Thorne 1992). Similarly, in spite of the celebration of the suburbs and the denigration of the city, people's concrete living patterns and ideals complicate this simple dichotomy. One principal trend, for example, has been the gentrification and renewal of urban centers (Zukin 1991). More important, many people abhor the isolation, anomie, and homogeneity of suburbs. Most American suburbs are not places, in Reagan's idealized imagery, "where neighbors help one another," but instead resemble the stereotyped cold and impersonal city.

The American dream presents a problematic ideal of individual life and community. More crucially for our purpose, however, the constellation of attitudes and institutions that constitutes the American dream has found a powerful articulation in the contrast between the model minority and the urban underclass: Korean Americans embody the

American dream, while African Americans betray its promise. The ideological constitution and construction of the "black-Korean conflict" should alert us not only to the importance of the broader political economy but also to the necessity of rethinking dominant American ideologies.

We cannot make sense of the heterogeneous voices of both conflict and cooperation, racism and solidarity, unless we see that they are the very ground on which ideologies work. In particular, an attempt to understand Korean American responses to the riots and the "black-Korean conflict" requires us to consider their transnational context and their heterogeneity. In so doing, we place American ideologies on trial. The complexities and contradictions of Korean American responses—indeed, the gritty reality of individual immigrant lives—require nothing less than an appreciation of themes at the heart of this book.

Conclusion

During the early morning of April 17, 1993, a federal jury convicted the Los Angeles Police Department officers Stacey Koon and Laurence Powell of violating Rodney King's civil rights, while acquitting the other two officers—Timothy Wind and Theodore Briseno. The verdicts, nearly one year after the original verdict that touched off the L.A. riots, satisfied Attorney General Janet Reno, who stated: "Justice has prevailed in Los Angeles" (Church 1993, p. 18). President Clinton observed: "Surely the lasting legacy of the Rodney King trial ought to be a determination to reaffirm our common humanity and to make a strength of our diversity" (Gerth 1993, p. 32). There was a celebration at the African Methodist Episcopal Church, while Koreatown and the rest of Los Angeles seemed to emit a collective sigh of relief.

A week of tension had surrounded Los Angeles as the whole world focused on the second verdict, if only as a potential catalyst for a reprise of the 1992 riots. The journalist Michael Rezendes called it "one of the most intensely watched trials of the century" (1993a, p. 1). Politicians and local leaders articulated their various pleas for peace, while the media lavished an inordinate amount of attention on every aspect of the trial. The fear of another riot was widespread. A *Los Angeles Times* poll, taken immediately after the L.A. riots, reported that over two-thirds of the respondents believed that they had "not seen the end of the sort of violence that swept through" Los Angeles (Clifford and McMillan 1992, p. A1). In anticipation of another riot, the Los Angeles

Police Department reportedly spent $1 million on riot gear (Serrano 1993). One Wilshire resident told the *New York Times*: "A lot of people are planning to leave. . . . I expect everything will be under control, but I'd rather be prepared for the worst, especially with children" (Reinhold 1993a, p. 14). As the jury deliberated for a week, rumors circulated and heightened the tension (Indiana 1993).

The wide gulf between the media gaze and inner-city reality manifested itself in the contrast between the intense anticipation and fear in the suburbs and the diffused concern and indifference in the inner city.[1] Reacting to the media hoopla over the impending riot, Milton Mallory, "an unemployed black construction worker," observed: "The only people I've seen that's so damned worried about it is Koreans and reporters" (Reinhold 1993a, p. 14). Michael Ventura noted ironically: "If you're not in one of the Designated Flashpoints like Koreatown (kept 'hot,' kept scared, by TV coverage), then your odds of getting through [the possible riots] unscathed aren't just good, they're great. Of course, the media doesn't emphasize this. It would spoil everybody's party" (1993, p. 9).

Neither rioting nor looting followed the 1993 verdicts. Harold Meyerson wrote: "So relax, we didn't have a riot—just an outburst of paranoia suggesting that L.A. has lost the minimal cohesion of postwar America" (1993a, p. 12; see also Martínez 1993, p. 24). Others were more sanguine. Los Angeles County Supervisor Yvonne Brathwaite Burke said: "People came here from all over the world to find hatred and to find disturbance, and they left having found an example of love and peace" (Rezendes 1993b, p. 1). Norma Johnson, a city official, observed: "There was so much tension. Now justice is done, and we can get some sleep" (Mashberg and Gorov 1993b, p. 10). To be sure, not all concerned parties were satisfied. Ira M. Salzman, Koon's lawyer, stated: "I cry for them. It's justice, not a circus. Stacey Koon is not some sacrificial animal to be cast aside for peace in Los Angeles" (Mydans 1993a, p. A1). The *Economist* (1993, p. 18) wrote: "Whatever the verdict, the principle of a fair trial has taken a beating." Some complained, in contrast, that all four should have been convicted.

The dominant tenor of post-verdict Los Angeles was relief, remembrance, and rebuilding. On the first anniversary of the 1992 riots, there were private ceremonies and public gatherings—church services and candlelight vigils—across Los Angeles.[2] By the time of the 1993 verdict, the 1992 L.A. riots, perhaps the largest civil disturbance in the

United States this century, had largely become part of history, albeit a matter of continuing contention and debate.

The Second Media Framing of Korean Americans

Unlike the reporting on the 1992 verdict, Korean Americans figured centrally in most accounts of the tension leading up to the 1993 verdicts. They were shown in panic, as they prepared for another riot—photos and articles depicted the brisk sale of guns and rifles among Korean Americans intent on defending their stores. The *New York Times* reported: "In Koreatown, Mike Kim vows to protect the convenience store he rebuilt after last year's riots, with a new gun. 'I don't leave this time,' he said" (Reinhold 1993a, p. 14). Incendiary comments were printed and broadcast; a Korean American man guarding his brother's store was quoted as saying: "Ninety percent of [the looters] are all thugs and crooks. . . . If they had stepped into my brother's store, without hesitation I would have blasted them away" (Goodman 1993, p. C18). The media framing of Koreatown and Korean Americans seemed stuck in the canonized image of armed vigilantes and rude shopkeepers.[3] At the same time, the "black-Korean conflict" resurfaced in many accounts as the hidden subtext of the L.A. riots.

Concerned Korean Americans felt framed by the media once again. To the media barrage, Angela Oh, who had emerged as the leading spokesperson for the Korean American community in Los Angeles, retorted: "You'd think from the media that these Koreans are just out of control, buying guns for no reason. . . . But there are reasons. They were targeted last time, and they have reason to feel like they could be targets again" (Mashberg and Gorov 1993a, p. 17). In a different vein, Charles Kim, a Korean American man going on a tour to Yosemite at the time of the 1993 verdicts, defied journalists: "I know you'd like me to say I'm leaving because of all this Rodney King business. . . . I'm just entertaining guests from Korea, and I wanted to take them out of town" (J. H. Lee 1993, p. 25).

Many Korean Americans continued to resist the dominant media portrait of Korean Americans and the "black-Korean conflict" frame. As we have argued, unless we analyze the ideological context of these media frames—and place them in their larger political economic context—Korean Americans continue to be unidimensional cardboard figures, rather than the multidimensional people they really are.

After the L.A. Riots

Given the diverse nature of the Korean American population, Korean American responses to the tension leading to the April 1993 verdict and its aftermath were, not surprisingly, extremely varied. For some suburban Korean Americans who suffered no direct damage, the memory of the L.A. riots had become something akin to a natural disaster—an event to be discussed from time to time. Their response was to go to Koreatown less frequently.

Yet the 1992 L.A. riots had, as we have seen, a tremendous impact on many Korean Americans. Those bearing the most visible scars of the riots remain the victims—those who suffered damage or lost their business altogether. The Korean American Inter-Agency Council, in a survey of over 1,500 respondents ten months after the riots, found that "approximately 75 percent of the Korean American victims of the Riots have not recovered from its after effects" (1993, p. 1). Less than 28 percent of those surveyed had been able to reopen their businesses.[4] In spite of being declared a federal disaster area, the first riot site to be so designated, federal relief was lagging.[5] The damages were not simply material; post-traumatic stress disorders remained common a year later. One such victim "suffered such a severe case that he has had temporary memory loss. He also has nightmares where African Americans and Latinos/as are attacking him and setting things on fire. The victim replays the Riot scenes over and over in his dreams" (Korean American Inter-Agency Council 1993, p. 6). The immigrant dream—materialism, modernity, mobility—burned with the flames of the 1992 L.A. riots.

The Lees represent a particularly tragic case. Their six-year-old store was looted and torched during the riots. In the year that followed, their relief money long depleted, Hi Soon Lee, with a depressive husband, "battles depression, nightmares, indigestion and heart palpitations, [and] has taken the only job she can find—waiting tables in a Koreatown restaurant. She works six days a week, from 9:30 A.M. to 11 P.M., for $600 per month plus tips" (Hamilton 1993, p. J9). She says: "For 20 years, I worked on my American dreams. . . . We saved money by not eating what we wanted to eat. By not spending our money. We worked even on Sunday. I had all that taken away from me in a matter of hours" (ibid.). Quite clearly, the L.A. riots will cast a long shadow on the lives of Korean Americans who suffered damage during the riots.[6]

The most profound effect of the 1992 L.A. riots for the wider Korean

American community, however, was the politicization of many, especially second-generation, Korean Americans. A Korean American in his thirties stated: "Through the riots we realized that we didn't have leaders, that we lacked political pull. . . . The [Korean American] community is going through an adolescent stage; these are growing pains and we need to find stability. We may have needed the riots, although it is tragic because of the loss of businesses, they brought a lot of good." Significant shifts have occurred in the politics and consciousness of Korean Americans: a new articulation of their transnational spaces and an effort to resituate themselves in the United States. It remains to be seen which directions and tendencies will prevail: essentialist nationalism, multiethnic alliance politics, cultural conservatism, labor solidarity, or perhaps even a return to political quietism. The complexities and confusions of Korean American politics refract the major political and ideological struggles of our times: the persisting divides of ethnicity and class, the meaning and morality of community, and conflicts over gender and multiculturalism.

A fundamental lesson of the L.A. riots for many Korean Americans was the need to shift their focus from South Korea to the United States. The transition from "Korean Korean" to "Korean American" implies not only a generational transfer of power but new articulations of the South Korean–U.S. relationship—from the first generation with its irrevocable ties to the homeland to the second generation with its firm footing in the United States. Many Korean Americans therefore seek to organize the community for better representation in U.S. politics and media. Yet not surprisingly, this scheme, trumpeted by younger Korean Americans, is not so simple. Members of the first generation do not somehow disappear; they do not stop working. Moreover, as we have seen, "Korean American" is not a monolithic identity.

In this regard, the state abandonment and media distortion during and following the riots constituted a clarion call for Korean American political and media participation. Those desiring improved representation for Korean Americans in the media were mindful of the media as a powerful social and political agent. The nationwide television appearance of Angela Oh signaled the heretofore absence of such figures and the dire need for media representatives. One Korean American found himself one of three Asian Americans in an otherwise all African American group on a television talk show; terrified, he didn't say a word. This man, tired of Korean Americans being "left, right—destroyed" by the pitiful media stunt in which a well-educated first-generation Korean immigrant interviewee, stumbling over simple English phrases—"I come long, work hard"—is pitted against an articulate African American activist whose answers are fluent and powerful, was exhilarated by the appearance of Angela Oh on *Nightline*. He was thrilled that she didn't mince words: " 'Listen to me, I have something to say,' she told them."

Others stress the importance of political representation for Korean Americans after the official riot response shattered their covenant with the United States. One of the organizers of the Koreatown peace rally following the riots said that, abandoned by the city, the police, firemen, and Police Chief Gates, "now we must mobilize in politics."

> This is the beginning of politics in this community. We've been good citizens. We've supported the police. We've given money to [Los Angeles Mayor Tom] Bradley. What did it get us? When these people came to steal from us and burn our stores, where were the police? Where were the firemen? Where was Gates?. . . . If there was a Korean on the city council, this never would have happened to us. (Rutten 1992, p. 53)

One immigrant explained that via the riots and the subsequent neglect of Korean Americans by the U.S. government, she understands even more the "racism and exclusion that blacks have been living with in this country." She noted: "We have no city council member—there was no one there for us—what are we supposed to do, just show up there? Sure! We only think about our kids becoming doctors and lawyers—people aren't interested in sending their kids into politics because in Korea politics has been so unstable and from one day to the next you could lose your job—in a single morning it can all go bad." She added: "What hurts the most is that we have no links to the government, no one to talk through. *We can't speak.*"

There was a definable surge in Korean American political participation after the riots. Several young Korean Americans we met were so deeply affected that they quit or abandoned plans for more lucrative jobs in order to enter community service—as representatives of Korean American organizations, volunteers in advocacy groups, or staff members of community organizations. Beyond these individual responses was the emergence of new organizations: Asian Pacific Americans for a New Los Angeles, the Korean American Inter-Agency Council, and the Asian Pacific Planning Council (Kwoh, Oh, and Kim 1993, p. B7; E. H. Kim 1993c, pp. 98–100).

The moves toward media or political representation do not, however, imply a consensus among Korean Americans. We have seen that Korean Americans are politically, economically, and ideologically diverse. Against the widespread assumption of ethnic or national solidarity, held passionately by some Korean American leaders, lies the unalterable reality of class divides and other cleavages. In the facile assumption of Korean American ethnic homogeneity, the concerns of poor and unemployed or working-class Korean Americans are passed over. Jay Kim, in 1992 the first Korean American to be elected to the U.S. Congress, is a conservative Republican who represents wealthy, predominantly European American, Orange County voters. His concerns, not surprisingly, are far from those of working-class or unemployed Korean Americans.

Neither the future of Koreatown nor the rebuilding of Korean American concerns in South Central Los Angeles is a simple matter. What will Koreatown become? Will recent efforts to Anglicize shop signs make symbolic space for its Latino majority? Will the city center's post-riot economic decline and suburban flight hasten its demise? Will it transform into a symbolic commercial center like Little Tokyo? And what of the victims, fading from public view with the passage of time and the emergence of new victims from other disasters? Some Korean American riot victims have already departed, returning to Seoul or fleeing for "whiter" suburbs and states; others struggle to rebuild and fight city hall. Will burgeoning second-generation groups continue to embrace the victims' increasingly unpopular cause? In the post-riot landscape these queries compose the terrain of public discourse, with its mountains and valleys of diaspora debate and ideological contest.

The Verdict on American Ideologies

The mainstream depiction of the Korean American story in conjunction with the L.A. riots celebrated the model minority while highlighting its conflict with the underclass. Others lambasted Korean American merchants for exploiting African Americans. Neither version, as we have seen, captures the complexity of the Korean American story or the diversity of Korean Americans in Los Angeles.

Indeed, our rendition of the Korean story challenges comfortable illusions concerning the American dream. The conservative celebration of individual entrepreneurship that denies systemic barriers, such as racism, is contradicted by the Korean experience in the United States. Corporate and governmental neglect of the inner city channeled Korean mobility strategies into businesses in the poorest areas of Los Angeles. The political economic underpinning of the interethnic conflict makes a mockery of various efforts to reduce the "black-Korean conflict" to ethnic or cultural differences. Korean Americans are irrelevant to the deindustrialization and governmental neglect of the inner city. Simultaneously, African American residents' efforts toward community control of South Central Los Angeles face the recalcitrant reality of the multiethnic population and class divisions among African Americans. Gang-related violence, in addition, mars a struggling community (Katz 1993, p. A23). Korean American merchants are thus irrelevant to the most pressing concerns, albeit useful as scapegoats.

Although many people insist on the irreducibility of ethnic or cultural differences, racial or ethnic generalizations obfuscate as much as they illuminate. Ethnic solidarity makes little sense in light of middle-class African American withdrawal from the inner city. The problem is class differentiation—successful Korean Americans do not live in Koreatown, either. The romantic vision of ethnic solidarity evaporates in the cold atmosphere of class division and mobility.

Blue Dreams I

David Rieff, an astute observer of Los Angeles, was shocked to discover that barely a half-year later, the L.A. riots seemed to have left almost no trace. "So the great riot turns out to have been both what it was, a great riot, and also an event with no particularly lasting consequences on the way the prosperous live" (1992, p. 8).[7] Noting that the prosperous have seceded into the suburbs, he goes on to say: "If a country can experience a riot like the one that took place in L.A., and see it driven off the front-pages of the newspapers by the controversy over whether the television show 'Murphy Brown' was immoral or not, then it is clear that except for those who are its victims, even riots are just a different, slightly unsettling form of spectacle" (pp. 8–9). He ends his reflections dramatically: "While there will be more L.A. riots, from Lyon to Seattle, they too will quickly become part of the background noise of our new world order, no more audible or visible to the bourgeoisie than the slaughter of animals or the crushing destiny of the poor. If this age had a motto, it would be 'out of sight, out of mind' " (pp. 9–10).

The efforts to "Rebuild LA," in spite of widespread media attention, seemed symptomatic of the crisis facing Los Angeles. Headed by Peter Ueberroth, the engineer of the successful 1984 L.A. Olympics, "Rebuild LA" sought a partnership between corporations and the government. Yet it primarily generated publicity, rather than economic growth in South Central Los Angeles, and Ueberroth resigned under heavy criticism in May 1993 (Davis 1993b, pp. 48–49; Johnson, Farrell, and Jackson 1994, pp. 20–21). Meanwhile, federal, state, or local government funding for urban renewal failed to materialize. Only half of the promised $1.2 billion in riot relief was dispensed (Mydans 1994, p. C20). Just one year after the 1992 riots, Michael Woo, an Asian American Democrat, lost to Richard Riordan, a European American Republican, in a hotly contested Los Angeles mayoral election (Meyerson 1993b). The poet June Jordan noted: "Nothing basic has changed" (1993, p. 12).

Indeed, the present and the future of the United States augur dark scenarios. The trends we described in Chapter 4—the division of Los Angeles into affluent suburbanites and impoverished inner-city residents; deindustrialization and the loss of urban manufacturing jobs; and class polarization within and across ethnic groups—wreak havoc on the body politic and commonweal. Tragedies in impoverished neighborhoods remain invisible, their cries muffled, and only violent outbursts capture fleeting moments of attention among the comfortable. In the "culture of contentment," eloquently described by John Kenneth Galbraith, self-serving ideas justify inequality and poverty, while they seek to secure their privileged existence—even at the cost of potential long-run disasters (Reich 1991; Galbraith 1992). The American dream, then, appears to be a promise that excludes the toiling majority.[8] As Langston Hughes rhapsodized in "Same in Blues": "There's liable / to be confusion / in a dream deferred" (1959, p. 271).

For many Korean Americans, especially the looted merchants, the L.A. riots shattered their faith in the United States and the American dream for which they left their homeland. In a few days, the material

embodiment of their dreams virtually went up in flames; at the heart of
the riot flames sizzled Korean American merchants' hopes. It is a fabled
ending as in the classic novel of Los Angeles, *The Day of the Locust,* where
violence is the climax to the promise of luxurious life in Southern
California (West 1962). To be sure, Korean American entrepreneurs
did not seek sun and surf in Los Angeles; yet they relentlessly pursued
their rendition of the American dream.[9] What riches they gained
burned between the cracks of the capitalist urban economy and the
weight of racist oppression. At the end of the American dream—its
path paved with sweat and tears—lay fire and mayhem.

Blue Dreams II

Yet if material dreams and tragedies are features of the current U.S.
economy and ideology, so too are boundless optimism and hope a
recognizable part of the American dream. If dreams are illusions, they
are also springs for that utopian impulse which makes possible the
impossible. If blue denotes depression and despair—the color of the
abyss—it is also the color of the heaven above, the splendor and
sunshine of the blue sky—the reason that dreams are considered blue
in Korea.

The dreams of sisterhood and brotherhood are not empty ideals but
real forces at work; the possibility of redemption is visible in unexpected places, in surprising forms. Paula Bellamy-Franklin, an African
American gospel singer, was touched by the singing of "We Shall
Overcome" in Korean at a joint African American–Korean American
service to mark the anniversary of the riots. "Everybody is so beautiful. . . . We are all of one blood" (Wallace and Kang 1993, p. A26;
Rodriguez 1993, p. 20). This impulse is not new, of course. Mary Paik
Lee, whose life as an early Korean immigrant was marked by poverty
and discrimination, developed a keen sense of the injustices of the
United States without losing hope for a better future. One solace was
minority solidarity: "Our black friends . . . were in the same situation as
Orientals. They spoke English, but that did not help them in their
struggle for a better life. . . . The Mexican people were here first, but
they were in the same hopeless state. Due to our mutual problems, all
minorities felt a sympathetic bond with one another. We patronized
one another's stores, to help out" (M. P. Lee 1990, p. 103; cf. Mura
1992, p. 14). She writes that in her old age, "I attend a church regularly

where most of the members are black, because it is there I feel most comfortable" (M. P. Lee 1990, p. 130).

These yearnings for human solidarity remain a powerful undercurrent, even as the reality seems to be one of ethnic hatred and misunderstanding. It would be the height of folly to blind oneself to the fires of nationalism, ethnocentrism, and racism that ravage Los Angeles (Martínez 1992, p. 2; see also Patterson 1977). Yet it would be equally unrealistic to close our eyes to the hankerings for fraternity.

The longing for community, however, cannot be for a simple return to the past, for a time and a place that no longer exist. Los Angeles, like the United States at large, is irremediably multiethnic, frustrating the efforts of European American suburbanites, African American inner-city nationalists, and Korean American ethnic purists alike to find a place of their own. The need for solidarity, as John Berger reminds us, is never-ending precisely because we can return neither to the pristine past nor to the primordial village. The impossibility of return, then, makes all the more urgent the efforts for fraternity and solidarity.

Notes

1. The Los Angeles Riots, the Korean American Story

1. In the light of later events, it is ironic that Rodney King was driving a South Korean–made car at the time of the beating and had earlier been arrested for robbing a Korean American-owned store. On Rodney King, the beating, and the Los Angeles Police Department, see Dunne (1991); and Los Angeles Times (1992c), pt. i.

2. See the editorials of various U.S. newspapers collected in Trager (1992), pp. 28–33. On the excessive force against King, see Amnesty International (1992); see also Davis (1990), chap. 5; Leibowitz (1993); and Skolnick and Fyfe (1993).

3. Laurence Powell, who was the most violent toward Rodney King, was put on another trial, while civil rights charges were made against all four (see Mydans 1992b). In April 1993, Powell and Koon were found guilty, while Wind and Briseno were acquitted, of violating Rodney King's civil rights. Racism was part of the motive for the beating: "Twenty minutes before he beat Mr. King senseless, Mr. Powell mocked a black family by saying in a message from his patrol car computer that they were right out of 'Gorilla in the Mist.' He described Mr. King as a sort of subhuman, saying under cross examination that Mr. King was not an animal but was 'acting like one' " (Cannon 1992, p. 18; see also Cooper 1992).

4. See, respectively, Bielski and Cochran (1992); Johnson (1992); Morris and Harrelson (1992); and Scigliano (1992). Strikingly, New York was relatively silent: "The impression was spread that when it's race against race New York is the most violent and also the most volatile of cities—an impression that was confounded when New York remained relatively calm in its reaction to the verdict in the Rodney King trial" (Logan 1992, p. 90).

5. Wheeler (1993), p. 274. For other estimates, see, for example, Senate Office of Research (1992), pp. 4–6; and Reinhold (1992), p. 14.

6. According to the Los Angeles Times (1992a, p. 8), it was "the worst civil disturbance of the century," while for Hazen (1992b, p. 10): "the most deadly and destructive riots in American history." For a summary narrative of the L.A. riots, see, among the earliest accounts, Hazen (1992a) and Los Angeles Times (1992a). On the New York City Draft Riots, see Bernstein (1990).

7. Davis (1992a), p. 5. Paul Delaney (1993, p. 11) wrote: "Years from now, writers, sociologists and politicians may well mark the beating of Rodney King and the 1992 Los Angeles riots as a defining moment for black Americans much like the 1955 lynching of Emmett Till, a black teenager who supposedly whistled at a white woman, or the 1965 riots in Watts. Surely black Americans will." Conservative Charles Murray (1992c, p. 10) noted: "The Los Angeles riots are likely to prove a watershed event in American race relations."

8. See, for example, Patterson and Winship (1992). In fact, mainstream media—TV especially—flattened the discourse on and the framing of the L.A. riots, which was, in itself, a telling reflection on the state of the Union. "A violent kaleidoscope of bewildering complexity was flattened into a single, categorical scenario: legitimate black anger over the King decision hijacked by hard-core street criminals and transformed into a maddened assault on their own community" (Davis 1992a, p. 4).

9. In terms of what the riots signified for radical political movements, *Political Affairs*, a Communist Party USA publication, was euphoric: "As our people confront monopoly, they will draw deeper conclusions about the system, with the help of the *People's Weekly World* and the Communist Party USA. The movement for socialism USA will grow in Los Angeles and across our nation" (Alarcon 1992, p. 24). Anderson Thompson (1993, p. 49) stated: "The Los Angeles Rebellion was fundamentally grounded in the ongoing worldwide African Liberation Movement." Cf. Meyerson (1992, p. 2): "Even on the wacko nether reaches of what remains of the American left, this will be a hard riot to romanticize."

10. Walker (1992b), p. 10. As the *New York Times* reported: "The White House said today that the riots last week in Los Angeles were a result of social welfare programs that Congress enacted in the 1960's and 70's" (Wines 1992, p. A1). Cf. Murray (1992b).

11. Rutten (1992), p. 52. See also Peter Kwong (1992), p. 88 ["the first multicultural riots"]; Davis (1992a), p. 1 ["the nation's first multiracial riot"]; West (1993), p. 1 ["a multiracial, trans-class, and largely male display of justified social rage"]; etc.

12. Although there are similarities between the upheavals in 1965 and 1992, they should not be overemphasized. Audacious comparisons may span across centuries and continents and may reveal remarkable similarities, such as between an eighteenth-century Parisian riot and the 1992 L.A. riots. The his-

torian Robert Darnton (1992, p. 46) notes that both shared "the previous histories of rioting, the settings of poverty, the influx of immigration, the prevalence of homelessness, the influence of gangs, the resentment of oppression, and the provocation of police. . . :" Fixating on formal similarities, however, effaces specificities and thereby risks a Pyrrhic victory.

13. See the prevalent imageries of "black and white" in the titles of Blauner (1989); Hacker (1992); Sonenshein (1993); and Terkel (1992). The concerns of such books and the United States have, however, become increasingly multiethnic.

14. This tendency exists among Asian American, including Korean American, writers as well. Cf. Joan Lee (1992), p. 229.

2. Reckoning via the Riots

1. There is a growing body of Korean and Korean American fiction, drama and poetry which also engages this contest. See, for example, S. H. Chang (1990) and T. Y. Chang (1992).

2. John Berger (1984, p. 55) notes that the immigrant is the paradigmatic figure of our age: "Never before our time have so many people been uprooted. Emigration, forced or chosen, across national frontiers or from village to metropolis, is the quintessential experience of our time" (see also Schiller, Basch, and Blanc-Szanton 1992, p. 13). Across the academic disciplines, new vocabularies challenge conceptions of identity and ethnicity, homes and displacements, and e- and im-migrations. These terms insist that many of us do not occupy fixed spaces, literally or metaphorically: "cosmopolitanism" (Rabinow 1986, p. 258), "global ethnoscapes" (Appadurai 1990), a "transnational public sphere" (Gupta and Ferguson 1992, p. 9), "global mass culture" (Hall 1991, p. 28), and a "new cartography of social space" (Rouse 1991, p. 12). Alongside new terms, new writing tactics refuse to translate, moving across languages and imageries. As Gloria Anzaldúa (1990, p. 379) proclaims across two idioms: "En unas pocas centurias, the future will belong to the mestiza."

3. A middle-aged Korean American man asked Abelmann where she was from. "Boston," she replied. He asked again: "No, but where are you from?" "My father was brought up in Switzerland after leaving Germany when the Nazis came to power." He then asked again. Abelmann said: "My father is a Jew born in Germany, my mother a Jew born in Boston." Finally, he said: "Oh, so you are from Israel—Israel, I see."

4. The notion that Koreatown, L.A., is but a ward of Seoul is often repeated both in Seoul and in Los Angeles.

5. Lim's comments, however, belie the complexity of class and status hierarchies in South Korea, where pre–Korean War rural status hierarchies have been superseded by contemporary hierarchies of wealth, education, and professional achievement.

6. Tae Sam Park became a return immigrant as he left Los Angeles for Seoul on March 20, 1993. The *Korea Times* reported his comment: "I want to say thank you to the Korean community for helping me when my troubles began and apologize for leaving without repaying them, but I am relieved because I feel as if I am leaving a war zone" (M. Cho 1993, p. 1).

7. Elaine Kim (1993a, p. 230) notes that the persistence of Korean "cultural nationalism" in the United States can be attributed to both the Japanese colonial legacy and the experience of racism in the United States. Kim (1993a, p. 229) professes that although she has been critical of cultural nationalism, she realizes that it is perhaps the only refuge: "[*Sa-i-gu,* the Los Angeles riots] makes me think again [about cultural nationalism]: what remains for those who are left to stand alone?"

8. Both written and spoken Korean combine so-called "pure Korean" words and Chinese character–based words.

9. Both of these terms, the purported spirit behind the name they chose, are "pure" Korean. In other words, they are Korean-language vocabulary which is not based on Chinese characters. However, the name they chose, *tongp'o,* is a term based on Chinese characters.

10. See Roh (1983) for an informative discussion of South Korean government control of Korean American journalism. In Los Angeles, a now discontinued independent weekly, the *Korean Street Journal,* challenged the received views of the South Korea–controlled ethnic media (E. Chang 1988, p. 63). Under the Park regime, the *New Korea,* an independent Korean community newspaper dating from 1905, was severely harassed by South Korean government officials, who hounded advertisers to withdraw their ads and merchants to remove the paper from their stands (New Korea 1976, pp. 140, 141). Throughout the 1960s and 1970s and even after the Kwangju Uprising, Korean Americans who engaged in anti-government activities were harassed by South Korean officials.

11. Some journalists portrayed this incident as exemplary of a "crazed" Korean nationalism. Ian Buruma (1988) even drew parallels to the infamous 1936 Berlin Games. See also Appadurai (1991), p. 204.

12. Kwangju is the capital city of the South Chŏlla Province, which, together with the North Chŏlla Province, makes up the Honam region. Located in southwestern Korea, these provinces have been less developed, and at points outright neglected, over the last thirty years. They are known to be a hotbed of radical activity, and Kim Dae Jung has been an important dissident and opposition party activist and politician.

13. Many Korean Americans, however, live entirely unfettered by the colonial mentality that Ryu detailed. Los Angeles Korean American minister Pyung Soon Im, one of the many 1993 L.A. mayoral candidates, entered the race "on a platform of brotherhood, sisterhood and wider merging lanes on the L.A. freeways." He joined the ministry after closing his "Hollywood Boulevard

gift shop that sold Elvis guitar clocks and miniature replicas of the Hollywood sign." When a *Los Angeles Times* reporter asked Im why he was qualified to "bring racial harmony to L.A."—his stated motivation to seek office—"he noted that he [had] three brothers-in-law—one Korean, one Caucasian and one African-American—and he gets along fine with all of them" (Los Angeles Times 1993a, p. A23). His rainbow image of multicultural Los Angeles is worlds away from the colony Ryu decries.

14. While some yearned to return to South Korea, others were skeptical. A wholesaler laughed at the absurdity of people's post-riot thoughts of returning to South Korea, and he couldn't get over the countless "emotional" people calling Radio Korea during the riots urging "all" Korean Americans to "go home." A one-year anniversary program on the L.A. riots in South Korea depicted dismayed Korean Americans who had discovered that you cannot go home again, that South Korea was by now closed to them.

15. We were never able to find the source of or any print reference to this frequently mentioned survey.

16. The Korean American Inter-Agency Council (1993, p. 6) reported that among the victims: "There is evidence of an increase in family conflict, domestic violence, child abuse and substance abuse." Counselors explain that since the riots many victims' families are experiencing difficulties: "Problems that were there already get out of hand."

17. One of the most frequently reprinted AP photographs shows a young bespectacled man in a striped business-type shirt holding a cigarette in one hand and a rifle in the other; in the background stands another well-groomed young man smoking a cigarette and holding a gun (New York Times 1992c, p. 2). For an example of a 1993 photo (prior to the April 1993 retrial), see Greenhouse (1993), p. 14; the caption reads, "Jay Shin (center) stands outside his liquor store with armed security guards yesterday, still on edge amid the calm in Los Angeles Koreatown."

18. Some, however, responded differently. Elaine Woo (1992, p. 155), a Chinese-American reporter, recounts that while she was troubled by the televised image of gun-toting Korean Americans, her Korean American colleague "was not embarrassed by the Korean vigilantes and did not believe other Asians should be, either. 'I think we need to have that image instilled in mainstream culture,' he said, 'so they don't think we could be taken as wimpy Asians. What is America? It was won with guns. It was built by individuals who defended their dignity with guns. These Korean vigilantes may help balance the view of Asians. Some are gentle, some are tough enough to stand up for themselves." These comments can be seen in part as a reaction against the stereotype of "geeky" feminized Asian American men (see Allis 1991).

19. The Korean American Inter-Agency Council (1993, p. 2) reported in March 1993: "Government bureaucracies are frustrating and tiring for native-

born, English-speaking Americans but for the non-English speaking victims, the experience is overwhelming."

20. According to the Korean American Inter-Agency Council (1993, p. 5), only 35 percent of the 527 riot victim respondents "had effective insurance on their business."

21. The Korean American Inter-Agency Council (1993, p. 6) reported: "Although so many victims suffer from severe anxiety and poor health, a great deal of suspicion and shame attached to mental health related services inhibit them from readily receiving counseling."

22. By 1993, however, the story had made the press (Mydans 1993b, p. E9).

3. Diaspora Formation: Modernity and Mobility

1. It is important to note that many immigrants do not reach the United States directly. For a comprehensive discussion of "contemporary migration in a rimless world," see Barkan (1992).

2. In 1945, "fully 20 percent of all Koreans were either abroad or in a province other than that in which they were born" (Cumings 1984, p. 25).

3. See *Song of Ariran* (Wales and Kim 1941) for a remarkable autobiographical account of such a life. Translated into Korean, this book is standard reading for student activists in South Korea today.

4. Most young people, and certainly the dissenting cohort in South Korea, do not question the identification of *Kim* Il Sung as a great guerrilla independence fighter.

5. These opposed ideological lineages were center stage in the Korean War when it was "at least in part . . . a matter of Japanese-trained military officers fighting Japanese-spawned resistance leaders" (Cumings, 1984, p. 23).

6. Kingsley Ryu notes: "To know the Korean political activities in America [during the colonial era] is therefore to know Korean politics in Korea" (quoted in Gee 1976, p. 126). See also W. Kim (1971).

7. In considering their disproportionate numbers, we must also note the large percentage of Christians, because northern Korea and particularly the largest city Pyŏngyang (North Korean capital) were strongholds of Christianity; Linda Pomerantz (1984, p. 291) estimates that in 1904 one quarter of the city's population, 15,000, were Christian. In 1977 North Korean refugees and their descendants accounted for about 14 percent of the population in South Korea (Light and Bonacich 1988, p. 113); during the 1960s Korean refugees from the North represented approximately 50 percent of those who emigrated from Korea to Latin America (I. Kim 1987, pp. 337–338). Most estimates for the United States are more conservative: Eui-Young Yu's figures, for example, indicate that 22 percent of the Korean American population is northern Korean while only 2 percent of the South Korean population is northern Korean (Yu 1983, p. 30).

8. I. Kim (1981), p. 35. Sǒnu Hwi's (1990, p. 213) 1965 short story, "Thoughts of Home," suggests the profound displacement of northern Koreans in South Korea. An older man sets out to re-create his old home from the North in a southern village chosen for its similar topography and vistas, and laments: "The trouble is that once I set out to imitate the old house, I found myself more and more caught up in minor details. Just placing a stone step. I would think it went one place but when I put it there it seemed wrong. So I'd stick it here and then there and after setting it and digging it up five or six times I would even end up going back to the spot where I had started." Over time he became troubled because there were no rats in the rafters of *this* house so he purchased rats and scattered food for them. Time passed and he took to drinking, sobbing of his older sister left behind in the North, and pointing here and there with an arrowroot cane, murmuring "No, no. This isn't the way it was" (1990, p. 214). The story ends as the old man dies while fishing in a nearby swamp, a favorite northern pastime; in a note he asked to be buried in a pine grove resembling his family's burial spot in the North.

9. Ubiquitously displayed telephone numbers on Seoul's public surfaces, its lamp posts, subway cars, and buses, urge residents to report any suspects. With the political upheavals in South Korea of the late 1980s and the global dismantling of cold war ideologies and borders, these spy posters have been increasingly defaced, often entirely blackened.

10. Sparse but sensational apertures in the civilian silence between South and North Korea include newspaper efforts over the 1960s and 1970s, the 1964 Tokyo Olympics when a few North Koreans were able to meet South Korean relatives, and September 1985 when "fifty dispersed family members, fifty folk singers and dancers, thirty reporters, and their support personnel, visited the capital city of the other regime" (C. S. Kim 1988, p. 107).

11. See C. S. Kim (1988) for a fascinating ethnography of South Korea's sundered families. Many of the poor refugees were illiterate and thus had been unable to take advantage of prior print media formats for family reunification. See also Ty Pak's (1983) *Guilt Payment* for short stories on the personal price of division, and particularly on the fate of split couples and their children.

12. Patterson (1988), p. 177. Lee and Chang-Su Houchins (1976, p. 135) suggest that the Korean emigration itself presented a threat to Japan's growing control over Korea.

13. INS (1990), app., A.1-5. The legacy of this policy can be found in the Chinese Exclusion Laws. See Chan (1991b) for a detailed discussion of the workings of these 1882–1904 laws.

14. As Hy-Sop Lim (1978, p. 8) notes, Koreans "accepted liberalism and democracy through Protestantism." In a different vein, "the sentiments of hostility of Koreans toward Japan implicitly reinforced the positive image of Americans" (Kang 1976, p. 23).

15. The Christian character of the March First Movement, however, has

been widely contested in contemporary South Korea. Increasingly, many scholars think of a hegemonic Christian and conservative leadership and a much more radical and popular movement that outstripped the plans and vision of the movement's more pacific leaders (Abelmann 1987).

16. In the account of the revolutionary *Kim* San (Wales and Kim 1941, p. 83), he was propelled into revolutionary action because of his rejection of his mother's deep Christian convictions, which had taught him to "bear with" the injustices of colonialism, and the failure of the March First Movement: "Before March First I had attended church religiously. . . . After this debacle [the suppression of the March First Uprising] my faith had been broken. I thought there was certainly no God and that the teachings of Christianity had little application for the world of struggle into which I had been born. One thing in particular made me angry. That was hearing an American missionary tell the people, 'God is punishing Korea for the mistakes she has made. . . . When God wills, Korea will get her independence, not before.' " Kim also recalled: "There was no Christianity in the methods the Japanese used [to suppress the March First Uprising]" (Wales and Kim 1941, p. 82). We also find an example of the quietism of Christianity that Kim abhors in Mary Paik Lee's immigrant memoir (1990, p. 12); when her family arrived in San Francisco from Hawaii in 1906 and "['a group of young white men'] laughed at us and spit in our faces," her father explained "that we deserved what we got because that was the same kind of treatment that Koreans had given to the first American missionaries in Korea."

17. Many of the women were somewhat educated and hailed from families in exile in China, Manchuria, and Siberia (Yang 1984, p. 8).

18. Yim (1989), p. 55. See Cathy Song's (1983, pp. 3–4) poem about her grandmother, a picture bride, for an illustration of the way in which contemporary diaspora identities are stitched from the stories of Korean displacement. In a comprehensive review of Korean American literature, J. K. Lee (1990, p. 198) suggests that Korean American women writers who descend from picture brides find "an inexplicable union with [their] immigrant forebears."

19. Kang (1947), p. 182. Elaine Kim (1982, pp. 34,43) cautions that *The Grass Roof* is a "justification of Kang's departure from Korea" and that he and his novel's protagonist are neither representative Koreans nor representative emigrants of their times. See also Yun (1992), pp. 80–86.

20. See W. Kim (1971); Shim (1977), p. 168; E. H. Kim (1989), p. 82; Son (1991); and Yang (1992). The early Korean independence movement in the United States, like the March First Movement in Korea, was inspired by Woodrow Wilson's declaration of the self-determination of nations in his 1918 "Fourteen Points" speech (Houchins and Houchins 1976, p. 156). As the United States allowed Japan's formal colonization of Korea, and never answered the passionate Korean and Korean American cries for independence,

however, the racial exclusivity of these ideologies became clear. *Kim San's* sense of profound betrayal is emblematic: "I believed that I was an important part of a great world movement and that the millennium had come. The shock of the betrayal from Versailles . . . was so great that I felt as though the heart had been torn out of me. What pathetic, naive creatures we Koreans were then, believing in words" (Wales and Kim 1941, p. 78).

21. A 1963 study of a twenty-five family Korean American community in Gresham, Oregon, noted that the March First commemoration, at which the [Korean] declaration of independence is read aloud, was the most important holiday of the year (Gregor 1963, p. 83).

22. See Givens (1939); Choy (1979); Yu (1983), p. 26; Chun (1987). For a fictional account of nationalist and church activities see *Clay Walls* (R. Kim 1987).

23. Gayn (1981), p. 353. His (1981, p. 429) indictment of the occupation is far-reaching: "I found . . . with shame and anguish, that under our flag—and often with our active encouragement—there had come into being a police-state so savage in its suppression of man's elemental liberties that it was difficult to find a parallel for it. I had found in our zone only the shallow verbiage of democracy, and none of its practices. I had found administrative and political ineptness, and an alliance with the darkest reaction." Gayn's observations accord with the analysis of Bruce Cumings (1981a) who, based on an exhaustive survey of U.S. military records, concludes that the United States mistook an indigenous impulse for independence and social reform as radical and pro-Soviet, and systematically suppressed it. By the late 1980s Cumings's *Origins of the Korean War*, Vol. 1, already twice translated into Korean, had become one of the canonical texts of South Korean student activists.

24. Hahm (1984), p. 42. Korean American novelist Richard Kim (1966, p. 109) traveled to South Korea in 1966 and similarly noted the popularity of the maxim: "You can't trust anybody [any nations]."

25. William Watts notes that the program "shows Koreans in positions of inferiority and servitude," and that it characterizes Korea as barren, backward, and poor (Y. Koo 1984, p. 367). Interestingly, in the same volume, Hellman (1984, p. 84) writes about the show: "Koreans are invariably portrayed with sympathy and humanity and the tragedy of the war for the country is poignantly evident."

26. Many children of military unions, including orphans, remain in South Korea. Won Moo Hurh (1972, pp. 17–18) reported on 1,541 such children in South Korea in 1966, noting their "marginal social status" from "*multiple* stigma labeling factors," and "that Black-Koreans carry the heaviest burden of these stigmas." One Afroasian American we interviewed recalls the visits to his mother's village in South Korea when he and his sister were kept inside, hidden from the villagers' gaze.

27. In 1975 an anthology of short stories on South Korean prostitutes

servicing American soldiers, *Ch'ŏn Sŭng-se's The Yellow Bitch's Scream* (Hwanggu ŭi pimyŏng), won a literary prize (Hahm 1984, p. 44).

28. This racist slur has, until quite recently, been widely and unself-consciously used in both South Korea and among first-generation immigrants in the United States; today, however, people are increasingly self-conscious about the term.

29. Another important group of immigrants emerging from wartime dislocations, interracial unions, and poverty, has been the children adopted in the United States, over 45,000 between 1962 and 1983 (I. Kim 1987, p. 331). Korean ideologies of patrilineage and consanguinity have made adoption difficult in South Korea; while intra-Korea adoptions are increasing today, the resistance is still considerable. See Janelli and Janelli (1982, pp. 53–57) on the historical context and persistence of this resistance.

30. Women, including military wives, adopted female children, and nurses, are disproportionately represented in INS immigration statistics, although the proportion has declined consistently since the 1950s. Women represented 81 percent of the total in 1965, 67 percent in 1970, 58 percent in 1975, and 55 percent by 1990.

31. Hy-Sop Lim (1978, p. 9) argues: "GI culture represents many elements of the lower class culture of American society . . . [it] could hardly be considered the capitalistic social morals of America based on Protestantism—It was considered rather a distortion of the materialistic and individualistic way of living." See also Raban (1991), pp. 276–277.

32. In highlighting South Korea's ambivalent relationship with the United States, however, it is important to note that South Korea's popular consumption of Japan is equally multifaceted, balancing the legacy of colonial hatred with contemporary envy and imitation of Japan's model of industrialization.

33. See Junghyo Ahn's (1992) *Hŏlliudŭ k'idŭ ŭi saengae* (The Life of a Hollywood Kid), an autobiographical novel whose 1950s protagonist is obsessed with Hollywood films, for a fascinating portrait of Hollywood in South Korea.

34. In *The Film Encyclopedia*, Terry Moore is described as a "busty Hollywood 'sexpot,'" who "generally got less press coverage for her film roles than for her romantic escapades, which included . . . Howard Hughes [and] Henry Kissinger" (Katz 1982, p. 826).

35. Raban (1991), p. 284. In the 1985 South Korean film, *Kipko p'urŭn pam* [Deep Blue Night]—which depicts the underside of the American immigration, including illegal contract marriages to procure green cards and violence against women—the Korean American contract wife who originally immigrated as a military bride notes the bitter irony of her pre-immigration "American dream": "I thought that everyday I would be going to parties at houses where I could see the ocean. Everyone would wear long dresses and I would dance . . . like I had seen in American movies." Later in the film the illegal

immigrant protagonist puts a twist on his Korean surname, and decides to call himself Gregory Paek.

36. Sterngold (1992), p. 6. Not unlike 1980s U.S. films on the Vietnam War, *White Badge* highlights the long-standing personal trauma of veterans.

37. Indeed, U.S. military aid to South Korea doubled after South Korea committed troops (Han 1978, p. 907).

38. Princeton Lyman (1968, p. 572) suggests that "they felt genuinely that a compromise settlement in Viet Nam would produce no more—and probably less—lasting peace and security than Korea could point to along its own DMZ [demilitarized zone]." For many, the participation "evoked a strong sense of patriotism as well as a feeling of national pride" (S. Kim 1970, p. 577). The fearlessness of the South Korean troops was widely reported in South Korea and the United States. In 1967, *Newsweek's* headline read: "Why the Korean Troops Are So Effective in Vietnam"; *U.S. News & World Report* featured "Korean General Tells How to Beat the Vietcong" (Han 1978, p. 910). In President Johnson's autumn 1966 travels through Asia, South Korea was the only country where he did not meet demonstrations protesting the U.S. involvement in Vietnam (Lyman 1968, p. 576).

39. Hattori (1987), p. 93. The boost was from "military commodity procurements, war risk insurance premiums, contracts for services, construction contracts, remittances of military and civilian personnel and commercial exports" (Han 1978, p. 898).

40. Lyman (1968), p. 577. At the same time, however, South Korean soldiers provided a mercenary opportunity for the United States because the price of keeping a poorly treated South Korean soldier was well under half that of supporting an American (Han 1978, pp. 897,899).

41. In an October 1989 address to the U.S. Congress, "Partners for Progress: ROK-US Relations in a Changing World," the President of South Korea, *Roh Tae Woo* (1990, p. 12), referred directly to his years in Vietnam: "For my part, I feel a particularly deep affinity for the United States. When my country was in flames [in the Korean War], I volunteered, still wearing a student uniform, to fight for our liberty. At that time many American soldiers fought alongside me and my colleagues. Many gave their lives so that Korea might be free. Later I fought in Vietnam together with young American soldiers. I know that there are many of my fellow soldiers among the members of the House and Senate present here today." He concluded his address: "God bless America and I thank you all." Ronald Reagan struck a similar chord in 1981 when he welcomed the South Korean President *Chun* Doo Hwan—the president whose lack of legitimacy culminated in nationwide struggles in 1987—to the White House: "Our young men have fought side by side, not only in Korea, but in Vietnam, and again there the cause was freedom, and today we are committed to each other's defense against aggression" (Larson 1990, p. 89). In *White Badge*, the Korean War and the Vietnam War similarly meet, but in a tortuous

fashion: "My life had been a succession of wars. When I was born in December of 1941, the Japanese were bombing Pearl Harbor and attacking the Philippines. Born during the Great War, I spent my childhood in the Korean War, and then a part of my youth fighting in Vietnam. . . . When I looked back at the garbage truck as our truck was grunting up the steep ridge, I saw Vietnamese villagers gathered where a truck had just unloaded refuse. The Vietnamese picking through the crumpled cans and stained leavings were grotesque. In these people I saw Korea twenty years ago" (Ahn 1989, pp. 8, 51).

42. See Reimers (1985). A *Los Angeles Times* editorial proclaimed after the L.A. riots that "the Immigration Reform Act of 1965 may come to seem the twin and equal of the Civil Rights Act of 1964" (Los Angeles Times 1992d, p. M4).

43. INS (1990), app. A.1-12. A ceiling for the entire Eastern hemisphere was set at 170,000 (app. A.1-12). This was amended in 1978 when a worldwide limit was set at 290,000 (A.1-17). The 1990 Immigration Act increased the total immigration to 675,000 beginning in 1995, and 700,000 for 1992 through 1994 (app. A.1-20). Barringer, Gardner, and Levin (1993, p. 35) suggest that in part the 1990 act aimed to limit family reunification's centrality in immigration.

44. Among Asian and Pacific Islanders, Koreans, after Vietnamese and tied with Asian Indians, account for the largest percentage change in immigration rates from 1980 to 1990, namely 125 percent (Barringer, Gardner, and Levin 1993, p. 4).

45. See Fuchs (1990) and Bailey and Morain (1993) for a report on the California anti-immigration bills in 1993. Ellis Cose (1992, p. 219) writes: "American history is one of absorbing successive waves of immigrants, [but] it is also a history of intermittent outbreaks of anti-immigrant hysteria, and of unremitting friction with racial minorities, whether native or foreign-born."

46. Eui-Hang Shin and Kyung-Sup Chang (1988, p. 622) demonstrate that "immigrant physicians are peripheralized as compared to both their homeland-staying cohort physicians and the native physicians of the host society."

47. Hall (1991), p. 28. *Kim* Chi Ha (1974, pp. 72–73), a 1970s literary, cultural and religious activist, offers an ironic description of the inscriptions of global capitalism on the body of a South Korean official in "Ko Kwan" (*Kogwan* or "High Official"):

> Ko Kwan puts on his clothes.
> He starts with U.S.-made jockey shorts and
> undershirt . . .
> Then long woolen underwear, camel hair socks
> and a white shirt, white as the snow
> "Daimaru" or "Takashimaya" [Japanese department stores] brand,
> A necktie bought in Paris, Chinese green jade cuff

links, as green as China's West Lake,
Oh! I forgot cologne. One drop of "Tabu"! . . .
Then he gets into his black-as-a-black-leopard
eight-cylinder Mercedes Benz 71. . . .

48. Koo (1987, pp. 108–109) calls South Korea's new middle class "contradictory," divided between its conservative elements aspiring to upward mobility under the status quo and its liberal or radical elements—primarily the intelligentsia—who side with labor and work to promote a more democratic, egalitarian society. Members of both groups have made their way to the United States.

49. Park et al. (1990), pp. 60–61. See also Hurh and Kim (1984), p. 67, and Min (1992), p. 228. We do not mean to suggest, however, that Korean American Christianity should be seen exclusively as an extension of South Korean Christianity.

50. P. Park (1982), p. 143. In South Korea today there are really two Christianities, which represent opposite reaches of the political spectrum. One is preached in middle-class neighborhoods and lavish churches that boast more members than churches anywhere else around the globe. South Korean capitalists and political elites meet at Seoul's conservative churches for an anticommunist celebration of Christianity. The other Christianity is practiced in modest buildings by small numbers in the factory districts of Seoul, where ministering to the needs of the poor takes precedence over formal doctrine. By the 1980s this South Korean variant of Liberation Theology (haebang or minjung [people's] sinhak) was a viable cultural and political movement, although the numbers remained small (Commission on Theological Concerns of the Christian Conference on Asia 1981). For a review of the various faces of Christianity in South Korea see Clark (1986).

51. People draw connections between Christianity and gender equality because missionaries played central roles in establishing many women's schools, most notably Ewha Woman's University.

52. I. Kim (1981); Shim (1977); and Min (1992). In fact, the influence of Christianity extends to Buddhists, whose religious practices are "Christianized" (Yu 1988).

53. Alfred Kazin's (1991, pp. 15–18) observation about Jewish immigration strikes a similar note: "The ideology of the family in Jewish literature can be far from the actual facts, Jews from Eastern Europe did not always emigrate because of anti-semitism. The enmity sometimes lay within the family itself."

54. Some would argue that Confucian ideology, which accords lower value to manual and mercenary activities, is relevant to these distinctions. As we turn to consider the numerous Korean Americans in small business in Chapter 5, however, we will see that the salience of this cultural argument wanes. That manual labor is looked down upon in South Korea, however, is undeniable.

55. By the end of the 1970s, college graduates' incomes easily doubled high

school graduates' and were more than four times those of primary school graduates (Koo 1984, pp. 1033–1034).

56. Over the last decade it has been popular among the very rich to send their children abroad for high school or even junior high school. In many cases the father remains in Seoul while the mother shuttles between her children and her husband (Seo 1993, p. 14).

57. Koo and Hong (1980), p. 62. Koo (1987, p. 109) notes: "The South Korean middle class seems to suffer a strong sense of relative deprivation with reference to the upper class."

58. Hagen Koo and Eui-Young Yu (1981, p. 19) suggest that South Koreans' "skills and aspirations cannot be absorbed in Korean society."

59. Yunshik Chang (1991) discusses the "personalism" entailed in these personal networks. The 1987 film *Sŏnggong sidae* [The Age of Success] offers a satirical portrait of a South Korean corporation and the unseemly side of rising up the corporate ladder.

60. Some have suggested that burgeoning white-collar labor unions, for teachers and bank employees among others, represent a polarization among the middle classes and a proletarianization of the lower echelons of white-collar workers, who find themselves excluded from middle-class lifestyles.

61. It remains, however, extremely difficult to gauge the social composition of the immigration because many enter with no occupation, including children and housewives. By the 1980s, 80 percent did not declare an occupation.

62. In a 1986 comparative study of Filipino and Korean immigration, Fred Arnold and colleagues (1989, p. 833) interviewed 1,834 South Koreans prior to departure to the United States about their family networks, and found that each immigrant represented an average of 17.4 living relatives who became eligible for immigration (father, mother, spouses, children, sons-in-law, daughters-in-law, siblings, siblings' spouses, and children of siblings). Only 4.3 people became newly eligible through each immigrant, however, and in turn from this group only .7 persons are at all likely to emigrate. The comparable figures for the Philippines are: 25.3 kin, 5.3 newly eligible, and 1.8 predicted immigrants. Although these figures were certainly higher in the past, they remind us that few potential family-network immigrants actually immigrate.

63. Park et al. (1990), p. 30. This does not reveal the region of origin of the Seoul residents, a considerable number of whom are likely to be first-generation migrants to Seoul.

64. A 1992 article reports: "[Immigrant] Lee Soo-yul was to have married on Sunday, but his bride's family canceled the wedding. They said they didn't want their only daughter moving to California. . . . The bride's parents said the Los Angeles riots had soured their image of America as a land of opportunity. . . . Lee, 35, who plans to become an American citizen, was heartbroken by the decision but said his future is in the West. He returned to California

alone Wednesday to divide his time between clothing stores in Fresno and Los Angeles" (Tunney 1992, p. 8).

65. James Larson (1990, p. 87) notes that the American coverage of Kwangju had a "dramatically different and greater impact in South Korea itself than in the U.S." The stark contrast between the official and unofficial stories illuminated the politically controlled South Korean media, dramatically mocking the nightly television spectacle of "Communist" student demonstrators. By the 1980s, a dissident journal *Mal* (Word) published verbatim the government directives to the media that instructed how to present various news events: which words to use, which words not to use, which images to include, which images to exclude, and so on.

66. The Kwangju Uprising did not pass unnoticed among Korean Americans, and made ripples in diaspora politics. The L.A. response challenged what Edward Chang (1988) calls the "tripartite alliance" of the consulate and KCIA (Korean Central Intelligence Agency), the ethnic media, and the Korea Federation. In short, as South Koreans demonstrated against the state's bloody suppression of a civilian uprising, some Korean Americans went to the streets protesting the events in their homeland, South Korean state intervention in their lives, and the United States's relationship to these goings-on. One North Chŏlla immigrant who arrived just after the Kwangju Uprising explained that the character of the Korean American Honam Association changed after the uprising from a friendship organization to a more political organization: "With Kwangju, with my 'brothers and sisters' [metaphorically] being killed, we couldn't be quiet. The press [in South Korea] distorted things so crazily, saying this was about North Koreans coming down." See Chang (1988) for a comprehensive discussion of responses to the Kwangju Uprising in Los Angeles.

67. This contrasts with the overwhelmingly negative South Korean response to President Carter's 1976 proposal to cut the number of troops in South Korea.

68. This cultural rejection, however, did not begin in the 1980s, but picked up the torch from cultural activists of the repressive 1970s, such as the song writer and singer *Kim* Min-gi and the poet *Kim* Chi Ha, important forebears of the *minjung* or people's movement.

69. See S. K. Kim (1991) on cultural politics in contemporary South Korea. In an interesting struggle for hegemony, the state appropriates "traditional" Korean culture in its expressions of Korean cultural identity as well. In spring 1993 *Sŏp'yŏnje*, a feature-length movie depicting the life of *p'ansori* (traditional Korean ballads) singers, surpassed all sales records for South Korean movies; considerable media attention addressed the popularity across age, gender, and class of this seemingly esoteric film on an increasingly remote indigenous genre (see Im 1993).

70. Seong-Kon Kim (1991, p. 114) goes so far as to proclaim that: "With its

dynamic energy and forceful movements, this [1980s] new dance played an important role in the democratization of Korea."

4. Mapping the Korean Diaspora in Los Angeles

1. Weinstock (1947), p. 2. W. W. Robinson (1968, p. 4) writes: "Everytime I find myself in Los Angeles I wonder what I've done to displease God."

2. Robert Heizer and Alan Almquist (1971, p. 202) write: "But history tells us that no more sorry record exists in the Union of inhuman and uncivil treatment toward minority groups than in California." For an overview of Asian labor in the making of Los Angeles, see Bonacich (1984).

3. Griswold del Castillo (1979), p. 6. "Los Angeles was founded in 1781 as an agricultural supply center for Alta California" (Starr 1985, p. 13).

4. Saxton (1990). On the ascent of Los Angeles as the center of Southern California, see Fogelson (1967), chap. 3.

5. See, for example, Kahrl (1982) and Gabler (1988) for the politics of water and of Hollywood, respectively.

6. Richard White (1991, p. 417) writes: "By 1890 Los Angeles had a chamber of commerce whose high-pressure efforts to sell the city nationwide became a model of their kind." See also Lotchin (1992), chap. 4.

7. Joan Didion (1992, p. 222) writes: "The extent to which Los Angeles was literally invented by the *Los Angeles Times* and by its owners, Harrison Gray Otis and his descendants in the Chandler family, remains hard for people in less recent parts of the country to fully apprehend." Mike Davis (1990, p. 101) observes: "For the half century between the Spanish-American and Korean wars, the Otis-Chandler dynasty of the [Los Angeles] Times did preside over one of the most centralized—indeed, militarized—municipal power-structures in the United States." See also Kotkin and Grabowicz (1982).

8. "The persistent strength of anti-union employers groups and their supportive public sector allies has been central to the twentieth-century industrialization of Los Angeles" (Soja 1989, p. 195).

9. McWilliams (1949), p. 22. The costs of the urban sprawl have been amply documented. For some, Los Angeles is a vast ecological wasteland, a metaphor for humanity's blind belief in progress. Richard Lillard (1966, p. 315), in one of the earliest polemics, concluded: "Southern California speeds from one brilliant improvisation . . . to another, valuing means, neglecting ends. Here is an engrossing and portentous foreshadowing of what mankind's heedless, headlong, onward plunge will do to landscape and to civilization." Hildegarde Flanner (1980, p. 22) wrote in the 1950s: "Our particular day has witnessed one of the West's most intense and ruthless replacements of agriculture with population, housing, industry, and freeways." The manifest political and aesthetic failings of Los Angeles led Lewis Mumford (1961, p. 510) to write: "The absurd belief that space and rapid locomotion are the chief

ingredients of a good life has been fostered by the agents of mass suburbia. That habit of low density building is the residual bequest of the original romantic movement, and by now it is one of the chief obstacles to reassembling the parts of the city and uniting them in a new pattern that shall offer much richer resources for living than either the congested and disordered central metropolis or the outlying areas reached by its expressways. The *reductio ad absurdum* of this myth is, notoriously, Los Angeles." Cf. Banham (1971), p. 243; and Bottles (1987), p. 254.

10. It should be noted that "Okies," or southwesterners, were also subjected to considerable prejudice and discrimination, including residential segregation (Gregory 1989, chap. 3).

11. This ethnic myth affects even progressive writers; Paul Jacobs and Saul Landau (1971, pp. xxxi–xxxii) note: "New Little Tokyos are growing up in the cities where most of the Japanese-Americans live, while . . . Chinese-Americans . . . clump together in what will soon be Little Chinatowns. . . . What America is witnessing is a new kind of clustering together of ethnic groups. They are perhaps afraid of being isolated from the familiar and reassuring." Bruce Cumings (1981b, p. 197) comments: "Our Chinatowns, successive generations of Americans believed, were populated by inscrutable deviants given to Tong wars, nefarious conspiracies, sleazy double-dealing, mayhem, and general depravity. Asians, whether here or there, lacked the requisites of freedom and civility."

12. Christopher Rand (1967, p. 102) observed: "L.A. has an exceptionally rich mixture of those human types that seem to be unmeltable, or meltable only with difficulty, in our culture." In fact, as Fogelson (1967, p. 198; see also p. 147) wrote: "Unfortunately, the white majority so subordinated and segregated the colored minorities—though, admittedly, not each group in the same way or to the same degree—that they were completely frustrated in their modest aspiration."

13. In 1930, of the total population of little over 1.2 million in the City of Los Angeles, there were approximately 21,000 Japanese Americans, 3,000 Chinese Americans, 51,000 "Mexican-born," and 39,000 African Americans (Modell 1977, p. 23).

14. Carey McWilliams (1990, p. 202) writes: "The oldest settlers in Los Angeles, Mexicans were pushed aside and swept under the extraordinary velocity and volume of Anglo-American migration after the first great 'land booms' in the 'eighties."

15. In the 1900s: "Residential dispersal did not bring improved housing. Restrictive racial covenants typically excluded the Spanish-speaking from desirable suburbs. The new barrios were established in sections of town that other more affluent groups refused to inhabit" (Ríos-Bustamante and Castillo 1986, p. 127; see also Camarillo 1979, pp. 117–126,199–210).

16. John Modell (1977, p. ix) writes: "The 'modal' Japanese American moved

to Los Angeles if he moved anywhere." Most writers agree that Japanese Americans received relatively better treatment compared with other minority groups (see, for example, McWilliams 1973, p. 322; Modell 1977, p. 32). On the history and contemporary situation of Japanese Americans, see, respectively, O'Brien and Fugita (1991) and Fugita and O'Brien (1991).

17. Japanese Americans resisted the law by various means, such as registering the land under the names of their U.S.-born children. Many, however, sought service jobs, such as gardening and domestic service (see, respectively, Tsuchida 1984 and Glenn 1984). On Japanese American agriculture, see Modell (1977), pp. 94–108.

18. Modell (1977), p. 71. On Japanese American small businesses in prewar Los Angeles, see Bonacich and Modell (1980), pp. 38–40.

19. Barry Bluestone and Bennett Harrison (1982, p. 6) describe deindustrialization as "a widespread, systematic disinvestment in the nation's basic productive capacity . . . [such that capital] has been diverted from productive investment in our basic national industries into unproductive speculation, mergers and acquisitions, and foreign investment. Left behind are shuttered factories, displaced workers, and a newly emerging group of ghost towns."

20. Soja (1989), p. 192. He (1989, p. 228) also writes that since 1930 "Los Angeles has probably led all other major metropolitan areas in the USA, decade by decade, in the accumulation of new manufacturing employment."

21. A study of the electronics and garment industries in Southern California reported: "Employers frankly state their preference for Hispanics, particularly the foreign-born, for direct production. These groups are perceived by employers as being more 'diligent,' 'hard-working,' and 'loyal' than native-born Americans. To a large extent, the same generalizations are made about Asians" (Fernández Kelly 1989, p. 156). Cf. Miles (1992, pp. 59–60): "Unskilled Latino immigration may be doing to American blacks at the end of the twentieth century what the European immigration that brought my own ancestors here did to them at the end of the nineteenth." See also Fuchs (1990).

22. "Orange County epitomizes the industrial and urban geography of the Sunbelt with its transaction-intensive economy, deeply segmented local labor markets, regressive labor relations, and high tech defense-related industries" (Soja 1992, p. 97).

23. Moffat (1993), p. B3. The Los Angeles Daily News reported: "Indeed Bradbury, with nine hundred inhabitants and ten miles of gated private roads, is so obsessed with security that its three city officials will not return phone calls from the press, since 'each time an article appears, . . . it draws attention to the city, and the number of burglaries increases' " (Davis 1992e, p. 172).

24. "So we built the outer walls of our castles. And inside them we built inner walls to protect each member of the family from the proximity of others" (Frayn 1968, p. 26).

25. Even freeways become class segregated; the accesses to freeways often bypass poorer areas (see Brodsly 1981, pp. 38–40).

26. For portraits of "Black L.A.," see George (1992); and Charles and Igus (1993).

27. McWilliams (1973), p. 324. W. E. B. DuBois, for example, stated in 1913: "Out here in this matchless Southern California there would seem to be no limit to your opportunities, your possibilities" (Bunch 1990, p. 101).

28. Bunch (1990), p. 110. "In the 1930s and 1940s Central Avenue (south of King and north of Manchester) was home for about 90 percent of L.A.'s black community" (Hamilton 1992, p. 5).

29. Starr (1990), p. 149. "After 1916 a sizable Negro community developed in Mud Town, or Watts, on the outskirts of Los Angeles, made up largely of migrants from rural areas in Mississippi, Georgia, and Alabama" (McWilliams 1973, p. 325).

30. Soja (1989), p. 201. Mike Davis (1990, p. 305) writes: "Young Black working-class men . . . have seen their labor-market options . . . virtually collapse as the factory and truckdriving jobs that gave their fathers and older brothers a modicum of dignity have either been replaced by imports, or relocated to white areas far out on the galactic spiral-arms of the L.A. megalopolis. . . ." See in general Wilson (1987).

31. Hubler (1992), pp. A1, A22. The changing ethnic composition of South Central Los Angeles has not resulted in cohesive organizations. There are, for example, virtually no interethnic organizations. Sergio Muñoz, the executive editor of the Spanish-language daily *La Opinion*, told the *New York Times*: "When the rioting exploded . . . [I] was among the leading Hispanic figures who gathered to call for calm, only to discover that they did not know the names of any Hispanic community leaders in the South Central area" (Mydans 1992c, p. D7; see also Oliver, Johnson, and Farrell 1993, pp. 130–132).

32. Givens (1939), p. 68. During World War II, one hundred Korean Americans in Southern California formed a special unit of the California National Guard (Shin 1971, p. 205).

33. Oh (1983, p. 37) has observed: "The Los Angeles branches of these Korean banks provide financial support for Korean firms conducting businesses in Southern California and to a limited extent local Korean businesses." See also D. O. Lee (1992), p. 264.

34. Yu (1990a), pp. 1–2. By 1979, the *Los Angeles Times* reported: "Los Angeles now has the largest population of Koreans outside of Korea—about 150,000 to 170,000. . . . So are their real estate holdings in an area that has come to be known as Korean Town." It had "5 shopping centers, 10 small strip shopping centers, 30 Korean restaurants, 5 supermarkets, 10 nightclubs, 80 churches, 4 Buddhist temples, 3 clinics and several schools" (Sherman 1979, p. 1). Eui-Young Yu (1982b, p. 28), however, estimated the number of Korean Americans in Los Angeles County at 55,000 in 1979.

35. J. W. Lee (1986), p. 36. Cf. Nee and Nee (1986, p. xxi): "The boundaries of Chinatown are not clearly demarcated." The expectation of clear boundaries is a figment of planners' desire, which counters the natural anarchy of urban life. On the nature of the ethnic built environment, see Noble (1992).

36. Koreatown became erroneously known as the second-largest Korean city (see, for example, Nelson 1983, p. 241; and Rieff 1991, p. 171). This is only one example of the kind of false information contained in most media accounts of Koreatown.

37. In Alexander Cockburn's (1992b) *tour d'horizon* of Los Angeles in the early 1990s Koreatown remains unmentioned. Davis (1990) is also largely silent on Koreatown.

38. Reichl (1993), p. 33. The 1993 *Zagat Los Angeles/So. California Restaurant Survey* lists only one Korean restaurant (Shindler and Berk 1992).

39. Cf. Rieff's (1991) title: *Los Angeles: Capital of the Third World.*

40. Kyung Lee (1969, p. 65) wrote: "A known, but seldom-stated factor in the suburbanization of Koreans was the progressive encroachment of the Negro population in the southern sector of the city."

41. Sherman (1979), p. 27. In the early 1980s, Eui-Young Yu (1982a, p. 30) noted: "Within Los Angeles County, there appears to be an increasing tendency for the Korean population to decentralize." See also Yu (1985), p. 39.

42. Yu (1990a), p. 34. The low home ownership figure for Koreatown stems in part from the preponderance of rental apartments.

43. Jonathan Raban (1991, p. 258) reports: "On his first day in Seattle, Mr. Han had learned that the Shoreline School District was 'much better, no comparison!' than the Seattle School District, and that the Syre Elementary School was just the place for his daughters to set foot on the ladder to academic stardom. So he bought a house in Richmond Beach. He had no Korean neighbors. The closeness of the house to the school was all that mattered."

44. H. S. Lee (1982). Yung-Hwan Jo (1982, p. 206) observes that many Korean American voluntary organizations are conflict-ridden.

45. Pyong Gap Min (1991a, pp. 236–237) argues that Korean American employees assume that they will become employers and hence express little working-class consciousness.

46. Angela Oh explained her ambivalence about her media role: "It's kind of tragic that Angela Oh [referring to herself] becomes the spokesperson, in some ways, because there are people who have been working for years, decades in some instances, building some very fundamental pillars in our community, who because of language differences can't express their experiences" (Asian American Policy Review 1993, p. 61). Media representatives, needless to say, are not always representative. The sociologist Todd Gitlin (1980, chap. 5) points out that the media, at a loss without spokespeople, sets about identifying them, and in so doing, the media effectively creates them.

47. Here she refers explicitly to the conclusions drawn by Light and Bonacich (1988).

5. Korean American Entrepreneurship

1. This chapter relies on many important works on Korean American entrepreneurship. In particular, Light and Bonacich (1988) is a milestone in this literature. Our emphasis in this chapter is different from that of their well-documented volume. In particular, we focus less on the significance of U.S. capital in structuring Korean American entrepreneurship and on the extent of Korean American merchants' ethnic solidarity. For a critical exchange on the book's findings and conclusions, see Min (1989, 1990b) and Bonacich (1989).

2. We interviewed the first three men with their wives; indeed, many of our interviews took place in offices and stores where both wife and husband were working together. In accepting such "natural" stages for our interviews, however, we unwittingly reproduced the patriarchal power structure in conversation such that the men's voices became dominant.

3. The protagonist continues: "All this time I thought I was getting those grades for him and Mom. And Mom and Father just wanted to set me up for a better life" (M. G. Lee 1992, p. 145).

4. See, *inter alia*, Hurh, Kim, and Kim (1979), p. 49; Kim, Lee, and Kim (1981), p. 5; Choi (1982), p. 155; Yu (1982b), p. 69; and Hurh and Kim (1984), p. 115. David S. Kim (1975, p. 52) states: "It is generally believed in the Korean community that only 10% speak English well."

5. Cf. Ivan Light's comment in his study (1972, pp. 4–5) of Chinese and Japanese immigrant entrepreneurs: "Compared to the native born, the foreign born have received less schooling and hold less impressive educational credentials. They possess fewer high-priced salable skills. They experience discrimination because of their accents and ethnicity. Hence the foreign born find in self-employment relatively better income and status rewards than do native-born persons who have advantages in the labor market."

6. In a 1975 Koreatown study, 51 percent of Korean men with college degrees and 60 percent of women with college degrees were employed as operatives or craft workers (D. S. Kim 1975, p. 53). In a 1978 study of Southern Californian Korean Americans, 58 percent had been professionals in South Korea, but only 21 percent in the United States (Yu 1982b, p. 60).

7. A 1984 study of Korean Americans in Los Angeles reports that although close to 90 percent of those surveyed had professional, managerial, or white-collar jobs in South Korea, about 63 percent had taken blue-collar jobs as their first job in the United States (Hurh and Kim 1984, p. 105). Pyong Gap Min's (1990a, p. 445) study shows a decline in occupational prestige in the first job after immigration. Although there is a consequent steady rise, even after seven

years, occupational prestige remains much lower than the job held in South Korea at the time of emigration.

8. Peter Kim told the *Los Angeles Times:* "[Korean immigrants] find out they're having a hard time getting a good job because of the language problem. They have no other option than to open their own business, if they have some kind of savings" (Millican 1992, p. B7).

9. Many Korean Americans realize that they will be more successful in small business even if they are able to become white-collar workers (Min 1984a, pp. 343–348, 1984b, p. 8).

10. Calvin Trillin, reflecting on his Jewish immigrant father, writes: "In the grocery business, it's accepted that one measure of a man's success is raising a son with enough sense to go into another line of work . . . It was a given in our family that my father was a grocer so that I wouldn't have to be. He hated it" (Trillin 1954, p. 59). Compare Bonacich and Modell (1980), p. 152.

11. Yoon (1990), p. 308. The immigrants surveyed in 1986 expected to triple their income upon arrival in the United States, and achieve a nine-fold increase after five years. Most planned to launch a business within three years (Park et al. 1990, pp. 87, 95).

12. In a study of New York greengrocers, Illsoo Kim stresses family labor and long working hours, in addition to capital, as the ingredients of mercantile success (1981, pp. 121–143).

13. See Min (1988a), p. 127. Ivan Light and Edna Bonacich (1988, p. 173) report 46.2 hours per week as the average for Korean American entrepreneurs.

14. J. Y. Lee (1983), p. 14. Illsoo Kim (1981, pp. 114–115), in his study of New York greengrocers, also stresses the importance of family labor and long working hours.

15. See, for example, Bang (1983), p. 86 (74 percent from personal, family, and relatives); and Min (1988b), p. 160 (63 percent from personal). Cf. Light and Bonacich (1988), pp. 243–272. Kwang Chung Kim and Won Moo Hurh (1985, p. 90) distinguish among "Korean accumulators," "American accumulators," and "dual accumulators."

16. Hyung-chan Kim (1977b, p. 104) claims that Korean Americans generally do not rely on *kye.* In Heeduk Bang's (1983, p. 86) study, only one out of fifty interviewees relied on *kye* as a main source of start-up capital. Our claim is tentative, however. As Ivan Light, Im Jung Kwuon, and Deng Zhong (1990, pp. 40–43) observe, there are considerable difficulties in ascertaining the extent of *kye;* some count *kye* earnings as savings, while others are worried about the *kye's* legality. See also Park et al. (1990), p. 89. Furthermore, there are pitfalls. We heard several stories of Koreans running off with *kye* money. The theft provided a springboard for a new life in the United States in some cases, and for a new beginning in another American city in other instances.

17. Comparing Korean with Filipino immigrants, Pyong Gap Min (1986–

87, p. 65) argues that the export-oriented South Korean economy has given Korean Americans an advantage in their economic endeavors.

18. Among the entrepreneurs studied by Bang (1983, p. 93), 75 percent of business information came from family members, relatives, and friends.

19. In Min's (1984b, p. 15) 1982 survey of Korean American merchants in Atlanta, 63 percent believed that they would not be successful in a "white area," and 24 percent said that it would be absolutely impossible.

20. "High labour costs push [supermarkets] out, as well as high insurance premiums, low sales volume, high levels of stock loss (from pilfering, pricing and checkout errors, and damage), high rents and low profits" (Economist 1992c, p. 30). See also Los Angeles Times (1991), p. B4; Shiver (1991); and Silverstein and Brooks (1991).

21. In Min's (1984b, p. 15) study of Atlanta merchants, "black consumption patterns" were cited by nearly 90 percent of them as a draw to opening stores in predominantly African American neighborhoods.

22. Edward T. Chang (1990, p. 104) notes that all the liquor stores sold between 1983 and 1988 passed from one Korean American to another.

23. Barbara J. Stanton, executive director of the Entrepreneur Educational Center in Los Angeles, said: "I'm not particularly fond of the swap meets. . . . They treat you like a suspect instead of a customer" (Shiver 1992, p. A12).

24. See, for example, K. C. Kim, Hurh, and Kim (1993). While the first generation faced problems in acquiring English, the problem for their children is to learn or retain their Korean (see Hau 1991).

25. Hong (1982b), p. 40. Eui-Young Yu (1987, p. 65) found that most juvenile delinquents came from families living in Koreatown where fathers were blue-collar workers or shopkeepers and mothers were seamstresses or working in the family business.

6. American Ideologies on Trial

1. There is by now a growing literature on the "black-Korean conflict"; see, for example, E. Chang (1990, 1993a, 1993b); Abelmann (1991); Ahn (1991); Chen (1991); S. Kim (1991); Min (1991b); Yi (1992); S. K. Cho (1993); and E. H. Kim (1993b). For literary works, see Lew (1993) and Min (1994).

2. Quoted in Rieder (1990), p. 17. Jan Sunoo states that Korean Americans "are captives of their own prejudices because of their narrow exposure to African-American culture and lifestyles. They get it the same way the majority of Americans get it—from movies" (George 1992, p. 83).

3. As Edward Chang summarizes, Korean Americans "despise what they believe to be black laziness and welfare dependency. Koreans can't understand why blacks aren't working harder to improve their status" (1990, p. 250).

4. The Korean American Grocers' Association purchased and distributed

1,000 copies of Edward Chang's (1993) Korean-language history of African Americans (Matzek 1993, p. 35).

5. Indeed, an African American woman complained that then presidential candidate Clinton and President Bush both visited Koreatown before meeting with African Americans and Latinos. "I think the riots sent out the right message, but I don't think the folks are comprehending the message. . . . When he [Clinton] came to the city, where did he go first? He went to Koreatown first. He met with those people before he met with the black and Mexican community. Bush done the same thing this morning. He went to Koreatown" (Scheer 1992, p. 8).

6. See J. Chang (1993). The media highlighted African American racism against Korean Americans; Christopher Hitchens writes: "The dislike among blacks for Koreans, and the euphemistic handling of this dislike by many black leaders, has to be one of the most dispiriting and demoralizing aspects not just of the Los Angeles crisis but of the current balkanization and tribalization of seemingly everything" (1992, p. 846).

7. The idea of "community control" has been important for many African Americans since the 1960s (see, for example, Feagin and Hahn 1973, pp. 306–317). Yet, as Marable writes: "The majority of Afro-American social institutions, from the Black churches to civic associations, were led by Blacks who were at best neutral, and more often than not positively hostile towards any form of racial separatism, whether imposed from without or created within their communities" (1985, p. 57).

8. Eui-Young Yu notes: "Korean shoppers think that non-Korean markets are more courteous, less expensive, carry more fresh vegetables, and have more choices" (1990a, p. 106).

9. Shaw (1990), p. A31. Edward Chang (1990, p. 244) asserts that Korean Americans "tend to be very cold toward people they do not know" and hence "there is a tendency . . . to disrespect their black customers."

10. New York Times (1992a). One effort forces individuals to crystallize and articulate "a compilation of negative, false stereotypes" about others (Njeri 1993, p. 22).

11. Charles Murray states: "The rhetoric had always proclaimed that affirmative action was needed to help minorities who were disadvantaged by the white majority. But Asians refused to exhibit the symptoms of disadvantage" (1992a, p. 32).

12. In Tikkun (1992), p. 42. In The Closest of Strangers, Sleeper writes: "Yet one 'means' never mentioned [by African American activists] is the recruitment and training of a few hundred young blacks prepared to work fifteen hours a day at low wages and in close family units, as the Koreans do, in order to pay their debts to immigrant lending societies [rotating credit associations]" (1990, p. 208).

13. Heterodoxy (1992), p. 10. In a similar vein, Midge Decter (1992,

pp. 21–22) charges that the "refusal of empathy with the Los Angeles Koreans on the part of America's liberal publicists has very deep roots," which include their advocacy of social welfare: "Assuming responsibility for one's life, for one's everyday choices as well as for one's moral conduct, is a practice that has been eroding in American life for a long, long time."

14. Andersen (1983), pp. 18, 20. The article continues by noting the less than enviable reputation of Korean Americans: "And everybody picks on the Koreans: Says U.C.L.A. Sociologist Harry Kitona [sic]: 'They regard the Koreans as the Mortimer Snerds of America. They cannot learn the language, their food smells and they cannot express themselves' " (p. 21). The article incited some Korean Americans to demonstrate at the local *Time* office in Beverly Hills (Chung 1983).

15. M. M. Kim (1989), p. 18; see also E. Lee, Kim, and Yim (1991), p. 582. In a *Doonesbury* cartoon, a perplexed student answers a teacher's query about Korea's location: "Isn't that a planet after Mars?"

16. See Chay (1984), p. 71 and Hellman (1984), p. 80. In the 1960s and 1970s, Korea was often mistaken for Vietnam, as the United States' two Asian wars became blurred into one pursuit: anticommunist war in Asia (see, for example, Hurh 1977, pp. 53–54). The popular image of South Korea in the 1970s, moreover, suffered from a series of infamous characters: Sun Myung Moon and the Unification Church, Tongsun Park and Koreagate, and General Park and repressive rule (see Hellman 1984, pp. 84–87).

17. The celebration of Korean American success was also heralded by insiders: "Despite language difficulties, cultural differences, and racial discrimination, Koreans are making progress in establishing a sound base in the United States. Many Koreans have gained national and international fame in their professions. In literature, Younghill Kang (author of *Grass Roof*), Richard Kim (author of *The Martyred, Lost Names*, and *The Innocent*), and Peter Lee (author of *Songs of Flying Dragons*) have made noticeable contributions. In music, Myung Hoon Chung (former Associate Conductor of the Los Angeles Philharmonic Orchestra), Myung Hwa Chung and Kyung Hwa Chung are among the top artists. Soon Taek Oh and Johnny Yoon are gaining popularity in the film and entertainment industry. An immigrant's daughter, Keung Suk Kim, was Miss Wisconsin of 1981. A Korean engineer turned businessman, K. T. Hwang is becoming the minicomputer king of California's Silicon Valley" (Yu 1983, p. 44).

18. In 1986: "*NBC Nightly News* and the *McNeil/Lehrer Report* aired special news segments on Asian Americans and their success. . . . Meanwhile, *U.S. News & World Report* featured Asian-American advances in a cover story, and *Time* devoted an entire section on this meteoric minority. . . . *Fortune* went even further, applauding them as 'America's Super Minority,' and the *New Republic* extolled 'The Triumph of Asian-Americans' as 'America's greatest success story' " (Takaki 1989, p. 474).

19. See K. C. Kim and Hurh (1983), p. 3. Probably the first popular articles on the Asian American model minority were Petersen (1966) and a 1966 *U.S. News & World Report* article reprinted in Tachiki et al. (1971). See also the special issue of *Journal of Social Issues* (Sue and Kitano 1973); and Osajima (1988).

20. U.S. Commission on Civil Rights (1992), p. 17. See also U.S. General Accounting Office (1990), pp. 20–28; Barringer, Gardner, and Levin (1993), pp. 267, 317–332; and Hing (1993), pp. 140–153.

21. See Yun (1989), pp. 33–52; and Chan (1991a), pp. 168–171. Not surprisingly, gender is an important axis of inequality (see, for example, Chu 1988).

22. Hurh and Kim (1989), pp. 525–526. For Korean Americans in particular, see Kim and Hurh (1983). "The inaccurate 'model minority' and 'foreigner' stereotypes, the misperception that Asian immigrants receive unfair subsidies from the government, and the public's unfamiliarity with the diverse histories, cultures, and socioeconomic circumstances of Asian Americans all contribute to anti-Asian feelings" (U.S. Commission on Civil Rights 1992, p. 24).

23. Vora Kanthoul comments: "The term *Asian-American* . . . was formed to show a unity that is not there. Most [immigrants and refugees] don't have that luxury, to think of the Asian-American movement. They are too busy making a living" (Moffat 1992, p. A21). See, however, Espiritu (1992) on the notion of emerging "Asian American panethnicity." See also Hing (1993), pp. 168–183; and Wei (1993).

24. Moffat (1992), p. A21. Jee Chin, a retired Hong Kong–born engineer, suggested: "People don't know if you're Korean or Chinese. [But] Chinese are friendly to [local people]" (p. A20).

25. Takaki (1989), p. 365. To be sure, the U.S. government was not as discriminating. "In 1940, the Alien Registration Act classified Korean immigrants as subjects of Japan; after the United States declared war against Japan, the government identified Koreans here as 'enemy aliens' " (ibid.).

26. See Roberta May Wong's artwork, "All Orientals Look Alike," in Lim and Tsutakawa (1989), pp. 74–75. Consider the following dialogue between "a WASP student and an Asian professor" reported by Won Moo Hurh (1977, p. 54):

> Student: "Hi! I thought I did fairly well on my final test, but you gave me a 'D'. Would you check my grade, please?"
> Professor: "Sure, but I haven't seen you before. Have you been attending my class? What's your name?"
> Student: "I am John Smith. I have never missed your class. You know, I am in your Sociology 100 class, Dr. Kim."
> Professor: "I think you are talking to the wrong person. I am not Dr. Kim."

Student: (with a shocked look) "Hmm . . . Are you sure?"

Professor: (a moment of silence) "Yes, I am dead sure. Dr. Kim's office is across the hall."

27. An older Korean American testified: "I know many forms and disguises of bigotry. When I came to Los Angeles from Hawaii in 1947 . . . [r]estrictive covenants against Asians were in effect. I have been refused jobs, housing and motel accommodations" (Hyun 1983, n.p.).

28. Ellen Stewart writes: "A surprising revelation in this study was that 80% of the merchants/employees interviewed indicated that they viewed being told to go back to Korea by Black patrons as inappropriate and often became very angry when told this" (1989, p. 91). It is puzzling why Korean American merchants' "anger" should be "a surprising revelation."

29. See the 1988 documentary by Christine Choy and Renée Tajima, *Who Killed Vincent Chin?* See also Wei (1993), pp. 194–196.

30. It is ironic that Harrison's solution prescribes the values of mainstream culture even as he decries them when he discusses the virtues of Confucian cultural values.

31. "By 1988, Peter Hamill was writing in *Esquire* that 'there is very little now that whites can do in a direct way for the maimed and hurting citizens of the Underclass.' In February of 1989, Morton Kondracke wrote in *The New Republic* that 'the crisis of the underclass is so great that probably nothing short of a spiritual renewal in black America would really solve the problem'. . . . In *The Washington Post* in April, Richard Cohen called for a 'war' in the inner city and denounced the 'pathetic lassitude' of 'the underclass' which militates against 'the dignity of honest work, the chance to move up the ladder'" (Cockburn 1989, p. 114).

32. Paul Peterson writes: "'under' suggests the lowly, passive, and submissive, yet at the same time the disreputable, dangerous, disruptive, dark, evil, and even hellish. And apart from these personal attributes, it suggests subjection, subordination, and deprivation" (1991, p. 3). See also Rieder (1985), pp. 57–79; and J. Jones (1992), pp. 54–55. See Jewell (1993) for a discussion of the gender dimension.

33. The centrality of deviant and antisocial behavior among chroniclers of the underclass is well captured by the political scientist Adolph Reed, Jr. (1990, pp. 23–24): "Mickey Kaus and Nicholas Lemann propose explicitly racialized, culture-of-poverty constructions. For Kaus the underclass is the 'black lower class' for whom 'the work ethic has evaporated and the entrepreneurial drive is channeled into gangs and drug-pushing' . . . In addition to the culture of poverty, he asserts the existence of a 'single-parent culture,' a 'welfare culture' . . . [Lemann] tells us that the underclass suffers from a 'strongly self-defeating culture.'" See also Glasgow's (1980) study of Watts.

34. Lewis (1966, p. xlv), with whom the idea of the culture of poverty was most closely associated, wrote in his best-selling *La Vida*: "By the time slum

children are age six or seven, they have usually absorbed the basic values and attitudes of their subculture and are not psychologically geared to take full advantage of changing conditions or increased opportunities which may occur in their lifetime." To be sure, Lewis himself stressed the adaptive functions of poverty culture and held some hope for social movements, which would achieve some reform. See especially Rigdon 1988; cf. Valentine 1968, chap. 3.

In terms of public policy, the single most important formulation was the so-called Moynihan Report. Daniel Patrick Moynihan (1981, p. 5) proclaimed that African American culture, particularly its family structure, was the root cause of African American poverty. He discussed "the tangle of pathology" said to exist in the inner city. Moynihan traced the historical roots of familial instability to the slavery that had destroyed African American families. One manifestation of the problem was the proliferation of female-headed house-holds. He explained: "In essence, the Negro community has been forced into a matriarchal structure which, because it is so out of line with the rest of the American society, seriously retards the progress of the group as a whole." (1981, p. 29). See also Frazier (1939, p. 290) and Clark (1965, p. 81).

35. "[N]eighborhoods with high concentration of poor blacks are politically viable communities. Poor blacks have a strong sense of community, and this characteristic seems to help propel them into the political arena" (Berry, Portney, and Thompson 1991, p. 371). See also Stack (1974); Jewell (1988); and Henry (1990). Cf. Jones (1992), p. 274.

36. In a related vein, even as the U.S. government waged a vigorous "just say no" campaign to deter drug use, the CIA was engaged in massive drug dealing (Chomsky 1991, pp. 114–120; see in general Scott and Marshall 1990).

37. The Reagan administration allowed "white-collar" criminals to run amuck: "In 1985 6,000 bank robberies netted gunmen about $50 million. The cost of assuming the liabilities of Lincoln Savings alone in 1989 totaled about *fifty times as much* money" (Schaller 1992, p. 115; see in general Stewart 1991).

38. According to Rothman (1994, p. 34), for every 100,000 Americans, 455 were incarcerated (289 for "white" and 1,860 for "black"; the figure for the Netherlands was 40, and Japan 45). The estimated annual cost for the prison system in 1992 was $25 billion. See also Shapiro (1992), p. 138.

39. On Reagan, see the indispensable work by Wills (1987). The best metaphor of denial comes from neurophysiologist Oliver Sachs: "Aphasias . . . experience an elevated understanding of . . . the quality of speech that com-municates an inner meaning rather than the mere assemblage of words. One cannot lie to an aphasiac because he cannot comprehend your words, and so is not deceived by them. . . . An aphasiac perceives the verisimilitude of a speaker's voice and cannot suspend disbelief. Reagan's 'grimaces, the histrion-isms, the false gestures, and above all, the false tones and cadences of the voice . . . rang false for these immensely sensitive patients'. . . . Normal audiences, 'aided doubtless by our wish to be fooled, were indeed well and truly fooled.'

The president's cunning and 'deceptive' use of words and tones assured that 'only the brain-damaged remained intact, undeceived' " (Schaller 1992, p. 59).

40. See, for example, Shapiro (1992). Stephen Graubard polemicizes: "The United States has become a victim of years of self-neglect, self-delusion, and self-praise. Once a quintessential model of a progressive society, it has become dowdy and old-fashioned, losing appreciation of its one remaining substantial resource—the heterogeneity of its people" (1992, p. 187).

41. See, for example, Edsall and Edsall (1991), p. 277. For expressions of conflicting visions, see, for example, Hunter (1991) and the pieces collected in Aufderheide (1992).

42. Kluegel and Smith (1986, p. 52) conclude their survey of ordinary Americans' beliefs about inequality thus: "A clear majority of the American population subscribes, largely unreservedly, to the characterization of America as the 'land of opportunity.' "

43. "The belief that all men, in accordance with certain rules, but exclusively by their own efforts, can make of their own lives what they will has been widely popularized for well over a century" (Weiss 1969, p. 3). See also Lipset (1979), p. 2.

44. Bellah and his colleagues note: "The self-sufficient entrepreneur, competitive, tough, and freed by wealth from external constraints, was one new American character" (1985, p. 44).

45. As Piven and Cloward (1993, chap. 11) argue, the anti-welfare ideology also functions to discipline workers.

46. Schwarz and Volgy (1992), p. 133. Although the transformation of social welfare into a social evil marked a tremendous shift in the terrain of political debate from the 1960s and 1970s, when Great Society programs and the alleviation of poverty were nearly consensual goals for U.S. citizens, the moral-philosophical foundation of social welfare in the United States remains less than secure and legitimate (see Katz 1989, chap. 3). Indeed, what Theodore Marmor and his colleagues call the "opportunity-insurance" state, which U.S. citizens broadly support, suffers from its conflation with the maligned welfare state (Marmor, Mashaw, and Harvey 1990, p. 49).

47. Benjamin DeMott writes: "America as a classless society is, finally, a deceit, and today, as yesterday, the deceit causes fearful moral and social damage" (1990, p. 12). Americans may be, however, class conscious in some ways; see Vanneman and Cannon (1987).

48. Indeed, neoconservative writers, especially in the 1980s, were emphatic on this point: to blame the lack of progress by some African Americans on racism was not only empirically wrong but morally objectionable. In so doing, they attempted to stem the tide of progressive "racial" legislation initiated by the civil rights movement of the 1950s and 1960s. Two African American intellectuals particularly influential in the 1980s articulated the ultimate irrelevance of race. Denying the impact of racism, the economist Thomas Sowell

notes: "The presence of Jewish and Japanese Americans at the top of the income rankings must undermine any simplistic theory that discrimination is an overwhelming determinant of socio-economic position" (1981b, p. 126). In his best-selling book *Ethnic America*, Sowell argues further that "perhaps the most striking difference among ethnic groups is in their attitudes toward learning and self-improvement" (1981a, p. 280). In other words, racism explains little of the disproportionate poverty experienced by African Americans. In another version of this argument, Shelby Steele highlights the fault with explaining African American problems with reference to racism. He writes: "Hard work, education, individual initiative, stable family life, property ownership—those have always been the means by which ethnic groups have moved ahead in America" (1990, p. 108). On this path to prosperity, it is necessary to assume an individual, not collective, perspective, and to shed the memory of past racism and the consciousness of victimization. "There will be no end to despair and no lasting solution to any of our problems until we rely on individual effort within the American mainstream (Steele 1990, p. 173). Thus Sowell and Steele articulated ideals that were enthusiastically endorsed by the Reagan and Bush administrations. But what is critical here is that this view—that "racism" is no longer an operative factor in the United States—resonates well with the dominant ideology. Again, Asian American successes controvert the claim that racism explains the failure of some African Americans to succeed in the United States.

49. Universal ethnicity also accentuates the irreducible import of culture in the sense that Michael Novak wrote: "Emotions, instincts, memory, imagination, passions, and ways of perceiving are passed on to us in ways we do not choose, and in ways so thick with life that they lie far beyond the power of consciousness (let alone of analytical and verbal reason) thoroughly to master, totally to alter. We are, in a word, ineffably ethnic in our values and our actions" (1972, p. xvi). Our "ineffably ethnic" self exists as a crucial precondition for the cultural explanation of ethnic groups' success and failure.

50. The shift from the older patriarchal norm to the new individualist ideal occurred as early as the late eighteenth century. Helena Wall writes: "Colonial society began by deferring to the needs of the community and ended by deferring to the rights of the individual" (1990, p. vii). The new ideal "was understood to be affectionate, voluntaristic, and private" (p. 138).

51. Claude Fischer writes: "Americans of the Left and of the Right esteem the local community. It rests in the pantheon of American civil religion paradoxically close to that supreme value, individualism. In our ideology, the locality is, following the family, the premier locus for 'community,' in the fullest sense of solidarity, commitment, and intimacy" (1991, p. 79). See also Gans (1988), p. 64.

52. Lewis Lapham notes: "The idea of a great city never has occupied a comfortable place in the American imagination. Much of the country's polit-

ical and literary history suggests that the city stands as a metaphor for depravity—the port of entry for things foreign and obnoxious" (1992, p. 4). See also White and White (1962).

53. The political scientist Edward Banfield writes: "The most conspicuous fact of life in the city is racial division. . . . The residential suburbs are mostly white—often 'lily-white'; the central cities, especially their older, more deteriorated parts, and above all their slums, are predominantly or entirely black" (1974, p. 77).

54. "Voices still trumpeting the nineteenth-century medley of stable independence and dynamic entrepreneurship have a patently disingenuous ring. The largest conglomerates regularly advertise their similarity to small business" (Berthoff 1980, pp. 42–43).

55. See, for example, Burstein (1985), p. 1. As Cornel West describes: "The chronic refusal of most Americans to understand the sheer absurdity that confronts human beings of African descent in this country—the incessant assaults on black intelligence, beauty, character, and possibility—is not simply a matter of defending white-skin privilege. It also bespeaks a reluctance to look squarely at the brutal side and tragic dimension of the American past and present" (1991, p. 35). See also Shklar (1991); Gould (1992); T. Morrison (1992); and Sundquist (1993).

56. Arlene Skolnick writes: "Contrary to the homogeneous, idealized family portrayed in the sitcoms, the most distinctive feature of American family life has always been its diversity" (1991, p. 3). She (pp. 51–54) also notes that the 1950s was in fact the "deviant decade." See also Coontz (1992).

Conclusion

1. Harold Meyerson noted: "The more distant and invisible the inner city, the more terrifying it seemed" (1993a, p. 10).

2. Stone (1993). The *Los Angeles Times* cover story on April 29, 1993 noted: "The city's soiled image is one of the enduring legacies of the riots, a scar as deep and ugly as the vacant lots in South-Central and Pico-Union" (Ferrell 1993, p. A1). See also Anna Deavere Smith's "documentary theater," *Twilight: Los Angeles, 1992* (1994).

3. "Given the number of journalists in Koreatown during the weeks leading up to the verdicts, there was a surprising lack of coverage beyond the beaten story path of vigilante patrols and firearm aficionados. Koreatown's only gun dealer, Western Gun Shop, hosted network news programs and print journalists from across the country. The impression given was that virtually all 7,000 Korean-American merchants in the county were girding for Armageddon, and Western Gun was their outfitter. The reality was that this tiny storefront on Western Avenue sold no more than 20 guns a day during the busiest post-riot buying sprees" (J. H. Lee 1993, p. 25). Joel Schumacher's film *Falling Down,*

which opened to much fanfare in Spring 1993, showed a rude Korean American shopkeeper, who lacked "the grace to learn my [the protagonist's] language [English]" (Brown 1993, p. 50).

4. Korean American Inter-Agency Council (1993), p. 1. Some were not insured, while others who were found their coverage to be bogus. Kibok Yoo's $280,000 policy is one example. "She had unknowingly bought from a gray market of policies sold widely in poor areas. She was shocked to hear that she might have to wait months or years to get money off her claims if she gets it at all" (Kerr 1992, p. F1). According to the Korean American Grocers' Association, only 6 of the 170 destroyed Korean American–owned stores in South Central Los Angeles were open by the time of the January 1994 earthquake (Emshwiller and Lubman 1994, p. A1).

5. Carla Rivera (1993, p. A1) reports that 50 to 60 percent of riot victims have been denied disaster aid.

6. See the video Sa-I-Gu (produced by Christine Choy, Dai Sil Kim-Gibson, and Elaine H. Kim) for an empathetic and engendered portrayal of riot victims. See also E. H. Kim (1993b), p. 31.

7. Mike Davis observes: "Yet within weeks, and before a single scorched minimall had actually been rebuilt, the second Los Angeles Riot, as well as the national urban-racial crisis that it symbolized, had been virtually erased from political memory banks" (1993a, p. 4).

8. "In an America more deeply divided by class, the American Dream . . . can not be a common enterprise and is transformed into multiple wilding agendas. . . . Among those at the bottom, the dream becomes pure illusion" (Derber 1992, p. 14).

9. Like the African American girl who yearns for blue eyes in Toni Morrison's (1970) The Bluest Eye, the Korean American version of the American dream overlooked the reality of racism.

References

Abelmann, Nancy. 1987. "The March First Movement: Nationalism and History." Paper presented at the American Anthropological Association meeting, Chicago, Ill.

——— 1990. "The Practice and Politics of History: A South Korean Tenant Farmers' Movement." Ph.D. dissertation, University of California, Berkeley.

——— 1991. "Transgressing Headlines: Reporting Race in the African American/Korean American Conflicts." Paper presented at the Association for Asian Studies meeting, New Orleans, La.

Against the Current. 1992. ". . . No Peace!" *Against the Current* 39 (July–Aug.): front cover.

Aguilar-San Juan, Karin, ed. 1993. *The State of Asian America: Activism and Resistance in the 1990s.* Boston: South End Press.

Ahn, Choong Sik. 1991. "An Alternative Approach to the Racial Conflict between Korean Small Business Owners and the Black-American Community in the New York Area." In Kwak and Lee, eds., *The Korean-American Community,* pp. 49–55.

Ahn, Junghyo. 1989. *White Badge: A Novel of Korea.* New York: Soho Press.

——— [An, Chŏng-hyo]. 1992. *Hŏlliudŭ k'idŭ ŭi saengae* [The Life of a Hollywood Kid]. Seoul: Minjok kwa Munhaksa.

Alan-Williams, Gregory. 1994. *A Gathering of Heroes: Reflections on Rage and Responsibility—A Memoir of the Los Angeles Riots.* Chicago: Academy Chicago.

Alarcon, Evelina. 1992. "The Los Angeles Rebellion." *Political Affairs* 71: 1–24.

Alba, Richard. 1990. *Ethnic Identity: The Transformation of White America.* New Haven, Conn.: Yale University Press.

Allis, Sam. 1991. "Kicking the Nerd Syndrome." *Time,* Mar. 25, pp. 64+.

Amnesty International. 1992. *USA: Torture, Ill-Treatment and Excessive Force by Police in Los Angeles, CA.* Washington, D.C.: Amnesty International.

Andersen, Kurt. 1983. "The New Ellis Island." *Time*, June 13, pp. 18+.

Andersen, Margaret L., and Patricia Hill Collins, eds. 1992. *Race, Class, and Gender: An Anthology.* Belmont, Calif.: Wadsworth.

Anderson, Elijah. 1978. *A Place on the Corner.* Chicago: University of Chicago Press.

———— 1990. *Streetwise: Race, Class, and Change in an Urban Community.* Chicago: University of Chicago Press.

———— 1992. "The Story of John Turner." *Public Interest* 108: 3–34.

Anzaldúa, Gloria. 1990. "La conciencia de la mestiza: Towards a New Consciousness." In idem, ed., *Making Face, Making Soul, Haciendo Caras: Creative and Critical Perspectives on Women of Color,* pp. 377–389. San Francisco: Aunt Lute Foundation.

Appadurai, Arjun. 1990. "Disjuncture and Difference in the Global Cultural Economy." *Public Culture* 2: 1–24.

———— 1991. "Global Ethnoscapes: Notes and Queries for a Transnational Anthropology." In Richard G. Fox, ed., *Recapturing Anthropology: Working in the Present,* pp. 191–210. Santa Fe, N.M.: School of American Research Press.

Arnold, Fred, Benjamin V. Cariño, James T. Fawcett, and Insook Han Park. 1989. "Estimating the Immigration Multiplier: An Analysis of Recent Korean and Filipino Immigration to the United States." *International Migration Review* 23: 813–838.

Asian American Policy Review. 1993. "An Interview with Angela Oh." *Asian American Policy Review* 3: 55–64.

Asian Women United of California, ed. 1989. *Making Waves: An Anthology of Writings by and about Asian American Women.* Boston: Beacon Press.

Aubry, Larry. 1993. "Black-Korean American Relations: An Insider's Viewpoint." *Amerasia Journal* 19(2): 149–156.

Aufderheide, Patricia, ed. 1992. *Beyond PC: Toward a Politics of Understanding.* Minneapolis, Minn.: Graywolf Press.

Auletta, Ken. 1982. *The Underclass.* New York: Random House.

Bailey, Eric, and Dan Morain. 1993. "Anti-Immigration Bills Flood Legislature." *Los Angeles Times*, May 3, pp. A3+.

Banfield, Edward C. 1974. *The Unheavenly City Revisited.* Boston: Little, Brown.

Bang, Heeduk. 1983. "The Self-Help/Mutual Aid Component in Small Business within the Korean-American Community." Ph.D. dissertation, University of Pennsylvania.

Banham, Reyner. 1971. *Los Angeles: The Architecture of Four Ecologies.* Harmondsworth: Penguin.

Baritz, Loren. 1989. *The Good Life: The Meaning of Success for the American Middle Class.* New York: Alfred A. Knopf.

Bark, Dong Suh. 1984. "The American-Educated Elite in Korean Society." In Koo and Suh, eds., *Korea and the United States*, pp. 263–280.

Barkan, Elliott Robert. 1992. *Asian and Pacific Islander Migration to the United States: A Model of New Global Patterns*. Westport, Conn.: Greenwood Press.

Barringer, Felicity. 1992a. "Census Data Show More U.S. Children Living in Poverty." *New York Times*, May 29, pp. A1+.

——— 1992b. "Census Reveals a City of Displacement." *New York Times*, May 15, p. A12.

——— 1992c. "As American as Apple Pie, Dim Sum or Burritos." *New York Times*, May 31, p. E2.

Barringer, Herbert R., and Sung-Nam Cho. 1989. *Koreans in the United States: A Fact Book*. Honolulu: Center for Korean Studies, University of Hawaii.

Barringer, Herbert R., Robert W. Gardner, and Michael Y. Levin. 1993. *Asians and Pacific Islanders in the United States*. New York: Russell Sage Foundation.

Bechhofer, Frank, and Brian Elliott, eds. 1981a. *The Petite Bourgeoisie: Comparative Studies of the Uneasy Stratum*. New York: St. Martin's.

Bechhofer, Frank, and Brian Elliott. 1981b. "Petty Property: The Survival of a Moral Economy." In Bechhofer and Elliott, eds., *The Petite Bourgeoisie*, pp. 182–200.

Bellah, Robert, et al. 1985. *Habits of the Heart: Individualism and Commitment in American Life*. Berkeley: University of California Press.

Bello, Madge, and Vincent Reyes. 1986–87. "Filipino Americans and the Marcos Overthrow: The Transformation of Political Consciousness." *Amerasia Journal* 13: 73–83.

Berger, John. 1984. *And Our Face, My Heart, Brief as Photos*. London: Readers and Writers.

Bernstein, Iver. 1990. *The New York City Draft Riots: The Significance for American Society and Politics in the Age of Civil War*. New York: Oxford University Press.

Berry, Jeffrey M., Kent E. Portney, and Ken Thompson. 1991. "The Political Behavior of Poor People." In Jencks and Peterson, eds., *The Urban Underclass*, pp. 357–372.

Bertaux, Daniel, and Isabelle Bertaux-Wiame. 1981. "Artisanal Bakery in France: How It Lives and Why It Survives." In Bechhofer and Elliott, eds., *The Petite Bourgeoisie*, pp. 155–181.

Berthoff, Rowland. 1980. "Independence and Enterprise: Small Business in the American Dream." In Stuart W. Bruchey, ed., *Small Business in American Life*, pp. 28–48. New York: Columbia University Press.

Bielski, Vince, and George Cochran. 1992. "The Emergency That Wasn't." In Hazen, ed., *Inside the L.A. Riots*, pp. 65–66.

Blauner, Bob. 1989. *Black Lives, White Lives: Three Decades of Race Relations in America*. Berkeley: University of California Press.

Bluestone, Barry, and Bennett Harrison. 1982. *The Deindustrialization of America: Plant Closings, Community Abandonment, and the Dismantling of Basic Industries.* New York: Basic Books.

Bonacich, Edna. 1984. "Asian Labor in the Development of California and Hawaii." In Cheng and Bonacich, eds., *Labor Immigration under Capitalism,* pp. 130–185.

————— 1989. "The Role of the Petite Bourgeoisie within Capitalism: A Response to Pyong Gap Min." *Amerasia Journal* 15: 195–203.

Bonacich, Edna, Ivan H. Light, and Charles Choy Wong. 1977. "Koreans in Business." *Society,* Sept.–Oct., pp. 54–59.

Bonacich, Edna, and John Modell. 1980. *The Economic Basis of Ethnic Solidarity: Small Business in the Japanese American Community.* Berkeley: University of California Press.

Boston, Thomas D. 1988. *Race, Class, and Conservativism.* Boston: Unwin Hyman.

Bottles, Scott L. 1987. *Los Angeles and the Automobile: The Making of the Modern City.* Berkeley: University of California Press.

Bradley, Bill. 1992. "The Real Lesson of L.A." *Harper's Magazine,* July, pp. 10–14.

Braun, Denny. 1991. *The Rich Get Richer: The Rise of Income Inequality in the United States and the World.* Chicago: Nelson-Hall.

Brodsly, David. 1981. *L.A. Freeway: An Appreciative Essay.* Berkeley: University of California Press.

Brown, Georgia. 1993. "Town without Pity." *Village Voice,* Mar. 2, pp. 50–52.

Buchanan, Patrick J. 1992. "The War for the Soul of America." *Human Events,* May 23, pp. 11+.

Bunch, Lonnie G., III. 1990. "A Past Not Necessarily Prologue: The Afro-American in Los Angeles since 1900." In Klein and Schiesl, eds., *20th Century Los Angeles,* pp. 101–130.

Burstein, Paul. 1985. *Discrimination, Jobs, and Politics: The Struggle for Equal Employment Opportunity in the United States since the New Deal.* Chicago: University of Chicago Press.

Buruma, Ian. 1988. "Playing for Keeps." *New York Review of Books,* Nov. 10, pp. 44–50.

Camarillo, Albert. 1979. *Chicanos in a Changing Society: From Mexican Pueblos to American Barrios in Santa Barbara and Southern California, 1848–1930.* Cambridge, Mass.: Harvard University Press.

Cannon, Lou. 1992. "A Different Story If Black Police Had Beaten a White." *Manchester Guardian Weekly,* May 10, p. 18.

Carson, Tom. 1993. "Sophist's Choice: Cornel West's Intellectual Agitprop." *L.A. Weekly,* Apr. 30–May 6, pp. 35–37.

Castells, Manuel. 1989. *The Informational City: Information Technology, Economic Restructuring, and the Urban-Regional Process.* Oxford: Blackwell.

Castuera, Ignacio, ed. 1992. *Dreams in Fire, Embers of Hope: From the Pulpits of Los Angeles after the Riots*. St. Louis, Mo.: Chalice Press.

Caughey, John, and Lauren Caughey, eds. 1976. *Los Angeles: Biography of a City*. Berkeley: University of California Press.

Center for Korean Youth Culture (CKYC). 1992. "Let's Get to Know: Center for Korean Youth Culture." Korean Immigrant Workers Advocates of Southern California Opening Ceremony and Fundraising Dinner Event. Mar. 21, p. 12.

Cha, Marn. 1975. "An Ethnic Political Orientation as a Function of Assimilation: With Reference to Koreans in Los Angeles." *Journal of Korean Affairs* 5: 14–25.

———— 1977. "An Ethnic Political Orientation as a Function of Assimilation: With Reference to Koreans in Los Angeles." In H. C. Kim, ed., *Korean Diaspora*, pp. 191–203.

Cha, Theresa Hak Kyung. 1982. *Dictee*. New York: Tanam Press.

Chai, Alice. 1992. "Picture Brides: Feminist Analysis of Life Histories of Hawai'i's Early Immigrant Women from Japan, Okinawa, and Korea." In Donna Gabaccia, ed., *Seeking Common Ground: Multidisciplinary Studies of Immigrant Women in the United States*, pp. 123–138. Westport, Conn.: Greenwood Press.

Chan, Sucheng. 1991a. *Asian Americans: An Interpretive History*. Boston: Twayne.

————, ed. 1991b. *Entry Denied: Exclusion and the Chinese Community in America, 1882–1943*. Philadelphia: Temple University Press.

Chang, Edward T. 1988. "Korean Community Politics in Los Angeles: The Impact of the Kwangju Uprising." *Amerasia Journal* 14: 51–67.

———— 1990. "New Urban Crisis: Korean-Black Conflicts in Los Angeles." Ph.D. dissertation, University of California, Berkeley.

———— 1991. "New Urban Crisis." In Hune, Kim, Fugita, and Ling, eds., *Asian Americans*, pp. 169–178.

———— 1993a. *Hŭg'in: Kŭdŭl ŭn nugunji* [Blacks: Who Are They?]. Seoul: Han'guk Kyŏngje Sinmunsa.

———— 1993b. "America's First Multiethnic 'Riots.'" In Aguilar-San Juan, ed., *The State of Asian America*, pp. 101–117.

———— 1993c. "Jewish and Korean Merchants in African American Neighborhoods: A Comparative Perspective." *Amerasia Journal* 19(2): 5–21.

Chang, Jeff. 1993. "Race, Class, Conflict and Empowerment: On Ice Cube's Black Korea." *Amerasia Journal* 19(2): 87–107.

Chang, Ryun. 1989. "Korean Churches in Los Angeles Metropolis in Relation to Present Status and Future Prospects." M.A. thesis, University of California, Los Angeles.

Chang, So-hyŏn. 1990. *Kkongt'ŭ Amerik'a* [Comic Skit America]. Seoul: Ch'aengnamu.

Chang, Tu-yi. 1992. *Amerik'a: kkumnara* [America: The Country of Dreams]. Seoul: Myŏngsang.

Chang, Yunshik. 1991. "The Personalist Ethic and the Market in Korea." *Comparative Studies in Society and History* 33: 106–129.

Charles, Roland, and Toyomi Igus, eds. 1993. *Life in a Day of Black L.A.: The Way We See It.* Los Angeles: Center for Afro-American Studies, University of California, Los Angeles.

Chay, John. 1984. "The American Image of Korea to 1945." In Koo and Suh, eds., *Korea and the United States*, pp. 53–76.

Chayanov, A. V. 1986. *The Theory of Peasant Economy.* Madison: University of Wisconsin Press. Originally published in English in 1966.

Chen, Elsa Y. 1991. "Black-led Boycotts of Korean-owned Grocery Stores." B.A. thesis, Princeton University.

Cheng, Lucie, and Edna Bonacich, eds. 1984. *Labor Immigration under Capitalism: Asian Workers in the United States before World War II.* Berkeley: University of California Press.

Cheng, Lucie, and Yen Espiritu. 1989. "Korean Businesses in Black and Hispanic Neighborhoods: A Study of Intergroup Relations." *Sociological Perspectives* 32: 521–534.

Chin, Frank. 1992. "Hello USA, This Is LA." In Hazen, ed., *Inside the L.A. Riots*, pp. 40–42.

Cho, Hae-joang. 1993. "Children in the Examination War in South Korea." Yonsei University. Manuscript.

Cho, Mindy. 1993. "Farewell America, Good-Bye Shattered Dreams." *Korea Times Weekly English Edition* 2(12), pp. 1+.

Cho, Myung Hyun. 1989. "The New Student Movement in Korea: Emerging Patterns of Ideological Orientation in the 1980s." *Korea Observer* 20: 93–110.

Cho, Soon Kyoung. 1985. "The Labor Process and Capital Mobility: The Limits of the New International Divison of Labor." *Politics and Society* 14: 185–222.

Cho, Sumi K. 1993. "Korean Americans vs. African Americans: Conflict and Construction." In Gooding-Williams, ed., *Reading Rodney King/Reading Urban Uprising*, pp. 196–211.

Choi, Keun-Hyuk, Tai-Hwan Kim, and Chan-Rai Cho. 1991. "The Impact of Anti-Americanism on U.S.-Korea Relations." *Korea Observer* 22: 311–333.

Choi, Kyung Soo. 1982. "The Assimilation of Korean Immigrants in the St. Louis Area." Ph.D. dissertation, Saint Louis University.

Choi, Sung-il. 1989. "Anti-Americanism in South Korea: From Kwangju to Reunification." *Korea Scope* 7: 1–16.

Choldin, Harvey M. 1973. "Kinship Networks in the Migration Process." *International Migration Review* 7: 163–176.

Chomsky, Noam. 1991. *Deterring Democracy*. London: Verso.

Choy, Bong-youn. 1979. *Koreans in America*. Chicago: Nelson-Hall.

Chu, Judy. 1988. "Social and Economic Profile of Asian Pacific American Women: Los Angeles County." In Okihiro, Hune, Hansen, and Liu, eds., *Reflections on Shattered Windows*, pp. 193–205.

Chun, Jinny. 1987. "The Ise and the Korean Independence Movement: Balancing between Social Reality and Social Goals." M.A. thesis, University of California, Los Angeles.

Chung, Min. 1993. "Activists Send Telegram to White House." *Koream*, Feb., p. 4.

Chung, Tong Soo. 1983. "Koreans in Los Angeles: Immigration and Misperceptions." In Los Angeles County Human Relations Commission, ed., *Rising Anti-Asian Bigotry*, n.p.

Church, George J. 1992. "The Fire This Time." *Time*, May 11, pp. 18–25.

———— 1993. "Cries of Relief." *Time*, Apr. 26, pp. 18–19.

Clark, Donald N. 1986. *Christianity in Modern Korea*. New York: Asia Society.

————, ed. 1988. *The Kwangju Uprising*. Boulder, Colo.: Westview Press.

———— 1991. "Bitter Friendship: Understanding Anti-Americanism in South Korea." In idem, ed., *Korea Briefing, 1991*, pp. 147–167. Boulder, Colo.: Westview Press.

Clark, Kenneth B. 1965. *Dark Ghetto: Dilemmas of Social Power*. New York: Harper & Row.

Cleage, Pearl. 1993. *Deals with the Devil and Other Reasons to Riot*. New York: Ballantine.

Clifford, Frank, and Penelope McMillan. 1992. "Most in L.A. Expect New Riots but Feel Safe." *Los Angeles Times*, May 14, pp. A1+.

Clifford, James. 1988. *The Predicament of Culture*. Cambridge, Mass.: Harvard University Press.

Cockburn, Alexander. 1989. "Beat the Devil: All in Their Family." *Nation*, July 24–31, pp. 113–114.

———— 1992a. "Ashes and Diamonds: The Voice of the Unheard." *In These Times*, May 13–19, p. 17.

———— 1992b. "On the Rim of the Pacific Century." In Reid, ed., *Sex, Death, and God in L.A.*, pp. 3–18.

Cole, Benjamin Mark. 1992. "Making Things Happen." In Los Angeles Business Journal, ed., *Beyond the Ashes*, pp. 63–67.

Colhoun, Jack. 1992. "The Family That Preys Together." *Covert Action Information Bulletin* 41: 50–59.

Collins, Keith E. 1980. *Black Los Angeles: The Maturing of the Ghetto, 1940–1950*. Saratoga, Calif.: Century Twenty One Publishing.

Commission on Theological Concerns of the Christian Conference on Asia. 1981. *Minjung Theology*. London: Zed Press.

Coontz, Stephanie. 1992. *The Way We Never Were: American Families and the Nostalgia Trap*. New York: Basic Books.

Cooper, Marc. 1992. "L.A.'s State of Siege." In Hazen, ed., *Inside the L.A. Riots*, pp. 12–19.

Cose, Ellis. 1992. *A Nation of Strangers: Prejudice, Politics, and the Populating of America*. New York: William Morrow.

———— 1993. *The Rage of a Privileged Class*. New York: HarperCollins.

Cumings, Bruce. 1981a. *The Origins of the Korean War*. Vol. 1: *Liberation and the Emergence of Separate Regimes*. Princeton, N.J.: Princeton University Press.

———— 1981b. "Chinatown: Foreign Policy and Elite Realignment." In Thomas Ferguson and Joel Rogers, eds., *The Hidden Election: Politics and Economics in the 1980 Presidential Campaign*, pp. 196–231. New York: Pantheon.

———— 1984. *The Two Koreas*. Washington, D.C.: Foreign Policy Association.

———— 1993. "Silent but Deadly: Sexual Subordination in the U.S.-Korean Relationship." In Sturdevant and Stoltzfus, eds., *Let the Good Times Roll*, pp. 169–175.

Daniels, Roger. 1962. *The Politics of Prejudice: The Anti-Japanese Movement in California and the Struggle for Japanese Exclusion*. Berkeley: University of California Press.

———— 1988. *Asian America: Chinese and Japanese in the United States since 1850*. Seattle: University of Washington Press.

Darnton, Robert. 1992. "Reading a Riot." *New York Review of Books*, Oct. 22, pp. 44–46.

Davis, F. James. 1991. *Who Is Black? One Nation's Definition*. University Park: Pennsylvania State University Press.

Davis, George, and Glegg Watson. 1982. *Black Life in Corporate America*. Garden City, N.Y.: Doubleday.

Davis, Mike. 1990. *City of Quartz: Excavating the Future in Los Angeles*. London: Verso.

———— 1992a. *L.A. Was Just the Beginning: Urban Revolt in the United States—A Thousand Points of Light*. Westfield, N.J.: Open Magazine Pamphlet Series.

———— 1992b. "*Chinatown*, Revisited? The 'Internationalization' of Downtown Los Angeles." In Reid, ed., *Sex, Death, and God in L.A.*, pp. 19–53.

———— 1992c. "The Empty Quarter." In Reid, ed., *Sex, Death, and God in L.A.*, pp. 54–71.

———— 1992d. "The L.A. Inferno." *Socialist Review* 22(1): 57–80.

———— 1992e. "Fortress Los Angeles: The Militarization of Urban Space." In Sorkin, ed., *Variations on a Theme Park*, pp. 154–180.

———— 1993a. "Who Killed L.A.? A Political Autopsy." *New Left Review* 197: 3–28.

———— 1993b. "Who Killed Los Angeles? Part Two: The Verdict Is Given." *New Left Review* 199: 29–54.

Davis, Mike, Manning Marable, Fred Pfeil, and Michael Sprinker, eds. 1987. *The Year Left 2: Toward a Rainbow Socialism—Essays on Race, Ethnicity, Class and Gender*. London: Verso.

Decter, Midge. 1992. "How the Rioters Won." *Commentary*, July, pp. 17–22.

Delaney, Paul. 1993. "An Optimist Despite the Evidence." *New York Times Book Review*, May 16, p. 11.

DeMott, Benjamin. 1990. *The Imperial Middle: Why Americans Can't Think Straight about Class*. New York: William Morrow.

DeParle, Jason. 1992. "1988 Welfare Act Is Falling Short, Researchers Say." *New York Times*, Mar. 30, pp. A1+.

Derber, Charles. 1992. *Money, Murder, and the American Dream: Wilding from Wall Street to Main Street*. Boston: Faber and Faber.

Didion, Joan. 1992. *After Henry*. New York: Simon and Schuster.

Doerner, William R. 1985. "To America with Skills." *Time*, July 8, pp. 42–44.

Dotson, John L., Jr. 1975. "The Pioneers." *Newsweek*, May 26, p. 10.

DuBois, W. E. B. 1986. "The Souls of Black Folk." In Nathan Huggins, ed., *W. E. B. DuBois: Writings*, pp. 357–547. New York: Library of America. Originally published in 1903.

Dunne, John Gregory. 1991. "Law and Disorder in Los Angeles," parts 1–2. *New York Review of Books*, Oct. 10, pp. 23–29, Oct. 24, pp. 62–70.

Eckert, Carter. 1990. "The South Korean Bourgeoisie: A Class in Search of Hegemony." *Journal of Koran Studies* 7: 115–148.

———— 1991. *Offspring of Empire: The Koch'ang Kims and the Colonial Origins of Korean Capitalism, 1876–1945*. Seattle: University of Washington Press.

Eckert, Carter, Ki-baik Lee, Young Ick Lew, Michael Robinson, and Edward W. Wagner. 1990. *Korea Old and New: A History*. Cambridge, Mass.: Korea Institute, Harvard University.

Economist. 1991. "America's Blacks: A World Apart." *Economist*, Mar. 30, pp. 17–21.

———— 1992a. "Getting Along." *Economist*, May 9, pp. 13–14.

———— 1992b. "Return of the Nativist." *Economist*, June 27, pp. 25–26.

———— 1992c. "A Sip of Something Good." *Economist*, Oct. 10, pp. 30–31.

———— 1993. "Justice in Los Angeles." *Economist*, Apr. 17, p. 18.

Edsall, Thomas Byrne, with Mary D. Edsall. 1991. *Chain Reaction: The Impact of Race, Rights, and Taxes on American Politics*. New York: W. W. Norton.

Elkholy, Sharin, and Ahmed Nassef. 1992. "Crips and Bloods Speak for Themselves." *Against the Current* 39 (July–Aug.): 7–10.

Ellis, David. 1992. "L.A. Lawless." *Time*, May 11, pp. 26–29.

Emshwiller, John R., and Sarah Lubman. 1994. "Shaken Faith: Small-Business Owners Say L.A. Is Murder, Even without Quakes." *Wall Street Journal*, Jan. 20, pp. A1+.

Enloe, Cynthia. 1990. *Bananas, Beaches, and Bases: Making Feminist Sense of International Politics*. Berkeley: University of California Press. Originally published in 1989.

Espiritu, Yen Le. 1992. *Asian American Panethnicity: Bridging Institutions and Ideologies*. Philadelphia: Temple University Press.

Farley, Reynolds. 1991. "Residential Segregation of Social and Economic Groups among Blacks, 1970–80." In Jencks and Peterson, eds., *The Urban Underclass*, pp. 274–298.

Fawcett, James T., and Benjamin V. Cariño, eds. 1987. *Pacific Bridges: The New Immigration from Asia and the Pacific Islands*. New York: Center for Migration Studies.

Feagin, Joe R., and Harlan Hahn. 1973. *Ghetto Revolts: The Politics of Violence in American Cities*. New York: Macmillan.

Ferguson, Thomas, and Joel Rogers. 1986. *Right Turn: The Decline of the Democrats and the Future of American Politics*. New York: Hill & Wang.

Fernández Kelly, M. Patricia. 1989. "International Development and Industrial Restructuring: The Case of Garment and Electronics Industries in Southern California." In Arthur MacEwan and William K. Tabb, eds., *Instability and Change in the World Economy*, pp. 147–165. New York: Monthly Review Press.

Ferrell, David. 1993. "World Sees Lotus Land as Badlands." *Los Angeles Times*, Apr. 29, pp. A1+.

Fischer, Claude S. 1991. "Ambivalent Communities: How Americans Understand Their Localities." In Wolfe, ed., *America at Century's End*, pp. 79–90.

Fishman, Robert. 1987. *Bourgeois Utopias: The Rise and Fall of Suburbia*. New York: Basic Books.

Flanner, Hildegarde. 1980. *A Vanishing Land*. Portola Valley, Calif.: No Dead Lines.

Fogelson, Robert. 1967. *The Fragmented Metropolis: Los Angeles, 1850–1930*. Cambridge, Mass.: Harvard University Press.

———, ed. 1969. *The Los Angeles Riots*. New York: Arno Press.

Fong, Katharine. 1992. "Looking for Hope." In Hazen, ed., *Inside the L.A. Riots*, pp. 93–94.

Franklin, Raymond S. 1991. *Shadows of Race and Class*. Minneapolis: University of Minnesota Press.

Frayn, Michael. 1968. *A Very Private Life*. New York: Viking.

Frazier, E. Franklin. 1939. *The Negro Family in the United States*. Chicago: University of Chicago Press.

Fredrickson, George M. 1987. *The Black Image in the White Mind: The Debate on Afro-American Character and Destiny, 1817–1914*. Middletown, Conn.: Wesleyan University Press. Originally published in 1971.

Fruto, Richard Reyes. 1992. "L.A. Slauson Reaches Out through Ad." *Korea Times Weekly English Edition*, June 3, p. 3.

Fuchs, Lawrence H. 1990. "The Reactions of Black Americans to Immigration." In Yans-McLaughlin, ed., *Immigration Reconsidered*, pp. 293–314.

Fugita, Stephen S., and David J. O'Brien. 1991. *Japanese American Ethnicity: The Persistence of Community*. Seattle: University of Washington Press.

Gabler, Neal. 1988. *An Empire of Their Own: How the Jews Invented Hollywood*. New York: Crown.

Gader, June Rose. 1980. *L.A. Live: Profiles of a City*. New York: St. Martin's Press.

Galbraith, John Kenneth. 1992. *The Culture of Contentment*. Boston: Houghton Mifflin.

Gans, Herbert J. 1988. *Middle American Individualism: The Future of Liberal Democracy*. New York: Free Press.

——— 1990. "Deconstructing the Underclass: The Term's Danger as a Planning Concept." *Journal of the American Planning Association* 56: 271–349.

Gates, Henry Louis, Jr. 1993. "Two Nations . . . Both Black." In Gooding-Williams, ed., *Reading Rodney King/Reading Urban Uprising*, pp. 249–254. Originally published in 1992.

Gayn, Mark. 1981. *Japan Diary*. Rutland, Vt.: Charles E. Tuttle Company. Originally published in 1946.

Gee, Emma, ed. 1976. *Counterpoint: Perspectives on Asian America*. Los Angeles: Asian American Studies Center, University of California, Los Angeles.

George, Lynell. 1992. *No Crystal Stair: African-Americans in the City of Angels*. London: Verso.

Georges, Kathi, and Jennifer Joseph, eds. 1992. *The Verdict Is In*. San Francisco: manic d press.

Gerth, Jeff. 1993. "Clinton Satisfied by Jury's Decision." *New York Times*, Apr. 18, p. 32.

Gitlin, Todd. 1980. *The Whole World Is Watching: Mass Media in the Making and Unmaking of the New Left*. Berkeley: University of California Press.

Givens, Helen Lewis. 1939. "The Korean Community in Los Angeles County." M.A. thesis, University of Southern California.

Glasgow, Douglas. 1980. *The Black Underclass: Poverty, Unemployment, and Entrapment of Ghetto Youth*. San Francisco: Jossey-Bass.

Glazer, Nathan. 1988. *The Limits of Social Policy*. Cambridge, Mass.: Harvard University Press.

Glenn, Evelyn Nakano. 1984. "The Dialectics of Wage Work: Japanese-American Women and Domestic Service, 1905–1940." In Cheng and Bonacich, eds., *Labor Migration under Capitalism*, pp. 470–514.

Goldsmith, William W., and Edward J. Blakely. 1992. *Separate Society: Poverty and Inequality in U.S. Cities*. Philadelphia: Temple University Press.

Gonzales, Paul. 1993. "Speaking Of: Foreign Students." *Los Angeles Times*, Jan. 19, p. H6.

Gooding-Williams, Robert, ed. 1993. *Reading Rodney King/Reading Urban Uprising*. New York: Routledge.

Goodman, Walter. 1993. "Talking about the Riots That Tore Los Angeles." *New York Times*, Apr. 27, p. C18.

Gorov, Lynda, and Tom Mashberg. 1993. "Peace in the Streets Source for Elation in an Anxious City." *Boston Globe*, Apr. 18, p. 15.

Gould, Mark. 1992. "The New Racism in the United States Society." In Paul Colomy, ed., *The Dynamics of Social Systems*, pp. 154–174. London: Sage.

Graubard, Stephen R. 1992. *Mr. Bush's War: Adventures in the Politics of Illusion*. New York: Hill & Wang.

Greenhouse, Pat. 1993. Photo. *Boston Globe*, Apr. 18, p. 14.

Gregor, Kyung Sook Cho. 1963. "Korean Immigrants in Gresham, Oregon: Community Life and Social Adjustment." M.A. thesis, University of Oregon.

Gregory, James N. 1989. *American Exodus: The Dust Bowl Migration and Okie Culture in California*. New York: Oxford University Press.

Grimond, John. 1982. "Somewhere Serious: Los Angeles—A Survey." *Economist*, Apr. 3, special survey section.

Griswold del Castillo, Richard. 1979. *The Los Angeles Barrio, 1850–1890*. Berkeley: University of California Press.

Gross, Jane. 1992. "Collapse of Inner-City Families Creates America's New Orphans." *New York Times*, Mar. 29, pp. A1+.

Gupta, Akhil, and James Ferguson. 1992. "Beyond 'Culture': Space, Identity, and the Politics of Difference." *Cultural Anthropology* 7: 6–23.

Gutman, Herbert G. 1976. *The Black Family in Slavery and Freedom, 1750–1925*. New York: Pantheon.

Hacker, Andrew. 1992. *Two Nations: Black and White, Separate, Hostile, Unequal*. New York: Scribner's.

Hahm, Pyong-choon. 1984. "The Korean Perception of the United States." In Koo and Suh, eds., *Korea and the United States*, pp. 23–52.

Hall, Peter. 1988. *Cities of Tomorrow*. Oxford: Blackwell.

Hall, Stuart. 1991. "The Local and the Global: Globalization and Ethnicity." In King, ed., *Culture, Globalization, and the World-System*, pp. 19–39.

Halliday, Jon, and Bruce Cumings. 1988. *Korea: The Unknown War*. New York: Pantheon.

Hamilton, Cynthia. 1992. *Apartheid in an American City: The Case of the Black Community in Los Angeles*. Van Nuys, Calif.: Labor/Community Strategy Center.

Hamilton, Denise. 1993. "Family Still Struggles a Year after Riots." *Los Angeles Times*, May 6, p. J9.

Han, Sungjoo. 1978. "South Korea's Participation in the Vietnam Conflict: An Analysis of the U.S.-Korean Alliance." *Orbis* 21: 893–912.

Harrison, Lawrence E. 1992. *Who Prospers? How Cultural Values Shape Economic and Political Success.* New York: Basic Books.

Hattori, Tamio, ed. 1987. *Kankoku no kōgyōka: hatten no kōzu* [Industrialization of South Korea: The Composition of Development]. Tokyo: Ajia Keizai Kenkyūsho.

———— 1992. *Kankoku: Nettowāku to seiji bunka* [South Korea: Networks and Political Culture]. Tokyo: Tokyo Daigaku Shuppankai.

Hau, Jong-Chol. 1991. "Teaching of Korean at Home: A Family's Experience." In Kwak and Lee, eds., *The Korean-American Community*, pp. 181–191.

Hayden, Dolores. 1984. *Redesigning the American Dream: The Future of Housing, Work, and Family Life.* New York: W. W. Norton.

Hazen, Don, ed. 1992a. *Inside the L.A. Riots.* New York: Institute for Alternative Journalism.

———— 1992b. "Foreword." In Hazen, ed., *Inside the L.A. Riots*, p. 10.

Heizer, Robert F., and Alan J. Almquist. 1971. *The Other Californians: Prejudice and Discrimination under Spain, Mexico, and the United States to 1920.* Berkeley: University of California Press.

Hellman, Donald C. 1984. "The American Perception of Korea: 1945–1982." In Koo and Suh, eds., *Korea and the United States*, pp. 77–88.

Henderson, Gregory. 1968. *Korea: The Politics of the Vortex.* Cambridge, Mass.: Harvard University Press.

Henry, Charles P. 1990. *Culture and African American Politics.* Bloomington: Indiana University Press.

———— 1992. "Understanding the Underclass: The Role of Culture and Economic Progress." In J. Jennings, ed., *Race, Politics, and Economic Development*, pp. 67–86.

Herman, Edward S., and Noam Chomsky. 1988. *Manufacturing Consent: The Political Economy of the Mass Media.* New York: Pantheon.

Hess, Darrel Eugene. 1990. "Korean Immigrant Entrepreneurs in the Los Angeles Garment Industry." M.A. thesis, UCLA.

Heterodoxy. 1992. June.

Hicks, Joe, Antonio Villaraigosa, and Angela Oh. 1992. "Los Angeles after the Explosion: Rebellion and Beyond." *Against the Current* 40: 44–48.

Higham, John. 1955. *Strangers in the Land: Patterns of American Nativism.* New Brunswick, N.J.: Rutgers University Press.

Hing, Bill Ong. 1993. *Making and Remaking Asian America through Immigration Policy, 1850–1990.* Stanford, Calif.: Stanford University Press.

Hitchens, Christopher. 1992. "Minority Report." *Nation*, June 22, p. 846.

Hoch, Charles. 1984. "City Limits: Municipal Boundary Formation and Class Segregation." In William K. Tabb and Larry Sawers, eds., *Marxism and the Metropolis: New Perspectives in Urban Political Economy*, 2nd ed., pp. 101–119. New York: Oxford University Press.

Hochschild, Arlie. 1989. *The Second Shift: Working Parents and the Revolution at Home.* New York: Viking.

Holley, David. 1985. "Koreatown Suffering Growing Pains." *Los Angeles Times*, Dec. 8, pp. 1+.

Hong, Doo-Seung. 1992. "Spatial Distribution of the Middle Classes in Seoul, 1975–1985." *Korean Journal of Population and Development* 21: 73–83.

Hong, Lawrence K. 1982a. "The Korean Family in Los Angeles." In E. Y. Yu, Phillips, and Yang, eds., *Koreans in Los Angeles*, pp. 99–132.

——— 1982b. "Perception of Community Problems among Koreans in the Los Angeles Area." In E. Y. Yu, Phillips, and Yang, eds., *Koreans in Los Angeles*, pp. 155–164.

Hong, Roy. 1992. "Korean Perspectives." *Against the Current*, July–Aug., p. 11.

Horowitz, Mark. 1992. "Givin' Good Riot." *Heterodoxy*, June, p. 16.

Houchins, Lee, and Chang-Su Houchins. 1976. "The Korean Experience in America, 1903–1924." In Norris Hundley, Jr., ed., *The Asian American: The Historical Experience*, pp. 129–156. Santa Barbara, Calif.: Clio Books.

Hsia, Jayjia. 1988. *Asian Americans in Higher Education and at Work.* Hillsdale, N.J.: Lawrence Erlbaum Associates.

Hubler, Shawn. 1992. "South L.A.'s Poverty Rate Worse Than '65." *Los Angeles Times*, May 11, pp. A1+.

Hughes, Langston. 1959. *Selected Poems of Langston Hughes.* New York: Vintage.

Hune, Shirley, Hyung-chan Kim, Stephen J. Fugita, and Amy Ling, eds. 1991. *Asian Americans: Comparative and Global Perspectives.* Pullman: Washington State University Press.

Hunter, James Davison. 1991. *Culture Wars: The Struggle to Define America.* New York: Basic Books.

Hurh, Won Moo. 1972. "Marginal Children of War: An Explanatory Study of American-Korean Children." *International Journal of Sociology of the Family* 2: 10–20.

——— 1977. *Comparative Study of Korean Immigration in the United States: A Typological Approach.* San Francisco: R & E Associates.

——— 1990. "The '1.5 Generation': A Paragon of Korean-American Pluralism." *Korean Culture* (Spring): 21–31.

Hurh, Won Moo, Hei Chu Kim, and Kwang Chung Kim. 1979. *Assimilation Patterns of Immigrants in the United States: A Case Study of Korean Immigrants in the Chicago Area.* Washington, D.C.: University Press of America.

Hurh, Won Moo, and Kwang Chung Kim. 1984. *Korean Immigrants in America: A Structural Analysis of Ethnic Confinement and Adhesive Adaptation.* Rutherford, N.J.: Fairleigh Dickinson University Press.

——— 1989. "The 'Success' Image of Asian Americans: Its Validity, and Its

Practical and Theoretical Implications." *Ethnic and Racial Studies* 12: 512–538.

———— 1990. "Adaptation Stages and Mental Health of Korean Male Immigrants in the United States." *International Migration Review* 24: 456–479.

Hyun, David. 1983. "Rising Anti-Asian Bigotry." In Los Angeles County Human Relations Commission, ed., *Rising Anti-Asian Bigotry*, n.p.

Im, Kwŏn-taek. 1993. *Sŏp'yŏnje yŏnghwa iyagi* [The Story of the Movie *Sŏp'yŏnje*]. Seoul: Hanŭl.

Immigration and Naturalization Service. 1990. *Statistical Yearbook of the Immigration and Naturalization Service.* Washington, D.C.: Immigration and Naturalization Service.

Indiana, Gary. 1993. "Closing Time." *Village Voice*, Apr. 20, pp. 25–27.

INS. *See* Immigration and Naturalization Service.

Irons, Peter. 1983. *Justice at War.* New York: Oxford University Press.

Jackson, Jesse. 1992. "Time to Invest in People." *Manchester Guardian Weekly*, May 10, pp. 1+.

Jackson, Kenneth T. 1985. *Crabgrass Frontier: The Suburbanization of the United States.* New York: Oxford University Press.

Jacobs, Brian D. 1992. *Fractured Cities: Capitalism, Community, and Empowerment in Britain and America.* London: Routledge.

Jacobs, Paul, and Saul Landau. 1971. *To Serve the Devil.* Vol. 1: *Natives and Slaves.* New York: Vintage.

James, Daniel. 1992. "Bar the Door." *New York Times*, July 25, p. 15.

Janelli, Roger L., and Dawnhee Yim Janelli. 1982. *Ancestor Worship and Korean Society.* Stanford, Calif.: Stanford University Press.

Jasso, Guillermina, and Mark R. Rosenzweig. 1990. *The New Chosen People: Immigrants in the United States.* New York: Russell Sage Foundation.

Jencks, Christopher. 1991. "Is the American Underclass Growing?" In Jencks and Peterson, eds., *The Urban Underclass*, pp. 28–100.

Jencks, Christopher, and Paul E. Peterson, eds. 1991. *The Urban Underclass.* Washington, D.C.: Brookings.

Jennings, James. 1992a. *The Politics of Black Empowerment: The Transformation of Black Activism in Urban America.* Detroit: Wayne State University Press.

————, ed. 1992b. *Race, Politics, and Economic Development: Community Perspectives.* London: Verso.

Jennings, Keith. 1992. "Understanding the Persisting Crisis of Black Youth Unemployment." In Jennings, ed., *Race, Politics, and Economic Development*, pp. 151–163.

Jewell, K. Sue. 1988. *Survival of the Black Family: The Institutional Impact of U.S. Social Policy.* New York: Praeger.

———— 1993. *From Mammy to Miss America and Beyond: Cultural Images and the Shaping of U.S. Social Policy.* London: Routledge.

Jo, Moon H. 1992. "Korean Merchants in the Black Community: Prejudice among the Victims of Prejudice." *Ethnic and Racial Studies* 15: 395–411.

Jo, Yung-Hwan. 1982. "Problems and Strategies of Participation in American Politics." In E. Y. Yu, Phillips, and Yang, eds., *Koreans in Los Angeles*, pp. 203–218.

Johnson, Dirk. 1992. "Las Vegas's Hope Leaves Blacks Bitter." *New York Times*, May 25, p. 7.

Johnson, Haynes. 1991. *Sleepwalking through History: America in the Reagan Years*. New York: W. W. Norton.

Johnson, James H., Walter C. Farrell, Jr., and Maria-Rosario Jackson. 1994. "Los Angeles One Year Later: A Prospective Assessment of Responses to the 1992 Civil Unrest." *Economic Development Quarterly* 8: 19–27.

Jones, Jacqueline. 1992. *The Dispossessed: America's Underclasses from the Civil War to the Present*. New York: Basic Books.

Jones, Mack. 1992. "The Black Underclass as Systemic Phenomenon." In Jennings, ed., *Race, Politics, and Economic Development*, pp. 53–65.

Jordan, June. 1992. "The Light of the Fire." *Progressive*, June, pp. 12–13.

———— 1993. "The Truth of Rodney King." *Progressive*, June, pp. 12–14.

Jordan, Winthrop D. 1968. *White over Black: American Attitudes toward the Negro, 1550–1812*. Chapel Hill: University of North Carolina Press.

Kahng, Anthony. 1992. "What Are the Lessons of Los Angeles?" *IMADR Bulletin* 16: 3–6.

Kahrl, William. 1982. *Water and Power: The Conflict over Los Angeles' Water Supply in the Owens Valley*. Berkeley: University of California Press.

Kang, Hyeon-dew. 1976. "Changing Image of America in Korean Popular Literature: With an Analysis of Short Stories between 1945–1975." *Korea Journal* 19–33.

Kang, Miliann, Juliana J. Kim, Edward J. W. Park, and Hae Won Park. 1993. *Bridge toward Unity*. Los Angeles: Korean Immigrant Workers Advocates of Southern California.

Kang, Younghill. 1947. *The Grass Roof*. New York: Charles Scribner.

Katz, Ephraim. 1982. *The Film Encyclopedia*. New York: Perigee Books. Originally published in 1979.

Katz, Jesse. 1993. "County's Yearly Gang Death Toll Reaches 800." *Los Angeles Times*, Jan. 19, pp. A1+.

Katz, Michael B. 1989. *The Undeserving Poor: From the War on Poverty to the War on Welfare*. New York: Pantheon.

————, ed. 1993. *The "Underclass" Debate: Views from History*. Princeton, N.J.: Princeton University Press.

Kazin, Alfred. 1991. "The Art of 'Call It Sleep.'" *New York Review of Books*, Oct. 10, pp. 15–18.

Kelley, Robin D. G. 1992. "Straight from Underground." *Nation*, June 8, pp. 793–796.

Kendall, Laurel. 1988. *The Life and Hard Times of a Korean Shaman: Of Tales and the Telling of Tales.* Honolulu: University of Hawaii Press.

Kerr, Peter. 1992. "Did Insurers Abandon the Inner City?" *New York Times,* May 31, pp. F1+.

Kerstein, Max. 1992. "Rebuilding Anew." *KAGRO Newsletter* 3(5/6): 18.

Kim, Bernice Bong Hee. 1934. "The Koreans in Hawaii." *Social Science* 9: 409–413.

Kim, Bok-Lim C. 1977. "Asian Wives of U.S. Servicemen: Women in Shadows." *Amerasia Journal* 4: 91–115.

———— 1978. *The Asian Americans: Changing Patterns, Changing Needs.* Montclair, N.J.: Association of Korean Christian Scholars in North America.

Kim, Chi Ha. 1974. *Cry of the People and Other Poems.* Hayama, Japan: Autumn Press.

Kim, Choong Soon. 1988. *Faithful Endurance: An Ethnography of Korean Family Dispersal.* Tucson: University of Arizona Press.

Kim, Chungmi. 1982. *Chungmi—Selected Poems.* Anaheim, Calif.: Korean Pioneer Press.

———— 1992. "My Silent Rage." *High Performance,* Summer, pp. 28–29.

Kim, David D., and Jeff Yang. 1992. "Koreatown Abandoned." *Village Voice,* May 12, pp. 33+.

Kim, David S. 1975. *Korean Small Businesses in the Olympic Area.* Los Angeles: School of Architecture and Urban Planning, University of California, Los Angeles.

Kim, David S., and Charles Choy Wong. 1977. "Business Development in Koreatown, Los Angeles." In H. C. Kim, ed., *The Korean Diaspora,* pp. 229–245.

Kim, Elaine H. 1982. *Asian American Literature: An Introduction to the Writings and Their Social Context.* Philadelphia: Temple University Press.

———— 1987. "Defining Asian American Realities through Literature." *Cultural Critique* 6: 87–111.

———— 1989. "War Story." In Asian Women United of California, ed., *Making Waves,* pp. 80–92.

———— 1993a. "Home Is Where the *Han* Is: A Korean-American Perspective on the Los Angeles Upheavals." In Gooding-Williams, ed., *Reading Rodney King/Reading Urban Uprising,* pp. 215–235.

———— 1993b. "Creating a Third Space." *Bay Guardian,* Mar. 10, pp. 31+.

———— 1993c. "Between Black and White: An Interview with Bong Hwan Kim." In Aguilar-San Juan, ed., *The State of Asian America,* pp. 71–100.

Kim, Elaine H., with Janice Otani. 1983. *With Silk Wings: Asian American Women at Work.* San Francisco: Asian Women United of California.

Kim, Eun Mee. 1988. "From Dominance to Symbiosis: State and *Chaebol* in Korea." *Pacific Focus* 3: 105–121.

Kim, H. Andrew. 1992. "It Cuts Both Ways." *Korea Times Weekly English Edition,* June 22, p. 6.

Kim, Hyung-chan. 1974. "Some Aspects of Social Demography of Korean Americans." *International Migration Review* 8: 23–42.

———, ed. 1977a. *The Korean Diaspora: Historical and Sociological Studies of Korean Immigration and Assimilation in North America.* Santa Barbara, Calif.: ABC-Clio.

——— 1977b. "Ethnic Enterprises among Korean Immigrants in America." In idem, ed., *The Korean Diaspora,* pp. 85–107.

Kim, Illsoo. 1981. *New Urban Immigrant: The Korean Community in New York.* Princeton, N.J.: Princeton University Press.

——— 1987. "Korea and East Asia: Premigration Factors and U.S. Immigration Policy." In Fawcett and Cariño, eds., *Pacific Bridges,* pp. 327–345.

Kim, Kong-On, Kapson Lee, and Tai-Yul Kim. 1981. *Korean Americans in Los Angeles: Their Concerns and Language Maintenance.* Los Alamitos, Calif.: National Center for Bilingual Research.

Kim, Kwang Chung. 1985. "Ethnic Resources Utilization of Korean Immigrant Entrepreneurs in the Chicago Minority Area." *International Migration Review* 19: 82–111.

Kim, Kwang Chung, and Won Moo Hurh. 1983. "Korean Americans and the 'Success' Image: A Critique." *Amerasia Journal* 10: 3–21.

——— 1985. "Ethnic Resources Utilization of Korean Immigrant Entrepreneurs in the Chicago Minority Area." *International Migration Review* 19: 82–111.

——— 1988. "The Burden of Double Roles: Korean Wives in the USA." *Ethnic and Racial Studies* 11: 151–167.

——— 1991. "The Extended Conjugal Family: Family-Kinship System of Korean Immigrants in the United States." In Kwak and Lee, eds., *The Korean-American Community,* pp. 115–133.

——— 1993. "Beyond Assimilation and Pluralism: Syncretic Sociocultural Adaptation of Korean Immigrants in the U.S." *Ethnic and Racial Studies* 16: 696–713.

Kim, Kwang Chung, Won Moo Hurh, and Shin Kim. 1993. "Generation Differences in Korean Immigrants' Life Conditions in the United States." *Sociological Perspectives* 36: 257–270.

Kim, Kwang Chung, Hei Chu Kim, and Won Moo Hurh. 1979. "Division of Household Tasks in Korean Immigrant Families in the United States." *International Journal of Sociology of the Family* 9: 161–175.

——— 1981. "Job Information Deprivation in the United States: A Case Study of Korean Immigrants." *Ethnicity* 8: 219–232.

Kim, Myung Mi. 1989. "Into Such Assembly." In Lim and Tsutakawa, eds., *The Forbidden Stitch,* pp. 18–19.

Kim, Richard E. 1966. "O My Korea!" *Atlantic,* Feb., pp. 106–117.

Kim, Richard, et al. 1992. "Asian Immigrant Women Garment Workers in Los Angeles: A Preliminary Investigation." *Amerasia Journal* 18: 69–82.

Kim, Ronyoung. 1987. *Clay Walls.* Seattle: University of Washington Press.

Kim, Sally. 1993. "The New Generation." *Pacific Ties* 16(5): 6–7.

Kim, Se Jin. 1970. "South Korea's Involvement in Vietnam and Its Economic and Political Impact." *Asian Survey* 10: 519–532.

Kim, Seong-Kon. 1991. "On Native Grounds: Revolution and Renaissance in Art and Culture." In Chong-Sik Lee, ed., *Korea Briefing, 1990,* pp. 97–117. Boulder, Colo.: Westview Press.

Kim, Shin. 1991. "Conceptualization of Inter-Minority Group Conflict: Conflict between Korean Entrepreneurs and Black Local Residents." In Kwak and Lee, eds., *The Korean-American Community,* pp. 29–48.

Kim, Warren Y. 1971. *Koreans in America.* Seoul: Po Chin Chai.

King, Anthony D., ed. 1991. *Culture, Globalization, and the World-System.* Binghamton, N.Y.: Department of Art and Art History, State University of New York at Binghamton.

Kinkead, Gwen. 1992. *Chinatown: A Portrait of a Closed Society.* New York: HarperCollins.

Kirschenman, Joleen, and Kathryn M. Neckerman. 1991. "'We'd Love to Hire Them, But . . .': The Meaning of Race for Employers." In Jencks and Peterson, eds., *The Urban Underclass,* pp. 203–232.

Klein, Norman M. 1990. "The Sunshine Strategy: Buying and Selling the Fantasy of Los Angeles." In Klein and Schiesl, eds., *20th Century Los Angeles,* pp. 1–38.

———— 1992. "Open Season: A Report on the Los Angeles Uprising." *Social Text* 34: 115–120.

Klein, Norman M., and Martin J. Schiesl, eds. 1990. *20th Century Los Angeles: Power, Promotion, and Social Conflict.* Claremont, Calif.: Regina.

Kluegel, James R., and Eliot R. Smith. 1986. *Beliefs about Inequality: Americans' Views of What Is and What Ought to Be.* New York: Aldine de Gruyter.

Kō, Chan Yū, and Sū Rī. 1993. *Amerika, Koriataun.* Tokyo: Shakai Hyōronsha.

Koo, Hagen. 1984. "The Political Economy of Income Distribution in South Korea: The Impact of the State's Industrialization Policies." *World Development* 12: 1029–1037.

———— 1987. "The Emerging Class Order and Social Conflict in South Korea." *Pacific Focus* 2: 95–112.

Koo, Hagen, and Doo-Seung Hong. 1980. "Class and Income Inequality in Korea." *American Sociological Review* 45: 610–626.

Koo, Hagen, and Eui-Young Yu. 1981. *Korean Immigration to the United States: Its Demographic Pattern and Social Implications for Both Societies.* Honolulu, Hawaii: East-West Center.

Koo, Youngnok. 1984. "The First Hundred Years and Beyond." In Koo and Suh, eds., *Korea and the United States,* pp. 353–371.

Koo, Youngnok, and Dae-Sook Suh, eds. 1984. *Korea and the United States: A Century of Cooperation.* Honolulu: University of Hawaii Press.

Korean American Inter-Agency Council (KAIAC). 1993. *KAIAC Press Packet.* Los Angeles: Korean American Inter-Agency Council.

Korean American Research Center. 1993. *"Mijutongp'o Sahoe Yŏn'guso ŭi sŏllip paegyŏng"* [The Background of the Founding of the Korean American Research Center]. Los Angeles: Korean American Research Center.

Korean Immigrant Workers Advocates of Southern California. 1992. Opening Ceremony and Fundraising Dinner Event (21 March). Los Angeles: Korean Immigrant Workers Advocates of Southern California.

Korea Times. 1992. "Letters to Ted Koppel." *Korea Times,* May 11, p. 7.

Kotkin, Joel. 1992. *Tribes: How Race, Religion, and Identity Determine Success in the New Global Economy.* New York: Random House.

Kotkin, Joel, and Paul Grabowicz. 1982. *California, Inc.* New York: Rawson, Wade.

Kwak, Tae-Hwan, and Seong Hyong Lee, eds. 1991. *The Korean-American Community: Present and Future.* Seoul: Kyungnam University Press.

Kwoh, Stewart, Angela E. Oh, and Bong Hwan Kim. 1993. "Don't Let Up Now That Verdicts Are In." *Los Angeles Times,* May 3, p. B7.

Kwon, Peter. 1972. "Report on the Needs of Korean Community and Churches in the United States." Paper presented at the meeting of the Asian American Presbyterian Caucus in Southern California, Los Angeles.

Kwong, Dan. 1992. "New Season." *High Performance,* Summer, p. 20.

Kwong, Peter. 1979. *Chinatown, New York: Labor and Politics, 1930–1950.* New York: Monthly Review Press.

——— 1987. *The New Chinatown.* New York: Hill & Wang.

——— 1992. "The First Multicultural Riots." In Hazen, ed., *Inside the L.A. Riots,* pp. 88–93.

Lacey, Mark. 1992. "Last Call for Liquor Outlets." *Los Angeles Times,* Dec. 14, pp. A1+.

La Ganga, Maria L. 1982. "Once-Booming Koreatown Goes Downhill." *Los Angeles Times,* Aug. 15, pp. 1+.

Lamott, Kenneth. 1971. *Anti-California: Report from Our First Parafascist State.* Boston: Little, Brown.

Lang, Curtis. 1992. "Legal Looting." *Village Voice,* May 19, p. 35.

Lapham, Lewis. 1992. "Notebook: City Lights." *Harper's Magazine,* July, pp. 4–6.

Larson, James F. 1990. "Quiet Diplomacy in a Television Era: The Media and U.S. Policy toward the Republic of Korea." *Political Communication and Persuasion* 7: 73–95.

L.A. Weekly. 1992. "Riot Chronology." In Hazen, ed., *Inside the L.A. Riots,* pp. 35–39.

Lee, Chantel. 1993. "Causes of Riots Remain Constant." *Daily Bruin News,* Apr. 29, pp. 8+.

Lee, Daniel Booduck. 1989. "Marital Adjustment between Korean Women and American Servicemen." *Korea Observer* 20: 321–351.

Lee, Don. 1992a. " 'We're Walking on a Blade's Edge.' " *Los Angeles Times,* May 13, pp. C5+.

——— 1992b. " 'I Felt Sad and Angry That We'd Come to This.' " *Los Angeles Times,* May 13, p. 12.

Lee, Don Chang. 1990. "Intermarriage and Spouse Abuse: Korean Wife–American Husband." *Korea Observer* 21: 43–60.

Lee, Dong Ok. 1992. "Commodification of Ethnicity: The Sociospatial Reproduction of Immigrant Entrepreneurs." *Urban Affairs Quarterly* 28: 258–275.

Lee, Eun-Ho, Hyung-chan Kim, and Yong Joon Yim. 1991. "Korea in American Kaleidoscope: What Americans Think of Her." *Korea Observer* 22: 555–583.

Lee, Hwa Soo [Yi, Hwa-su]. 1978. "Hanin tanch'e ŭi t'ŭkchil kwa lidŏswip munje" [The Special Characteristics and the Leadership Problem of Korean Organizations]. In Han'gukhak Yŏn'guhoe, ed., *Miguk an ŭi Hanin k'ŏmyunit'i* [The Korean Community in the United States], pp. 67–74. Los Angeles: Korean Pioneer Press.

——— 1982. "Korean-American Voluntary Associations in Los Angeles: Some Aspects of Structure, Function, and Leadership." In E. Y. Yu, Phillips, and Yang, eds., *Koreans in Los Angeles,* pp. 185–201.

Lee, Jin-Won. 1986. "The Ethnic Enclave as a 'Place': A Case Study of Koreantown of Los Angeles." M.A. thesis, University of California, Berkeley.

Lee, Joan Faung Jean. 1992. *Asian Americans.* New York: New Press. Originally published in 1991.

Lee, John H. 1992. "Looking at a Ravaged Koreatown . . ." In Los Angeles Times, *Understanding the Riots,* pp. 157–158.

——— 1993. "Stuck in the Middle." *L.A. Weekly,* Apr. 23–29, pp. 21–25.

Lee, John Kyhan. 1990. "The Notion of 'Self' in Korean-American Literature: A Sociohistorical Perspective." Ph.D. dissertation, University of Connecticut.

Lee, John Y. 1983. *A Study on Financial Structure and Operating Problems of Korean Small Businesses in Los Angeles.* Los Angeles: Mid-Wilshire Community Research Center.

Lee, Kapson Yim. 1992. "Civil Rights Commission Hears Community Criticism of Media." *Korea Times Weekly English Edition,* May 18, p. 6.

——— 1993. "Hate Crimes Propelled by Media." *Korea Times Weekly English Edition,* Mar. 31, pp. 1+.

Lee, Kyung. 1969. "Settlement Patterns of Los Angeles Koreans." M.A. thesis, University of California, Los Angeles.

Lee, Marie G. 1992. *Finding My Voice.* Boston: Houghton Mifflin.

Lee, Mary Paik. 1990. *Quiet Odyssey: A Pioneer Korean Woman in America,* ed. Sucheng Chan. Seattle: University of Washington Press.

Lee, Seong Hyong. 1988. "The Role of Korean Language Newspapers in the Korean-American Community." In Lee and Kwak, eds., *Koreans in America,* pp. 105–116.

Lee, Seong Hyong, and Tae-Hwan Kwak, eds. 1988. *Koreans in America: New Perspectives.* Seoul: Kyungnam University Press.

Lee, Sharon M. 1993. "Racial Classification in the U.S. Census, 1890–1990." *Ethnic and Racial Studies* 16: 75–94.

Leibowitz, Ed. 1993. "The Color of Justice." *L.A. Weekly,* Apr. 23–29, pp. 16–19.

Leong, Russell C. 1989. "Asians in the Americas: Interpreting the Diaspora Experience." *Amerasia Journal* 15: vii–xvii.

Levine, Lawrence. 1977. *Black Culture and Black Consciousness: African-American Folkthought from Slavery to Freedom.* New York: Oxford University Press.

Lew, Walter. 1993. "Black Korea." In Jessica Hagedorn, ed., *Charlie Chan Is Dead,* pp. 230–235. New York: Penguin.

Lewis, Oscar. 1966. *La Vida: A Puerto Rican Family in the Culture of Poverty—San Juan and New York.* New York: Random House.

——— 1968. *A Study of Slum Culture: Backgrounds for "La Vida."* New York: Random House.

Lie, John. 1992a. "The Political Economy of South Korean Development." *International Sociology* 7: 285–300.

——— 1992b. "The State as Pimp." Paper presented at the meeting of the American Sociological Association, Pittsburgh, Pa.

Lieberman, Paul. 1992. "Latinos Lead in Riot Arrests, Study Says." *Los Angeles Times,* June 18, p. B3.

Lieberman, Paul, and Richard O'Reilly. 1993. "Most Looters Endured Lives of Crime, Poverty." *Los Angeles Times,* May 2, pp. A1+.

Lieberson, Stanley. 1980. *A Piece of the Pie: Blacks and White Immigrants since 1880.* Berkeley: University of California Press.

Light, Ivan. 1972. *Ethnic Enterprise in America.* Berkeley: University of California Press.

——— 1988. "Los Angeles." In Mattei Dogan and John Kasarda, eds., *The Metropolis Era.* Vol. 2: *Mega-Cities,* pp. 56–96. Newbury Park, Calif.: Sage.

Light, Ivan, and Edna Bonacich. 1988. *Immigrant Entrepreneurs: Koreans in Los Angeles, 1965–1982.* Berkeley: University of California Press.

Light, Ivan, Im Jung Kwuon, and Deng Zhong. 1990. "Korean Rotating Credit Associations in Los Angeles." *Amerasia Journal* 16: 35–54.

Light, Ivan, Georges Sabagh, Mehdi Bozorgmehr, and Claudia Der-Martirosian. 1993. "Internal Ethnicity in the Ethnic Economy." *Ethnic and Racial Studies* 16: 581–597.

Lillard, Richard G. 1966. *Eden in Jeopardy: Man's Prodigal Meddling with His Environment: The Southern California Experience.* New York: Alfred A. Knopf.

Lim, Hy-sop. 1978. "A Study of Korean-American Cultural Relations, With Emphasis on Koreans' Perception of American Culture." *Korea Journal* (June): 4–14.

Lim, Kyung Kyu. 1992. "Los Angeles 'Urban Unrest': A Progressive Korean Perspective." *Korea Report* (Summer): 23–26.

Lim, Shirley Geok-lin, and Mayumi Tsutakawa, eds. 1989. *The Forbidden Stitch: An Asian American Women's Anthology.* Corvallis, Oreg.: Calyx Books.

Lipset, Seymour Martin. 1979. *The First New Nation: The United States in Historical and Comparative Perspective.* New York: W. W. Norton. Originally published in 1973.

Lo, Clarence Y. H. 1990. *Small Property versus Big Government.* Berkeley: University of California Press.

Logan, Andy. 1992. "Around City Hall: Two Cities." *New Yorker,* June 8, pp. 90–93.

Logan, John R., and Harvey L. Molotch. 1987. *Urban Fortunes: The Political Economy of Place.* Berkeley: University of California Press.

Los Angeles Business Journal, ed. 1992. *Beyond the Ashes.* Los Angeles: Los Angeles Business Journal.

Los Angeles County Human Relations Commission, ed. 1983. *Rising Anti-Asian Bigotry: Manifestations, Sources, Solutions.* Los Angeles: Los Angeles County Human Relations Commission.

Los Angeles Times. 1991. "A Market Looking for Legitimate Businesses." *Los Angeles Times,* Nov. 29, p. B4.

———— 1992a. *Understanding the Riots: Los Angeles before and after the Rodney King Case.* Los Angeles: Los Angeles Times.

———— 1992b. "An End to the Self-Destruction." *Manchester Guardian Weekly,* May 10, p. 9.

———— 1992c. "Understanding the Riots," parts 1–5. *Los Angeles Times,* May 11–16.

———— 1992d. "Globalization of Los Angeles: The First Multiethnic Riots." *Los Angeles Times,* May 10, p. M4.

———— 1993a. "Hopefuls: Many Seek to Be Mayor." *Los Angeles Times,* Jan. 23, pp. A1+.

———— 1993b. "Race Relations in L.A.: Attitudes toward Asian Americans." *Crosscurrents* 16(2): 1+.

Lotchin, Roger W. 1992. *Fortress California 1910–1961: From Warfare to Welfare.* New York: Oxford University Press.

Lowe, Lisa. 1991. "Heterogeneity, Hybridity, Multiplicity: Marking Asian American Differences." *Diaspora* 1: 24–44.

Lyman, Princeton N. 1968. "Korea's Involvement in Viet Nam." *Orbis* 12: 563–581.

Lyu, Kingsley K. 1976. "Korean Nationalist Activities in Hawaii and America, 1901–1945." In Gee, ed., *Counterpoint*, pp. 106–128.

Madhubuti, Haki R., ed. 1993. *Why L.A. Happened: Implications of the '92 Los Angeles Rebellion*. Chicago: Third World Press.

Mangiafico, Luciano. 1988. *Contemporary American Immigrants: Patterns of Filipino, Korean, and Chinese Settlement in the United States*. New York: Praeger.

Marable, Manning. 1983. *How Capitalism Underdeveloped Black America*. Boston: South End Press.

———— 1985. *Black American Politics: From the Washington Marches to Jesse Jackson*. London: Verso.

———— 1987. "The Contradictory Contours of Black Political Culture." In Davis, Marable, Pfeil, and Sprinker, eds., *The Year Left 2*, pp. 1–17.

———— 1991. "Multicultural Democracy: Toward a New Strategy for Progressive Activism." *Z Magazine*, Nov., pp. 89–95.

Marmor, Theodore R., Jerry L. Mashaw, and Philip L. Harvey. 1990. *America's Misunderstood Welfare State: Persistent Myths, Enduring Realities*. New York: Basic Books.

Marriott, Michael. 1992. "Fire of Anguish and Rage as Random Violence Spreads across Los Angeles." *New York Times*, May 1, p. A11.

Martin, Douglas. 1993. "Seeking New Ties and Clout, Korean Grocers Join Voices." *New York Times*, Mar. 22, pp. A1+.

Martin, Tony. 1993. "From Slavery to Rodney King: Continuity and Change." In Madhubuti, ed., *Why L.A. Happened*, pp. 27–40.

Martínez, Rubén. 1992. *The Other Side: Fault Lines, Guerilla Saints, and the True Heart of Rock 'n' Roll*. London: Verso.

———— 1993. "Muchachos in the Hood." *L.A. Weekly*, Apr. 23–29, pp. 20–24.

Mashberg, Tom, and Lynda Gorov. 1993a. "L.A. Mood: Training Hard, Buying Guns." *Boston Globe*, Apr. 11, p. 18.

———— 1993b. "After Seven Days, L.A. Calls It a Night." *Boston Globe*, Apr. 19, p. 10.

Massey, Douglas S., and Nancy A. Denton. 1993. *American Apartheid: Segregation and the Making of the Underclass*. Cambridge, Mass.: Harvard University Press.

Mattera, Philip. 1990. *Prosperity Lost: How a Decade of Greed Has Eroded Our Standard of Living and Endangered Our Children's Future*. Reading, Mass.: Addison-Wesley.

Matzek, Virginia. 1993. "Neighbors in the 'Hood." *California Monthly*, Nov., p. 35.

Mazón, Mauricio. 1984. *The Zoot-Suit Riots: The Psychology of Symbolic Annihilation.* Austin: University of Texas Press.

McClain, Leanita. 1992. "The Middle-Class Black's Burden." In Andersen and Collins, eds., *Race, Class, and Gender,* pp. 120–122. Originally published in 1986.

McKibbin, Ross. 1990. *The Ideologies of Class: Social Relations in Britain, 1880–1950.* Oxford: Clarendon Press.

McMillan, Penelope. 1992a. "Making a Grateful Pay-Back." *Los Angeles Times,* July 11, pp. B1+.

———— 1992b. "Merchants Find Political Quest for Riot Relief Frustrating." *Los Angeles Times,* June 30, p. 31.

———— 1992c. "Korean American Protesters Pelted from City Hall Windows." *Los Angeles Times,* July 8, pp. B1+.

———— 1992d. "Task Force on Liquor Stores Is Unveiled." *Los Angeles Times,* June 30, pp. B1+.

McNelis-Ahern, Margaret. 1992. "Agenda for Action." In Los Angeles Business Journal, ed., *Beyond the Ashes,* pp. 12–15.

McPhail, Clark. 1991. *The Myth of the Madding Crowd.* New York: Aldine de Gruyter.

McWilliams, Carey. 1944. *Prejudice: Japanese-Americans—Symbol of Racial Intolerance.* Boston: Little, Brown.

———— 1949. *California: The Great Exception.* New York: A. A. Wyn.

———— 1973. *Southern California: An Island on the Land.* Salt Lake City, Utah: Peregrine Smith. Originally published in 1946.

———— 1990. *North from Mexico: The Spanish-Speaking People of the United States.* New York: Praeger. Originally published in 1948.

Melendy, H. Brett. 1977. *Asians in America: Filipinos, Koreans, and East Indians.* Boston: Twayne.

Meyerson, Harold. 1992. "Casualties of the Los Angeles Riot." *In These Times,* May 13–19, p. 2.

———— 1993a. "Fear Takes the Primary." *L.A. Weekly,* Apr. 23–29, pp. 10–14.

———— 1993b. "The Death of Urban Liberalism?" *In These Times,* June 28, pp. 25–28.

Miles, Jack. 1992. "Blacks vs. Browns." *Atlantic,* Oct., pp. 41–68.

Miller, Gary J. 1981. *Cities by Contract: The Politics of Municipal Incorporation.* Cambridge, Mass.: M.I.T. Press.

Millican, Anthony. 1992. "Presence of Koreans Reshaping the Region." *Los Angeles Times,* Feb. 2, pp. B3+.

Min, Katherine. 1994. "K-Boy and 2 Bad." *TriQuarterly* 89: 38–51.

Min, Pyong Gap. 1984a. "From White-Collar Occupations to Small Business: Korean Immigrants' Occupational Adjustment." *Sociological Quarterly* 25: 333–352.

———— 1984b. "A Structural Analysis of Korean Business in the United States." *Ethnic Groups* 6: 1–25.

———— 1986–87. "Filipino and Korean Immigrants in Small Business: A Comparative Analysis." *Amerasia Journal* 13: 53–71.

———— 1988a. *Ethnic Business Enterprise: Korean Small Business in Atlanta.* New York: Center for Migration Studies.

———— 1988b. "Korean Immigrant Entrepreneurship: A Comprehensive Explanation." In Lee and Kwak, eds., *Koreans in America*, pp. 153–176.

———— 1989. "The Social Costs of Immigrant Entrepreneurship: A Response to Edna Bonacich." *Amerasia Journal* 15: 187–194.

———— 1990a. "Problems of Korean Immigrant Entrepreneurs." *International Migration Review* 24: 436–455.

———— 1990b. "The Role of a Social Scientist in Social Change: A Response to Edna Bonacich." *Amerasia Journal* 16: 55–60.

———— 1991a. "Cultural and Economic Boundaries of Korean Ethnicity: A Comparative Analysis." *Ethnic and Racial Studies* 14: 225–241.

———— 1991b. "Korean Immigrants' Small Business Activities and Korean-Black Interracial Conflicts." In Kwak and Lee, eds., *The Korean-American Community*, pp. 13–28.

———— 1992. "The Structure and Social Functions of Korean Immigrant Churches in the U.S." *International Migration Review* 26: 1370–1394.

Miranda, Gloria E. 1990. "The Mexican Immigrant Family: Economic and Cultural Survival in Los Angeles, 1900–1945." In Klein and Schiesl, eds., *20th Century Los Angeles*, pp. 39–60.

Modell, John. 1977. *The Economics and Politics of Racial Accommodation: The Japanese of Los Angeles, 1900–1942.* Urbana: University of Illinois Press.

Moffat, Susan. 1992. "Splintered Society: U.S. Asians." *Los Angeles Times*, July 13, pp. A1+.

———— 1993. "Both Sides of the Fence." *Los Angeles Times*, Jan. 25, pp. B1+.

Moon, Daniel Y. 1978. "Ministering to 'Korean Wives' of Servicemen." In Sunoo and Kim, eds., *Korean Women in a Struggle for Humanization*, pp. 97–116.

Moon, Hyung June. 1976. "The Korean Immigrants in America: The Quest for Identity in the Formative Years, 1903–1918." Ph.D. dissertation, University of Nevada at Reno.

Morgan, Edward. 1975. *American Slavery, American Freedom: The Ordeal of Colonial Virginia.* New York: W. W. Norton.

Morris, Robert, and Michael Harrelson. 1992. "A New Civil Rights Militancy." In Hazen, ed., *Inside the L.A. Riots*, pp. 54–55.

Morrison, Patt. 1992. "Symbol of Pain Survives Flames." *Los Angeles Times*, May 7, p. B3.

Morrison, Toni. 1970. *The Bluest Eye.* New York: Holt Rinehart & Winston.

———— 1992. *Playing in the Dark: Whiteness and the Literary Imagination.* Cambridge, Mass.: Harvard University Press.

Morrow, Lance. 1992. "Essay: Video Warriors in Los Angeles." *Time,* May 11, p. 68.

Moynihan, Daniel Patrick. 1981. *The Negro Family: The Case for National Action.* Westport, Conn.: Greenwood Press. Originally published in 1965.

Mumford, Lewis. 1961. *The City in History: Its Origins, Its Transformations, and Its Prospects.* New York: Harcourt Brace & World.

Muñoz, Carlos, Jr. 1987. "Chicano Politics: The Current Conjuncture." In Davis, Marable, Pfeil, and Sprinker, eds., *The Year Left* 2, pp. 35–52.

Mura, David. 1992. "Strangers in the Village." In Andersen and Collins, eds., *Race, Class, and Gender,* pp. 11–20.

Murchison, William. 1992. "We Are Searching for Irrelevant Solutions." *Human Events,* May 23, p. 12.

Murray, Charles. 1984. *Losing Ground: American Social Policy, 1950–1980.* New York: Basic Books.

———— 1992a. "Causes, Root Causes, and Cures." *National Review,* June 8, pp. 30–32.

———— 1992b. "The Legacy of the 60's." *Commentary,* July, pp. 23–30.

———— 1992c. "The Reality of Black America." *Times Literary Supplement,* May 22, p. 10.

Muwakkil, Salim. 1993. "Fight the Powerless." *In These Times,* Oct. 4, pp. 23–24.

Mydans, Seth. 1992a. "The Young Face of Inner City Unemployment." *New York Times,* Mar. 22, pp. A1+.

———— 1992b. "Los Angeles Policemen Acquitted in Taped Beating." *New York Times,* Apr. 30, pp. A1+.

———— 1992c. "An Invisible Presence Grows in the Barrios of Los Angeles." *New York Times,* May 24, p. D7.

———— 1993a. "2 of 4 Officers Found Guilty in Los Angeles Beating." *New York Times,* Apr. 18, pp. A1+.

———— 1993b. "Giving Voice to the Hurt and Betrayal of Korean-Americans." *New York Times,* May 2, p. E9.

———— 1994. "Awaiting Quake Aid, and Riot Aid, Too." *New York Times,* Jan. 27, p. C20.

Mydans, Seth, and Michel Marriott. 1992. "Riots Ruin a Business, and a Neighborhood Suffers." *New York Times,* May 18, pp. A1+.

Myrdal, Gunnar. 1962. *An American Dilemma: The Negro Problem and Modern Democracy.* New York: Harper & Row. Originally published in 1944.

Nash, Gerald D. 1985. *The American West Transformed: The Impact of the Second World War.* Bloomington: Indiana University Press.

National Advisory Commission on Civil Disobedience. 1988. *The Kerner Report: The Report of the National Advisory Commission on Civil Disobedience.* New York: Pantheon. Originally published in 1968.

Nee, Victor G., and Brett de Bary Nee. 1986. *Longtime Californ': A Documentary Study of an American Chinatown*. Stanford, Calif.: Stanford University Press. Originally published in 1972.

Nelson, Howard J. 1983. *Los Angeles Metropolis*. Dubuque, Iowa: Kendall/Hunt.

Nelson, Laura. 1994. "Driving Nationalism: The South Korean Automobile Industry and Consumer Nationalism." Paper presented at the Association for Asian Studies meeting, Boston.

New Korea. 1976. "KCIA Agents All Out to Get New Korea." In Gee, ed., *Counterpoint*, pp. 140–142.

Newman, Katherine S. 1993. *Declining Fortunes: The Withering of the American Dream*. New York: Basic Books.

New Yorker. 1992. "The Talk of the Town: Notes and Comment." *New Yorker*, May 11, pp. 27–28.

New York Times. 1992a. "Of 58 Riot Deaths, 50 Have Been Ruled Homicides." *New York Times*, May 17, p. 17.

———— 1992b. "Bridges between Blacks and Koreans." *New York Times*, May 18.

———— 1992c. Photo. *New York Times*, May 2, p. 2.

Njeri, Itabara. 1993. "The Conquest of Hate." *Los Angeles Times Magazine*, Apr. 25, pp. 20–21.

Noble, Allen G., ed. 1992. *To Build in a New Land: Ethnic Landscapes in North America*. Baltimore: Johns Hopkins University Press.

Noel, Peter. 1992. "When the Word Is Given." *Village Voice*, May 12, pp. 31+.

Norden, Edward. 1992. "South-Central Korea: Post-Riot L.A." *American Spectator*, Sept., pp. 33–40.

Novak, Michael. 1972. *The Rise of the Unmeltable Ethnics: Politics and Culture in the Seventies*. New York.

O, Chŏng-hŭi. 1989. "Chinatown." In Sŏk-kyŏng Kang, Chi-wŏn Kim, and Chŏng-hŭi O, *Words of Farewell: Stories by Korean Women Writers*, trans. Bruce and Ju-Chan Fulton, pp. 202–230. Seattle: Seal Press.

O'Brien, David J., and Stephen S. Fugita. 1991. *The Japanese American Experience*. Bloomington: Indiana University Press.

Ogbu, John U. 1978. *Minority Education and Caste: The System in Cross-Cultural Perspective*. New York: Academic Press.

Ogle, George E. 1990. *South Korea: Dissent within the Economic Miracle*. London: Zed.

Oh, Moonsong David. 1983. *An Analysis of the Korean Community in the Mid-Wilshire Area*. Los Angeles: Mid-Wilshire Community Research Center.

———— 1988. "A Survey of Korean Business in the Los Angeles Area." In Lee and Kwak, eds., *Koreans in America*, pp. 177–195.

Okihiro, Gary Y., Shirley Hune, Arthur A. Hansen, and John M. Liu, eds. 1988. *Reflections on Shattered Windows: Promises and Prospects for Asian American Studies*. Pullman: Washington State University Press.

Okubo, Miné. 1983. *Citizen 13660.* Seattle: University of Washington Press. Originally published in 1946.

Oliver, Melvin L., and James H. Johnson, Jr. 1984. "Inter-Ethnic Conflict in an Urban Ghetto: The Case of Blacks and Latinos in Los Angeles." *Research in Social Movements, Conflict, and Change* 6: 57–94.

Oliver, Melvin L., James H. Johnson, Jr., and Walter C. Farrell, Jr. 1993. "Anatomy of a Rebellion: A Political-Economic Analysis." In Gooding-Williams, ed., *Reading Rodney King/Reading Urban Uprising*, pp. 117–141.

Omi, Michael, and Howard Winant. 1986. *Racial Formation in the United States: From the 1960s to the 1980s.* New York: Routledge.

Ong, Aihwa. 1992. "Limits to Cultural Accumulation: Chinese Capitalists on the American Pacific Rim." In Schiller, Basch, and Blanc-Szanton, eds., *Toward a Transnational Perspective on Migration*, pp. 125–143.

Orfield, Gary, and Carole Ashkinaze. 1991. *The Closing Door: Conservative Policy and Black Opportunity.* Chicago: University of Chicago Press.

Osajima, Keith. 1988. "Asian Americans as the Model Minority: An Analysis of the Popular Press Image in the 1960s and 1980s." In Okihiro, Hune, Hansen, and Liu, eds., *Reflections on Shattered Windows*, pp. 165–174.

Pacific Ties. 1992. "Emergency Issue, Peace: Notes from the L.A. Uprising." *Pacific Ties*, May.

Paik, Irvin. 1971. "A Look at the Caricatures of the Asians as Sketched by American Movies." In Tachiki, Wong, Odo, and Wong, eds., *Roots*, pp. 30–36.

Paik, Sook Ja. 1991. "Korean-American Women's Underemployment and Dual Labor Burden." In Kwak and Lee, eds., *The Korean-American Community*, pp. 251–261.

Pak, Ty. 1983. *Guilt Payment.* Honolulu, Hawaii: Bamboo Ridge Press.

Palumbo-Liu, David. 1994. "Los Angeles, Asians, and Perverse Ventriloquisms: On the Functions of Asian America in the Recent American Imaginary." *Public Culture* 6: 365–381.

Pang, Morris. 1974. "A Korean Immigrant." In Hyung-chan Kim and Wayne Patterson, eds., *The Koreans in America, 1882–1974: A Chronology and Fact Book.* New York: Oceana Publications.

Park, Gary Wanki. 1988. "Koreans in Transition: The Evolution of the Korean Community in Los Angeles." B.A. thesis, University of California, Los Angeles.

Park, Hyoung Cho. 1973. "The Urban Middle Class Family in Korea." Ph.D. dissertation, Harvard University.

Park, Insook Han, James T. Fawcett, Fred Arnold, and Robert W. Gardner. 1990. *Korean Immigrants and U.S. Immigration Policy: A Predeparture Perspective.* Honolulu, Hawaii: East-West Center.

Park, Kyeyoung. 1989. " 'Born Again': What Does It Mean to Korean-Americans in New York City." *Journal of Ritual Studies* 3: 287–301.

——— 1990a. "The Korean American Dream: Ideology and Small Business in Queens, New York." Ph.D. dissertation, City University of New York.

——— 1990b. "Declaring War at Home: Different Conceptions of Marriage and Gender in the Korean American Community." Paper presented at the meeting of the American Anthropological Association, New Orleans, La.

——— 1991. "Conceptions of Ethnicities by Koreans: Workplace Encounters." In Hune, Kim, Fugita, and Ling, *Asian Americans*, pp. 179–190.

Park, Peter. 1982. Review of *Korean Immigrants in America* by Won Moo Hurh and Kwang Chung Kim. *Amerasia Journal* 9: 140–145.

Patterson, Orlando. 1977. *Ethnic Chauvinism: The Reactionary Impulse.* New York: Stein and Day.

Patterson, Orlando, and Chris Winship. 1992. "White Poor, Black Poor." *New York Times*, May 3, p. 17.

Patterson, Wayne. 1988. *The Korean Frontier in America: Immigration to Hawaii, 1896–1910.* Honolulu: University of Hawaii Press.

Patterson, Wayne, and Hyung-chan Kim. 1977. *The Koreans in America.* Minneapolis: Lerner Publications.

Petersen, William. 1966. "Success Story, Japanese American Style." *New York Times Magazine*, Jan. 6, pp. 20+.

Peterson, Paul E. 1991. "The Urban Underclass and the Poverty Paradox." In Jencks and Peterson, eds., *The Urban Underclass*, pp. 3–27.

Phillips, Gary. 1992. "Destructive Engagement." *CrossRoads* 22: 2–4.

Phillips, Kevin. 1991. *The Politics of Rich and Poor: Wealth and the American Electorate in the Reagan Aftermath.* New York: Harper Perennial. Originally published in 1990.

Piven, Frances Fox, and Richard A. Cloward. 1993. *Regulating the Poor: The Functions of Public Welfare*, updated ed. New York: Vintage.

Pomerantz, Linda. 1984. "The Background of Korean Emigration." In Cheng and Bonacich, eds., *Labor Immigration under Capitalism*, pp. 277–315.

Porter, Bruce, and Marvin Dunn. 1984. *The Miami Riot of 1980.* Lexington, Mass.: Lexington Books.

Portes, Alejandro, and Rubén Rumbaut. 1990. *Immigrant America: A Portrait.* Berkeley: University of California Press.

Portes, Alejandro, and Alex Stepick. 1993. *City on the Edge: The Transformation of Miami.* Berkeley: University of California Press.

Portes, Alejandro, and Min Zhou. 1992. "Gaining the Upper Hand: Economic Mobility among Immigrant and Domestic Minorities." *Ethnic and Racial Studies* 15: 491–522.

Raban, Jonathan. 1991. *Hunting Mister Heartbreak: A Discovery of America.* New York: HarperCollins.

Rabinow, Paul. 1986. "Representations Are Social Facts: Modernity and Post-Modernity in Anthropology." In James Clifford and George E. Marcus, eds., *Writing Culture: The Poetics and Politics of Ethnography*, pp. 234–261. Berkeley: University of California Press.

Rand, Christopher. 1967. *Los Angeles: The Ultimate City*. New York: Oxford University Press.

Reed, Adolph, Jr. 1990. "The Underclass as Myth and Symbol: The Poverty of Discourse about Poverty." *Radical America* 24(1): 21–40.

Reed, Ishmael. 1993. *Airing Dirty Laundry*. Reading, Mass.: Addison-Wesley.

Reich, Robert B. 1991. *The Work of Nations: Preparing Ourselves for 21st-Century Capitalism*. New York: Knopf.

Reichl, Ruth. 1993. "Grills, Chills, and Kimchee." *Los Angeles Times Magazine*, Jan. 17, pp. 33+.

Reid, David, ed. 1992. *Sex, Death, and God in L.A.* New York: Pantheon.

Reimers, David M. 1985. *Still the Golden Door: The Third World Comes to America*. New York: Columbia University Press.

Reinhold, Robert. 1992. "6 Months after Riots, Los Angeles Still Bleeds." *New York Times*, Nov. 1, p. A14.

———— 1993a. "An Edgy Los Angeles Awaits a Jury's Verdict." *New York Times*, Apr. 11, p. A14.

———— 1993b. "While Waiting for the Verdict, Los Angeles Troubled." *New York Times*, Apr. 18, p. E3.

Rezendes, Michael. 1993a. "L.A. Calm after Two Guilty Verdicts." *Boston Globe*, Apr. 18, pp. 1+.

———— 1993b. "L.A. Relaxes in Wake of a Riot That Wasn't." *Boston Globe*, Apr. 19, pp. 1+.

Ridgeway, James. 1992. "What Did You Do in the Class War?" *Village Voice*, May 12, pp. 11–12.

Rieder, Jonathan. 1985. *Canarsie: The Jews and Italians of Brooklyn against Liberalism*. Cambridge, Mass.: Harvard University Press.

———— 1990. "Trouble in Store." *New Republic*, July 2, pp. 16–20.

Rieff, David. 1991. *Los Angeles: Capital of the Third World*. New York: Touchstone.

———— 1992. "Homelands: Seeing, Not Seeing." *Salmagundi* 96: 4–10.

Rigdon, Susan M. 1988. *The Culture Facade: Art, Science, and Politics in the Work of Oscar Lewis*. Urbana: University of Illinois Press.

Ríos-Bustamante, Antonio, and Pedro Castillo. 1986. *An Illustrated History of Mexican Los Angeles, 1781–1985*. Los Angeles: Chicano Studies Research Center, University of California, Los Angeles.

Rivera, Carla. 1993. "Disaster Agency Probe Hit for Ignoring Riots." *Los Angeles Times*, Jan. 11, pp. A1+.

Robinson, W. W. 1968. *Los Angeles: A Profile*. Norman: University of Oklahoma Press.

Rodgers, Daniel. 1978. *The Work Ethic in Industrial America, 1850–1920*. Chicago: University of Chicago Press.

Rodriguez, Richard. 1992. "Multiculturalism with No Diversity." *Los Angeles Times*, May 10, pp. M1+.

———— 1993. "The Birth Pangs of a New L.A." *Harper's Magazine*, July, pp. 20–21.

Roediger, David R. 1991. *The Wages of Whiteness: Race and the Making of the American Working Class*. London: Verso.

Roh, Kil-Nam. 1983. "Issues of Korean American Journalism." *Amerasia Journal* 10: 89–102.

Roh, Tae Woo. 1990. *Korea: A Nation Transformed, Selected Speeches by Roh Tae Woo*. New York: Pergamon Press.

Rosaldo, Renato. 1989. *Culture and Truth: The Remaking of Social Analysis*. Boston: Beacon Press.

Rosenthal, Andrew. 1992. "Quayle Says Riots Sprang from Lack of Family Values." *New York Times*, May 20, pp. A1+.

Rosin, Hanna. 1994. "Boxed In." *New Republic*, Jan. 3, pp. 12–14.

Rothman, David J. 1994. "The Crime of Punishment." *New York Review of Books*, Feb. 17, pp. 34–38.

Rothstein, Richard. 1992. "Who Are the Real Looters?" *Dissent*, Fall, pp. 429–430.

Rouse, Roger. 1991. "Mexican Migration and the Social Space of Postmodernism." *Diaspora* 1: 8–23.

Rutten, Tim. 1992. "A New Kind of Riot." *New York Review of Books*, June 11, pp. 52–54.

Ryang, Sonia. 1992. "Indoctrination or Rationalization? The Anthropology of 'North Koreans' in Japan." *Critique of Anthropology* 12: 101–132.

Saari, Neil. 1992. "Letter." *Time*, June 1, p. 10.

Sakong, MyungDuk C. 1990. "Rethinking the Impact of the Enclave: A Comparative Analysis of Korean-Americans' Economic and Residential Adaptation." Ph.D. dissertation, State University of New York at Albany.

Sánchez, George J. 1993. *Becoming Mexican American*. New York: Oxford University Press.

Sassen, Saskia. 1991. *The Global City: New York, London, Tokyo*. Princeton, N.J.: Princeton University Press.

Saxton, Alexander. 1971. *The Indispensable Enemy: Labor and the Anti-Chinese Movement in California*. Berkeley: University of California Press.

———— 1990. *The Rise and Fall of the White Republic: Class Politics and Mass Culture in Nineteenth-Century America*. London: Verso.

Schaller, Michael. 1992. *Reckoning with Reagan: America and Its President in the 1980s*. New York: Oxford University Press.

Scharnhorst, Gary, and Jack Bales. 1985. *The Lost Life of Horatio Alger, Jr.* Bloomington: Indiana University Press.

Scheer, Robert. 1992. " 'Everybody Is Pointin' Their Finger at Everybody.' " *Los Angeles Times*, May 13, p. C8.

Schifrin, Matthew. 1988. "Horatio Alger Kim." *Forbes*, Oct. 17, pp. 92–96.

Schiller, Nina Glick, Linda Basch, and Cristina Blanc-Szanton. 1992. "Transnationalism: A New Analytic Framework for Understanding Migration." In idem, eds., *Toward a Transnational Perspective on Migration: Race, Class, Ethnicity, and Nationalism Reconsidered*, pp. 1–24. New York: New York Academy of Sciences.

Schlesinger, Arthur M., Jr. 1992. *The Disuniting of America: Reflections on a Multicultural Society*. New York: W. W. Norton.

Schlozman, Kay Lehman, and Sidney Verba. 1979. *Insult to Injury: Unemployment, Class, and Political Response*. Cambridge, Mass.: Harvard University Press.

Schoenberger, Karl. 1992. "Bridging the Gap between Two Worlds." *Los Angeles Times*, July 12, pp. A1+.

Schumpeter, Joseph. 1934. *The Theory of Economic Development: An Inquiry into Profits, Capital, Credit, Interest, and the Business Cycle*, trans. Redvers Opie. Cambridge, Mass.: Harvard University Press.

Schwarz, John E., and Thomas J. Volgy. 1992. *The Forgotten Americans: Thirty Million Working Poor in the Land of Opportunity*. New York: W. W. Norton.

Scigliano, Eric. 1992. "Seattle's Little Big Riot." In Hazen, ed., *Inside the L.A. Riots*, pp. 63–64.

Scott, A. J., and A. S. Paul. 1991. "Industrial Development in Southern California." In John Hart, ed., *Our Changing Cities*, pp. 189–217. Baltimore: Johns Hopkins University Press.

Scott, Peter Dale, and Jonathan Marshall. 1990. *Cocaine Politics*. Berkeley: University of California Press.

2nd Generation. 1992. Nov. 1.

See, Carolyn. 1992. "Melting." In Reid, ed., *Sex, Death, and God in L.A.*, pp. 75–107.

Senate Office of Research. 1992. *The South-Central Los Angeles and Koreatown Riots: A Study of Civil Unrest*. Sacramento, Calif.: Senate Office of Research.

Seo, Diane. 1993. "L.A. Threatens, Seoul Beckons: South Korean Emigration to the U.S. Has Reached a Turning Point." *Los Angeles Times*, Aug. 15, p. 14.

Serrano, Richard. 1993. "LAPD Seeks to Spend $1 Million on Riot Gear." *Los Angeles Times*, Jan. 20, pp. B1+.

Shao, Maria. 1991. "Suddenly, Asian-Americans Are a Marketer's Dream." *Business Week*, June 17, pp. 54–55.

Shapiro, Andrew L. 1992. *We're Number One*. New York: Vintage.

Shaw, David. 1990. "Asian-Americans Chafe against Stereotype of 'Model Citizen.'" *Los Angeles Times*, Dec. 11, p. A31.

Sherman, Diana. 1979. "Korean Town's Extent, Population Grows Daily." *Los Angeles Times*, Feb. 25, pt. 8, p. 1.

Shim, Steve S. 1977. *Korean Immigrant Churches Today in Southern California.* San Francisco: R & E Associates.

Shin, Eui-Hang, and Kyung-Sup Chang. 1988. "Peripheralization of Immigrant Professionals: Korean Physicians in the United States." *International Migration Review* 22: 609–626.

Shin, Eui-Hang, and Shin-Kap Han. 1990. "Korean Immigrant Small Businesses in Chicago: An Analysis of the Resource Mobilization Processes." *Amerasia Journal* 16: 39–60.

Shin, Eui-Hang, and Hyung Park. 1988. "An Analysis of Causes of Schisms in Ethnic Churches: The Case of Korean-American Churches." In Lee and Kwak, eds., *Koreans in North America,* pp. 231–252.

Shin, Linda. 1971. "Koreans in America, 1903–1945." In Tachiki, Wong, Odo, and Wong, eds., *Roots,* pp. 200–206.

Shindler, Merrill, and Karen Berk, eds. 1992. *Zagat Los Angeles / So. California Restaurant Survey 1993.* New York: Zagat Survey.

Shiver, Jube, Jr. 1991. "South L.A. Patrons Pay a Hefty Price as Banks Leave." *Los Angeles Times,* Nov. 26, pp. A1+.

——— 1992. "Tensions, Bargains Share Space at Indoor Swap Meets." *Los Angeles Times,* July 8, pp. A1+.

Shklar, Judith N. 1991. *American Citizenship: The Quest for Inclusion.* Cambridge, Mass.: Harvard University Press.

Shorris, Earl. 1992. *Latinos: A Biography of the People.* New York: W. W. Norton.

Silverstein, Stuart, and Nancy Rivera Brooks. 1991. "Shoppers in Need of Stores." *Los Angeles Times,* Nov. 24, pp. A1+.

Simmons, Charles E. 1993. "The Los Angeles Rebellion: Class, Race, and Misinformation." In Madhubuti, ed., *Why L.A. Happened,* pp. 141–155.

Sims, Calvin. 1994. "Vons Opens New Store in a City Torn by Riots." *New York Times,* Jan. 13, p. C3.

Skerry, Peter. 1993. *Mexican Americans: The Ambivalent Minority.* New York: Free Press.

Skolnick, Arlene. 1991. *Embattled Paradise: The American Family in an Age of Uncertainty.* New York: Basic Books.

Skolnick, Jerome, and James J. Fyfe. 1993. *Above the Law: Police and the Excessive Use of Force.* New York: Free Press.

Sleeper, Jim. 1990. *The Closest of Strangers: Liberalism and the Politics of Race in New York.* New York: W. W. Norton.

Smith, Anna Deavere. 1994. *Twilight Los Angeles, 1992.* New York: Anchor Books.

Sniderman, Paul M., and Thomas Piazza. 1993. *The Scar of Race.* Cambridge, Mass.: Harvard University Press.

Soja, Edward W. 1989. *Postmodern Geographies: The Reassertion of Space in Critical Social Theory.* London: Verso.

———— 1992. "Inside Exopolis: Scenes from Orange County." In Sorkin, ed., *Variations on a Theme Park*, pp. 94–122.

Son, Young Ho. 1991. "Korean Ethnic Institutions in America: The Church and Village Council." *Korea Observer* 22: 335–361.

Sonenshein, Raphael J. 1993. *Politics in Black and White: Race and Power in Los Angeles.* Princeton, N.J.: Princeton University Press.

Song, Cathy. 1983. *Picture Bride.* New Haven, Conn.: Yale University Press.

Song, Mia. 1993. "Defects of the Heart." *Transpacific*, Nov., pp. 64+.

Song, Young In. 1986. "Battered Korean Women in Urban America: The Relationship of Cultural Conflict to Wife Abuse." Ph.D. dissertation, Ohio State University.

———— 1989. "The Silent Suffering of Abused Korean Women." *Korea Observer* 20: 303–320.

Sŏnu, Hwi. 1990. "Thoughts of Home." In Peter Lee, ed., *Modern Korean Literature*, pp. 203–215. Honolulu: University of Hawaii Press.

Sorkin, Michael, ed. 1992. *Variations on a Theme Park: The New American City and the End of Public Space.* New York: Noonday Press.

Sowell, Thomas. 1981a. *Ethnic America: A History.* New York: Basic Books.

———— 1981b. *Markets and Minorities.* New York: Basic Books.

Spickard, Paul R. 1989. *Mixed Blood.* Madison: University of Wisconsin Press.

Stack, Carol. 1974. *All Our Kin: Strategies for Survival in a Black Community.* New York: Harper & Row.

Starr, Kevin. 1973. *Americans and the California Dream, 1850–1915.* New York: Oxford University Press.

———— 1985. *Inventing the Dream: California through the Progressive Era.* New York: Oxford University Press.

———— 1990. *Material Dreams: Southern California through the 1920s.* New York: Oxford University Press.

Steele, Shelby. 1990. *The Content of Our Character: A New Vision of Race in America.* New York: St. Martin's Press.

Steinberg, Stephen. 1989. *The Ethnic Myth: Race, Ethnicity, and Class in America,* updated ed. Boston: Beacon Press. Originally published in 1981.

Sterngold, James. 1992. "South Korea's Vietnam Veterans Begin to Be Heard." *New York Times*, May 10, p. 6.

Stewart, Ellen. 1989. "Ethnic Cultural Diversity: An Interpretive Study of Cultural Differences and Communication Styles between Korean Merchants/Employees and Black Patrons in South Los Angeles." M.A. thesis, California State University, Los Angeles.

———— 1993. "Communication between African Americans and Korean Americans: Before and after the Los Angeles Riots." *Amerasia Journal* 19(2): 23–53.

Stewart, James B. 1991. *Den of Thieves.* New York: Simon and Schuster.

Stone, Keith. 1993. "L.A. Will Mark Year since Riots." *Daily News*, Apr. 29, pp. 1+.

Sturdevant, Saundra Pollock, and Brenda Stoltzfus, eds. 1993. *Let the Good Times Roll: Prostitution and the U.S. Military in Asia*. New York: New Press.

Sue, Stanley, and Harry H. L. Kitano, eds. 1973. "Asian Americans: A Success Story?" *Journal of Social Issues*, special issue 29(2).

Suk, Chin-Ha, and James L. Morrison. 1987. "South Korea's Participation in the Vietnam War: A Historiographical Essay." *Korea Observer* 18: 270–316.

Sundquist, Eric J. 1993. *To Wake the Nations: Race in the Making of American Literature*. Cambridge, Mass.: Harvard University Press.

Sunoo, H. Cooke. 1974. "Koreans in Los Angeles: Employment and Education." Paper presented at the meeting of the Association of Korean Christian Scholars in the United States.

Sunoo, Harold Hakwon, and Dong Soo Kim, eds. 1978. *Korean Women in a Struggle for Humanization*. Memphis, Tenn.: Association of Korean Christian Scholars in North America.

Tachiki, Amy, Eddie Wong, Franklin Odo, and Buck Wong, eds. 1971. *Roots: An Asian American Reader*. Los Angeles: Asian American Studies Center, University of California, Los Angeles.

Takagi, Dana Y. 1992. *The Retreat from Race: Asian-American Admissions and Racial Politics*. New Brunswick, N.J.: Rutgers University Press.

Takaki, Ronald. 1989. *Strangers from a Different Shore: A History of Asian Americans*. Boston: Little, Brown.

Terkel, Studs. 1992. *Race: How Blacks and Whites Think and Feel about the American Obsession*. New York: New Press.

Thompson, Anderson. 1993. "The Los Angeles Rebellion: Seizing the Historical Moment." In Madhubuti, ed., *Why L.A. Happened*, pp. 49–59.

Thompson, E. P. 1978. *The Poverty of Theory and Other Essays*. New York: Monthly Review Press.

Thorne, Barrie. 1992. "Feminism and the Family: Two Decades of Thought." In Barrie Thorne and Marilyn Yalom, eds., *Rethinking the Family: Some Feminist Questions*, rev. ed., pp. 3–30. Boston: Northeastern University Press.

Tikkun. 1992. "Roundtable: Domestic Social Policy after the L.A. Uprising." *Tikkun*, July/Aug., pp. 39–44, 74–75.

Tilly, Charles. 1990. "Transplanted Networks." In Yans-McLaughlin, ed., *Immigration Reconsidered*, pp. 79–95.

Trachtenberg, Jeffrey A. 1986. " 'My Daughter, She Will Speak Better.' " *Forbes*, Oct. 6, pp. 68–70.

Trager, Oliver, ed. 1992. *America's Minorities and the Multicultural Debate*. New York: Facts on File.

Trillin, Calvin. 1994. "Personal History: Messages from My Father." *New Yorker*, June 20, pp. 56–78.

Tsuchida, Nobuya. 1984. "Japanese Gardeners in Southern California, 1900–1940." In Cheng and Bonacich, eds., *Labor Immigration under Capitalism*, pp. 455–469.

Tunney, Kelly Smith. 1992. "L.A. Riots Soured American Dream." *Korea Times*, June 15, p. 8.

Turner, Patricia A. 1993. *I Heard It through the Grapevine: Rumor in African-American Culture*. Berkeley: University of California Press.

Uchida, Yoshiko. 1982. *Desert Exile: The Uprooting of a Japanese-American Family*. Seattle: University of Washington Press.

UCLA Ethnic Studies Centers. 1987. *Ethnic Groups in Los Angeles: Quality of Life Indicators*. Los Angeles: Ethnic Studies Centers, University of California, Los Angeles.

Ugwu-Oju, Dympna. 1992. "Black and No Place to Hide." *New York Times*, May 17, p. 17.

United Nations. 1990. *United Nations Demographic Yearbook 1990*. New York: United Nations.

U.S. Commission on Civil Rights. 1975. *A Dream Unfulfilled: Korean and Pilipino Health Professionals in L.A.* Washington, D.C.: U.S. Commission on Civil Rights.

———— 1992. *Civil Rights Issues Facing Asian Americans in the 1990s*. Washington, D.C.: U.S. Commission on Civil Rights.

U.S. General Accounting Office. 1990. *Asian Americans: A Status Report*. Washington, D.C.: United States General Accounting Office.

Valentine, Charles A. 1968. *Culture and Poverty: Critique and Counter-Proposals*. Chicago: University of Chicago Press.

Vanneman, Reeve, and Lynn Weber Cannon. 1987. *The American Perception of Class*. Philadelphia: Temple University Press.

Ventura, Michael. 1993. "Riotous Dreams." *L.A. Weekly*, Apr. 23–29, p. 9.

Wada, Haruki. 1992. *Kin Nissei to Manshū kōnichi sensō* [Kim Il Sŏng and Manchurian Anti-Japanese War]. Tokyo: Heibonsha.

Wales, Nym, and San Kim. 1941. *Song of Ariran: A Korean Communist in the Chinese Revolution*. San Francisco: Ramparts Press.

Walker, Martin. 1992a. "Dark Past Ambushes the 'City of the Future.'" *Manchester Guardian Weekly*, May 10, p. 7.

———— 1992b. "Clinton Turns Tables on Bush over Riots." *Manchester Guardian Weekly*, May 17, p. 10.

Wall, Helena M. 1990. *Fierce Communion: Family and Community in Early America*. Cambridge, Mass.: Harvard University Press.

Wallace, Amy, and K. Connie Kang. 1993. "One Year Later, Hope and Anger Remain." *Los Angeles Times*, Apr. 30, pp. A1+.

Ward, Arvli. 1992. "24 Hours in the Life of the Rebellion." *Nommo*, May–June, pp. 18+.

Waters, Mary C. 1990. *Ethnic Options: Choosing Identities in America.* Berkeley: University of California Press.

Wei, William. 1993. *The Asian American Movement.* Philadelphia: Temple University Press.

Weiner, Michael. 1989. *The Origins of the Korean Community in Japan.* Atlantic Highlands, N.J.: Humanities Press.

Weinstock, Matt. 1947. *My L.A.* New York: A. A. Wyn.

Weiss, Richard. 1969. *The American Myth of Success: From Horatio Alger to Norman Vincent Peale.* New York: Basic Books.

Wellman, David T. 1993. *Portraits of White Racism,* 2nd ed. Cambridge: Cambridge University Press.

West, Cornel. 1991. "On Black Rage." *Village Voice,* Sept. 17, pp. 35–36.

————— 1993. *Race Matters.* Boston: Beacon Press.

West, Nathanael. 1962. *The Day of the Locust.* In idem, *Miss Lonelyhearts and The Day of the Locust,* pp. 59–185. New York: New Directions.

Wheeler, B. Gordon. 1993. *Black California: The History of African-Americans in the Golden State.* New York: Hippocrene Books.

White, Michael J., Ann E. Biddlecom, and Shenyang Guo. 1993. "Immigration, Naturalization, and Residential Assimilation among Asian Americans in 1980." *Social Forces* 72: 93–117.

White, Morton, and Lucia White. 1962. *The Intellectual vs. the City: From Thomas Jefferson to Frank Lloyd Wright.* Cambridge, Mass.: Harvard University Press.

White, Richard. 1991. *"It's Your Misfortune and None of My Own": A New History of the American West.* Norman: University of Oklahoma Press.

Whyte, William Foote. 1955. *Street Corner Society,* 2nd ed. Chicago: University of Chicago Press. Originally published in 1943.

Wideman, John Edgar. 1992. "Dead Black Men and Other Fallout from the American Dream." *Esquire,* Sept., pp. 149–156.

Wiley, Ralph. 1993. *What Black People Should Do Now: Dispatches from Near the Vanguard.* New York: Ballantine.

Wilkinson, Tracy, and John Lee. 1992. "Ethnic Media Serve as Lifeline amid the Chaos." *Los Angeles Times,* May 3, pp. A1+.

Wills, Garry. 1987. *Reagan's America: Innocents at Home.* Garden City, N.Y.: Doubleday.

Wilson, William Julius. 1987. *The Truly Disadvantaged: The Inner City, the Underclass, and Public Policy.* Chicago: University of Chicago Press.

————— 1991. "Public Policy Research and *The Truly Disadvantaged.*" In Jencks and Peterson, eds., *The Urban Underclass,* pp. 460–481.

Wines, Michael. 1992. "White House Links Riots to Welfare." *New York Times,* May 5, pp. A1+.

Wolfe, Alan, ed. 1991. *America at Century's End*. Berkeley: University of California Press.

Wong, Charles Choy. 1977. "Black and Chinese Grocery Stores in Los Angeles' Black Ghetto." *Urban Life* 5: 439–464.

Wong, Roberta May. 1989. "All Orientals Look Alike." In Lim and Tsutakawa, eds., *The Forbidden Stitch*, pp. 74–75.

Woo, Elaine. 1992. "A Third-Generation Chinese-American . . ." In Los Angeles Times, ed., *Understanding the Riots*, pp. 154–156.

Wright, Gwendolyn. 1981. *Building the Dream: A Social History of Housing in America*. Cambridge, Mass.: M.I.T. Press.

Yang, Eun Sik. 1984. "Korean Women of America: From Subordination to Partnership, 1903–1930." *Amerasia Journal* 11: 1–28.

———— 1990. "Korean Revolutionary Nationalism in America: Kim Kang and the Student Circle, 1937–1956." *California Sociologist* 13: 173–198.

Yang, Jeff. 1992. "Shooting Back." *Village Voice*, May 19, pp. 47–48.

Yans-McLaughlin, Virginia, ed. 1990. *Immigration Reconsidered: History, Sociology, and Politics*. New York: Oxford University Press.

Yi, Jeongduk. 1992. "Social Order and Protest: Black Boycotts against Korean Shopkeepers in Poor New York City Neighborhoods." Paper presented at the meeting of the American Anthropological Association, Chicago, Ill.

Yi, Kŭn-sik, and T'ae-dong Kim. 1991. *Ttang* [Land]. Seoul: Pibong Ch'ulp'ansa.

Yim, Sun Bin. 1978. "Korean Battered Wives: A Sociological and Psychological Analysis of Conjugal Violence in Korean Immigrant Families." In Sunoo and Kim, eds., *Korean Women in a Struggle for Humanization*, pp. 171–199.

———— 1984. "The Social Structure of Korean Communities in California, 1903–1920." In Cheng and Bonacich, eds., *Labor Immigration under Capitalism*, pp. 515–548.

———— 1989. "Korean Immigrant Women in Early Twentieth-Century America." In Asian Women United of California, ed., *Making Waves*, pp. 50–60.

———— 1991. "Kinship Networks among Korean Immigrants in the U.S.: Structural Analysis." In Kwak and Lee, eds., *The Korean-American Community*, pp. 135–154.

Yoo, Chul-In. 1993. "Life Histories of Two Korean Women Who Married American GIs." Ph.D. dissertation, University of Illinois at Urbana-Champaign.

Yoo, Jay Kun. 1979. *The Koreans in Seattle*. Elkins Park, Pa.: Philip Jaisohn Memorial Foundation.

Yoon, In-Jin. 1990. "The Changing Significance of Ethnic and Class Resources in Immigrant Businesses: The Case of Korean Immigrant Businesses in Chicago." *International Migration Review* 25: 303–332.

———— 1991. "Self-Employment in Business: Chinese-, Japanese-, Korean-Americans, Blacks, and Whites." Ph.D. dissertation, University of Chicago.

———— 1992. "The Social Origins of Korean Immigration to the United States, 1965–Present." Paper presented at the meeting of the American Sociological Association, Pittsburgh, Pa.

Yoshihashi, Pauline, and Sarah Lubman. 1992. "American Dreams: How the Kims of L.A. and Other Koreans Made It in the U.S." *Wall Street Journal,* June 16, pp. A1+.

Young, Philip K. Y. 1983. "Family Labor, Sacrifice, and Competition: Korean Greengrocers in New York City." *Amerasia Journal* 10: 53–71.

Yu, Eui-Young. 1982a. "Koreans in Los Angeles: Size, Distribution, and Composition." In E. Y. Yu, Phillips, and Yang, eds., *Koreans in Los Angeles,* pp. 23–47.

———— 1982b. "Occupation and Work Patterns of Korean Immigrants." In E. Y. Yu, Phillips, and Yang, eds., *Koreans in Los Angeles,* pp. 49–73.

———— 1983. "Korean Communities in America: Past, Present, and Future." *Amerasia Journal* 10: 23–51.

———— 1985. " 'Koreatown' in Los Angeles: Emergence of a New Inner-City Ethnic Community." *Bulletin of the Population and Development Studies Center* 14: 29–43.

———— 1987. *Juvenile Delinquency in the Korean Community of Los Angeles.* Los Angeles: Korea Times.

———— 1988. "The Growth of Korean Buddhism in the United States, with Special Reference to Southern California." *Pacific World: Journal of the Institute of Buddhist Studies,* new ser., 4: 82–93.

———— 1990a. *Korean Community Profile: Life and Consumer Patterns.* Los Angeles: Korea Times.

———— 1990b. "Regionalism in the South Korean Power Structure." *California Sociologist* 13: 123–144.

———— 1993. "The Korean American Community." In Donald N. Clark, ed., *Korea Briefing, 1993,* pp. 139–162. Boulder, Colo.: Westview Press.

Yu, Eui-Young, Earl H. Phillips, and Eun Sik Yang, eds. 1982. *Koreans in Los Angeles: Prospects and Promises.* Los Angeles: Koryo Research Institute.

Yu, Jin H. 1980. *The Korean Merchants in the Black Community: Their Relations and Conflicts with Strategies for Conflict Resolution and Prevention.* Elkins Park, Pa.: Philip Jaisohn Memorial Foundation.

Yun, Chung-Hei. 1992. "Beyond 'Clay Walls': Korean American Literature." In Shirley Geok-lin Lim and Amy Ling, eds., *Reading the Literatures of Asian America,* pp. 79–95. Philadelphia: Temple University Press.

Yun, Grace, ed. 1989. *A Look Beyond the Model Minority Image: Critical Issues in Asian America.* New York: Minority Rights Group.

Zhou, Min. 1992. *Chinatown: The Socioeconomic Potential of an Urban Enclave.* Philadelphia: Temple University Press.

Zukin, Sharon. 1991. "Hollow Center: U.S. Cities in the Global Era." In Wolfe, ed., *America at Century's End*, pp. 245–261.

Zweigenhaft, Richard L., and G. William Domhoff. 1991. *Blacks in the White Establishment? A Study of Race and Class in America.* New Haven, Conn.: Yale University Press.

Index